Screening #MeToo

Screening #MeToo

Rape Culture in Hollywood

Edited by

Lisa Funnell and Ralph Beliveau

Cover: Photofest image of the interrogation room from *The Invisible Man* (2020); Universal Studios.

Published by State University of New York Press, Albany

For information, contact State University of New York Press, Albany, NY
www.sunypress.edu

Library of Congress Cataloging-in-Publication Data

Names: Funnell, Lisa, editor. | Beliveau, Ralph, editor.
Title: Screening #MeToo: Rape Culture in Hollywood / Lisa Funnell and
    Ralph Beliveau, editors.
Description: Albany : State University of New York Press, [2022] | Includes
    bibliographical references and index.
Identifiers: ISBN 9781438487595 (hardcover : alk. paper) | ISBN 9781438487618
    (ebook) | ISBN 9781438487601 (pbk. : alk. paper)
Further information is available at the Library of Congress.

10 9 8 7 6 5 4 3 2 1

*This book is dedicated to
the survivors of sexual violence.*

Contents

Part II
Consequences and the Fixing Gaze:
Surveillance and Rape/Revenge

Part III
Teen Comedies and Women's Horror Stories
in the #MeToo Era

Acknowledgments

This book is dedicated to my family. First, I must thank my parents, Lorne and Mary Funnell, for your never-ending support and encouragement. Your unwavering belief in me gives me courage to tackle such challenging and meaningful projects as this book. Second, I need to thank my amazing family—my brother Dave, his wife Caren, and their three amazing children Tailor, Harrison, and Daniel. You are a constant source of love and laughter in my life. Finally, I am indebted to my sweet pup, Justice, who lay beside me so patiently as I edited multiple drafts of each chapter. I adore you, my little nugget!

—Lisa Funnell

My thanks to Lisa, my co-conspirator and friend. Thanks to Laura Bolf-Beliveau for her discussions and tolerance, and to Abby and Martha for giving me hope that in the future people will not tolerate depictions discussed here without a good dose of criticism. The challenge is to be better, do better, and reduce the level of misery in the world.

—Ralph Beliveau

We would both like to thank our contributors, whose insightful work is featured throughout this book. Additionally, we are grateful for receiving permission to reproduce sections from the following copyrighted material:

A portion of chapter 10—"Taking Consent into Account: American Teen Films amidst #MeToo"—appeared as "Exposing Flaws of Affirmative Consent through Contemporary American Teen Films" in *Girlhood Studies* 14, no. 1 (Spring 2021): 101–116. The article is reproduced here with the permission of Berghahn Books.

Introduction

The Promise of #MeToo as a Theoretical Lens

Lisa Funnell and Ralph Beliveau

Social justice initiatives require the development and adoption of new crit-ical lenses through which pervasive and pernicious systems of oppression (such as sexism, racism, heterosexism, and the like) can be recognized, interrogated, and subsequently dismantled. Media literacy—the ability to read, think about, and respond critically to texts—plays a key role in this transformative process. Mainstream culture in general and Holly-wood film specifically are designed to maintain the status quo; producers don't necessarily want you to think about how/why media is made, and the responses they seek, particularly in the digital era, are essentially extensions of marketing done with free labor. In term of context, the most influential filmmaking personnel—from director and producer to screenwriter and cinematographer—are largely white, middle-to-upper class, heterosexual, able-bodied cis-men, so it is not surprising that they relay narratives from a perspective of privilege. Despite efforts to diversify in terms of gender and race, the unseen unconscious advantages that make up privilege are disconnected from the narratives.

In terms of content, sexual violence—be it real, threatened, or suggested—and particularly against marginal/minority groups, has become so pervasive in Hollywood film that it is often goes unnoticed. This is deeply troubling given the way that mainstream culture binds individuals and institutions together, shapes public consciousness, and sends powerful messages about what is to be considered appropriate conduct. Over the last 100 years, Hollywood has played a key role in shaping social ideas associated with gender, sex, and power via effects that happen both in front of and behind the camera.

#MeToo Movement

The rise of the #MeToo movement has drawn attention to the sexual assault, coercion, and harassment experienced by many individuals, and especially cis-women. While there are a number of precursors and starting points for the movement, it's important to recognize the role Tarana Burke has played in its creation through her activism. Her experience with discussing sexual abuse with a thirteen-year-old girl not only resulted in a profound desire to help survivors but also alerted her to the power of shared voices (i.e., there is strength in numbers for survivors as well as in collectively challenging deniers/victim-blamers) (Garcia 2017). The movement went viral in October 2017 when actor Alyssa Milano posted on Twitter: "If you've been sexually harassed or assaulted write 'me too' as a reply to this tweet." The #MeToo hashtag exploded across Twitter as well as Facebook, Instagram, and other social media platforms around the world. The magnitude of sexual violence was finally rendered visible through the courageous posts of survivors sharing their experiences with sexual violence in professional, public, and private spaces.

The rapid expansion that followed Milano's tweet was a confluence of Burke's understanding of survivor solidarity, the power of social media to give voice to a mass movement, and the significance of celebrity attention. Many women working in Hollywood began speaking up about their experiences of sexual violence, condemning the industry for silencing survivors while safeguarding predators. Hollywood has arguably served as a microcosm for concentrated discussions of sexual assault, coercion, and harassment in the workplace. Fortunately, this conversation about sexual conduct and safe working spaces extended into other fields/industries via the #TimesUp movement as greater awareness was raised about abuse of power and the victimization of employees. At the time of this writing, we have seen several high-profile cases that have resulted in the public shaming, "cancelation," removal, and occasionally prosecution of powerful and predatory men working in film (e.g., Harvey Weinstein), news media (e.g., Bill O'Reilly), finance (e.g., Jeffrey Epstein), sports (e.g., Larry Nassar), and the law (e.g., Brett Kavanaugh). While these high-profile cases offer some justice, many other abusers have not been outed and continue to be safeguarded by power, money, and social privilege.

Efforts to reduce systematic sexual violence will require the sustainment of this crucial conversation as well as the extension of social, media, and scholarly attention and empathy to survivors in less privileged positions, who may not be celebrities, or be recognized for the injuries of class, economics, and marginalization. Part of sustaining the conversation, we argue, includes a consideration of *our* experience with all media, and especially film, utilizing the perspectives and issues raised by the #MeToo and #TimesUp movements.

Screening #Me Too

This anthology constitutes a step, albeit one of many, toward dismantling the deeply entrenched heteropatriarchy through the interrogation of Hollywood film. Chapters examine films released from the 1960s onward, a broad period defined by the end of the Production Code in Hollywood that resulted in more frequent and increasingly graphic images of sex and violence being included in mainstream films. Additionally, chapters in this collection cover a variety of film genres—spy films, teen comedies, kitchen sink dramas, coming-of-age stories, rape/revenge thrillers, horror flicks—in which surveillance and sexual violence figure prominently in the narratives. Our authors are not concerned only with the content of the films under scrutiny but also with the clear relationship between the stories, how they are being told, and the culture that produces them. The goal of *Screening #MeToo* is to challenge our readers to look at mainstream Hollywood film differently, in light of attitudes about art and power, sexuality and consent, and the pleasures and frustrations of criticizing "entertainment" film from this perspective.

We also hope that *Screening #MeToo* offers a variety of starting points that readers can use to reexamine their own histories of viewing. The varying perspectives brought forward in this collection are applicable to many other films. In truth, we consider this book to be a series of invitations to reexamine storytelling, and the power and privileges associated with it, in alternative lights. Readers are encouraged to consider how our understanding of consent has changed, how the roles of people and their gendered interactions can be understood differently, and how power manifests in film storytelling. Moreover, while films reflect contemporaneous attitudes, events, and agendas, our remembrance of them is often influenced by feelings of nostalgia and fandom. This anthology offers an opportunity to (re)think the meanings of these films utilizing different lenses and new critical approaches, thereby challenging our memory of them. We believe that this process of reexamination will result in deeper, more nuanced understandings of film while destabilizing the institutional privilege and power undergirding their creation.

Chapters in part I, "Sexual Politics and Violence in Established Genres," offer new and expansive ways to think about the bodily autonomy and sexual agency in well-known films and genres. Lisa Funnell explores the spectrum of violence featured in the James Bond films of the Sean Connery era (1962–1971) as well as their source novels and considers the influence of these foundational sexual politics on subsequent Bond films as well as other derivative spy narratives. Sabrina Moro examines the significance of the nonconsensual rape scene featured in *Last Tango in Paris* (1972), presenting the argument that the recent shift in media coverage of the accusation made by Maria Schneider is reflective of a broader change in social perception regarding the disclosure of sexual assault in the #MeToo era. Katherine Karlin challenges the nostalgia associated with *Saturday Night Fever* (1977), arguing that the film is a kitchen-sink drama centering on violence, racism, and rape. She discusses the depiction of two sexual assaults in relation to the changing social definition of rape at the time of the film's release. In his analysis of *The Howling* (1981), Brian Brems considers how the portrayal of Karen White as a victim of trauma parallels the experiences of sexual assault survivors. He contends that while the film predates the #MeToo era, it anticipates the trajectory of many women's stories that gained traction in the media beginning in the fall of 2017. Emily Naser-Hall discusses the historical connections between the figure of the witch and the laws governing sexual violence, especially the marital rape exception. She explores how American witchcraft films of the 1980s and 1990s—such as *The Witches of Eastwick* (1987) and *The Witches* (1990)—reflect both the rise of female sexual agency in the criminal justice system and the cultural backlash against it from deeply entrench patriarchal attitudes of male sexual license.

Part II, "Consequences and the Fixing Gaze: Surveillance and Rape/Revenge," draws attention to the range of sexual violence inflicted on women's bodies on and through film—from surveillance to assault—and the (ongoing) problem of presenting sexual violation/victimization as a narrative strategy that justifies women (temporarily) enacting violence on men (via revenge). Julia Chan explores the depiction of image-based sexual abuse and especially nonconsensual sexualized imaging and surveillance (or "revenge porn") featured in the classic frat body comedy *Revenge of the Nerds* (1984). Brittany Caroline Speller examines how maverick horror director Wes Craven addresses rape in his franchise work. Focusing on the *Scream* trilogy, Speller identifies a shift toward confronting the consequences of rape culture rather than simply the act of assault. Amanda Spallacci examines mimetic representations of trauma in *Monster* (2003), *The Girl with the Dragon Tattoo* (2011), and *Kill Bill: Volume 1* (2003). She argues that by focusing on the effects of trauma rather than the acts of sexual violence, each individual rape is presented as being part of a much larger chain of violence against women. Finally, Nicole Burkholder-Mosco discusses how the story of *The Girl with the Dragon Tattoo*—from the original novel to the Swedish and American films—depicts the classic disparity between violent men and the women they violate. Written or directed by men, these texts present the impression that women have no hope for official retribution or even the prevention of abuse, with vigilante justice being their only recourse.

Chapters in part III, "Teen Comedies and Women's Horror Stories in the #MeToo Era," explore the rising emphasis on affirmative consent and bodily autonomy in relatively recent Hollywood narratives. Michelle Meek traces the history of sexual consent in American teen films and discusses how such #MeToo-era releases as *Blockers* (2018), *The Kissing Booth* (2018), *Good Boys* (2019), and *Booksmart* (2019) highlight the importance and complexity of consensuality. Shana MacDonald explores the feminist counter-narratives featured in recent teenage romantic comedies written and directed by women. She argues that *To All The Boys I've Loved Before* (2018) and *Booksmart* (2019) reconfigure the sexual politics associated with the traditional rom-com by depicting both straight and queer women protagonists in formative and consensual sexual/romantic relationships. Michelle Kay Hansen discusses how Leigh Whannell's 2020 iteration of *The Invisible Man* updates the 1933 monster movie with a #MeToo horror spin and offers commentary on the ways in which the concerns of women (especially with respect to sexual violence) are often rendered invisible by systems of oppression designed to safeguard privilege.

Finally, we include a chapter that suggests two potentially transformative moves: first, the expansion of the Hollywood storytelling ethos moving to serial on-demand drama—what some might consider the end of television or maybe even a middle ground between television and film narratives—and, second, what it means when women storytellers occupy writing and directing chairs. Tracy Everbach discusses how the Netflix miniseries *Unbelievable* (2019) offers a feminist deconstruction of traditional rape and sexual assault portrayals featured in male-centered dramas that feature women as victims and men as cops and criminals. By focusing on the work of two women detectives, *Unbelievable* presents survivors being believed and treated with empathy and respect, and decreases the usually indulgent and underserved attention to the perpetrator, thereby making a powerful statement about conditions within rape culture.

To Be Continued . . .

As suggested earlier, we hope the critical directions explored here are an impetus and invitation to extend these critiques to other genres, other kinds of storytelling, and other possible uses of a transforming media sphere. We hope this collection offers moments of self-reflection, and also a recognition that these issues have been around for as long as the production of images has used sexual assault victims as aesthetic objects. In her 2019 book *Unspeakable Acts: Women, Art, and Sexual Violence in the 1970s*, Nancy Princenthal writes:

> What does rape look like? How can it be differentiated visually from an act of consensual sex? These questions pertain with special force to graphic imagery. As feminist scholar Sharon Marcus observes, the ambiguity of rape imagery can be seen to parallel the difficulties of adjudicating rape charges, so many of which require us to determine intentions—states of mind—that are invisible. The question is whether rape can be pictured—in paintings, say, or photographs—without being a form of involuntary and unwanted exposure, hence of harm. (para. 2)

As Princenthal points out, these discussions have been around for a long time, since rape was used as "allegorical" subject matter by male artists painting for male audiences. Many contemporary women artists, from the Guerilla Girls to Nancy Spero to Marina Abromović, have problematized the use and violation of women's bodies in visual culture. We acknowledge the efforts of artists and critics to contend with this issue in its complexity. We hope to add to the interrogation of these issues by focusing on similar questions in the context of film.

There is certainly something to celebrate in the high(er) profile that the #MeToo movement has offered to some media spheres. But much more work remains to be done. Sexual violence in relation to issues of race, class, and LGBTQIA+ inequality require further exploration on the screens, behind the productions, and in the world that films come from and are speaking to.

Included in this work is the need for a broader examination of the conditions experienced by victims of sexual assault outside of the usual scope of attention reproduced in legacy and digital culture. This is a continuing challenge because it requires attention at the intersection between focused, critical attention to the day-to-day practices that perpetuate much of this behavior away from the spotlight, and the questions of pleasure and desire produced in popular media. The participation of Milano and other high-profile individuals brought welcome attention to the issues in the #MeToo movement, but at the same time they revealed what conditions would need to be in place to garner such attention. It is possible to be grateful for the social justice that comes from high-profile and celebrity attention to such important issues, while at the same time critiquing how those conditions draw attention to disempowerment in an unbalanced way.

In the material world, victims of sexual harassment and assault span widely across intersections of class, race, and gender identity. Many people are still being victimized in unacknowledged locations. We need to extend to these individuals the attention that encourages them to speak out from all those places beyond the spotlight. The sincerity of our concern for these issues is measures not by the widely known and obvious cases but from how the most disempowered are cared for as a result. This means shedding additional light on indigenous people, Black and Brown people, people in the Trans community, and people who do hard work at low wages to play their part in our culture. They deserve our attention, and they deserve justice too.

But that lack of attention is partially a product of our media imaginaries as well. The treatment of a character in traditional Hollywood film elevates attention to stories that might appear to attend to other kinds of social marginalization, but this accomplishes what these chapters are trying to achieve only if such treatment inspires new ways of thinking about the real lives of the people represented through the hegemony of Hollywood storytelling. And the revision to our ways of consuming the present and the past of film (or television, or fiction, etc.) must be informed by the ability to acknowledge how these issues were marginalized in the past, how the conditions of harassment and assault have been used in media. Through the careful development and deployment of media literacy skills, it is possible in the future for young people to grow up acknowledging that media systems in the past can be understood in their own context but can also be reexamined for new and different ways of attending to the way ideologies of identity are manifested in popular media. We can use new critical lenses to bring attention where it has not previously been in focus, and to use our voices and our dollars to insist that media industries change the assumptions built into their traditional storytelling. One clear route to accomplishing this is expanding the range of creative talent to include previously marginalized people, to focus on previously underexamined areas of life, and to seek to end the reproduction of attitudes that give a pass to such behavior and its role in media storytelling. This has implications for how we understand and critique the history of these media forms, and how in the future we can insist that the issues that impact disempowered and exploited people receive the attention they deserve.

While some of these issues are more thoroughly depicted in nonfiction media like documentaries, news programs, reality television, and online storytelling of a wide variety of types, as well as independent film, the mainstream industry all too frequently sidesteps these projects or greenlights them to be created and/or performed by people who are not part of the communities being represented (e.g., trans* actors should play trans* characters). It not only matters what stories are being told but also who gets to tell and embody them. We hope that the reflection and reevaluation that occurs in this book inspires others to (re)consider the issues at stake as well as the importance of addressing these issues in relation to other identity categories, in other media spheres, and in other storytelling industries around the world as we continue to question power and how it is used.

Works Cited

Garcia, Sandra E. "The Women Who Created #MeToo Long Before Hashtags." *New York Times* October 20, 2017. www.nytimes.com/2017/10/20/us/me-too-movement-tarana-burke.html

Princenthal, Nancy. "Nancy Spero Depicted Sexual Violence in an Era When the Subject Was Unspeakable." *Art in America*, October 18, 2019. www.art news.com/art-in-america/features/nancy-spero-unspeakable-acts-art-sexual-violence-60210

CHAPTER 1

Delightful Duties?

Sexual Violence in the Connery-Era James Bond Films (1962–1971)

Lisa Funnell

As the longest film franchise in history, James Bond consists of twenty-five films released across a nearly six-decade period. With *No Time to Die* (Fukunaga 2021) marking the end of the Daniel Craig era, critics and fans continue to speculate about the direction of the series. While the orphan origin trilogy (*Casino Royale* [Campbell 2006], *Quantum of Solace* [Forster 2008], and *Skyfall* [Mendes 2012]) is revisionist and reworks key elements of the Bond brand, *Spectre* (Mendes 2015) is decidedly reversionist as the film is rooted in the gender politics and generic conventions of earlier works (Funnell and Dodds 2017; Funnell 2018). Although scholars have examined the importance of sex in the franchise in relation to Bond's libidinal masculinity and mission success (Black 107–109), limited attention has been directed toward the sexual politics of the early Bond films and the messages conveyed through them about sex, gender, and power. Bond is framed as a lover, but his sexual encounters with women are often violent and devoid of consent. These problematic scenes are framed within narratives that justify and normalize sexual assault, coercion, and harassment.

While sex plays a central role in spy culture, so too does sexual violence. Affirmative consent is often strikingly absent especially in the

early Bond films and novels, which have been influential in shaping
subsequent/derivative spy narratives. Through words *and* actions, a person—real or fictional—must be able to knowingly (i.e., not hindered by
age, substances, or cognitive impairments) and voluntarily (i.e., without
pressure, force, or coercion) agree to participate in sexual activity. When
affirmative consent is missing and sexual violence prevails, it influences
the way a character is perceived even if they are heroic by design. This
chapter explores the spectrum of sexual violence depicted across the
Connery-era films as well as their source novels. It considers how the
sexual misconduct of Bond and his predatory practices diminish his
heroic capacity, decrease his phallic masculinity, and mar his reputation
as a hero. Moreover, it raises questions about the adoption of these
foundational sexual politics in subsequent James Bond films as well as
other spy narratives.

In recent years, the #MeToo Movement has raised social awareness of the insidious and pervasiveness nature of sexual violence within
the workplace and especially the media industry. While focus has been
placed on the working conditions for women (cis and trans) as well as
trans-men, and nonbinary and queer individuals within the industry,
limited attention has been directed toward the content of the films on
which they are working. Sexual violence all too often plays a central
role in defining the identity of women on screen as well as their heteronormative relationships with men. These texts frequently convey
troublesome messages about gender, sex, race, identity, and power though
the normalization and naturalization of sexual harassment, coercion, and
assault, thereby influencing social consciousness. Utilizing a critical lens
informed by the #MeToo movement, this chapter draws attention to the
hegemonic invisibility of rape culture that has, for too long, defined the
world of James Bond and spy culture at large.

Literary Roots

James Bond is an icon of popular culture. As a character, Bond is defined
by his social locations and privilege. He is a white, cis-gender, able-bodied British man from the upper-middle class with an elite education
and burgeoning professional career. He is also defined by his sexuality.
As a heterosexual man, Bond is depicted as having an almost magnetic
appeal and women seem to gravitate toward him. His heroic identity

centers on a prominent stereotype of masculinity—the lover. According to Julia Wood, "being sexual is a way to perform and prove [heterosexual] masculinity" (176). Bond exudes a libido-based heroism that is rooted in the British lover literary tradition (Funnell, "I Know" 458), which brought forward glamorous gentlemen heroes who were willing to risk everything for both a higher cause and the women they love (Hawkins 29–30). By sleeping with women, Bond confirms his masculinity (as well as that of the British Secret Service) and convinces his lovers to support his missions (Black 107–109).

The inaugural Bond films starring Sean Connery were adaptations of a series of novels and short stories written by Ian Fleming. Published between 1953 and 1966, the texts convey some troubling messages about sex, gender, and power that have, in turn, influenced the representational politics in the Connery-era films. While an examination of each work is beyond the scope of this chapter, a consideration of how sexual violence factors into prominent characterizations and storylines is paramount. Although Fleming uses sexual violence—be it real, suggested, or threatened—in his framing of various characters, he offers a somewhat ambivalent impression. While rape and sexual exploitation are frequently included in the backstories of various figures, their framing in the narrative seems to be more dependent on the gender of the character and their relationship to Bond rather than the egregious nature of the act.

Sexual exploitation is often referenced in the backstories of men who are antagonists. In the first two novels, *Casino Royale* (1953) and *Live and Let Die* (1954), villains Le Chiffre and Mr. Big respectively run prostitution rings. This is included in their dossiers as a way to quickly establish their immorality via the sexual exploitation of women. In addition, villains frequently strip women of their clothing when holding them captive. Clothing is not only a powerful signifier of identity but also serves as a layer of protection concealing vulnerable areas including sex characteristics. As such, its forceful removal can be framed as a (sexual) violation. In *Live and Let Die*, Solitaire is stripped in front of Bond on the order of Mr. Big: "She stood pale and naked. She hung her head and the heavy black hair fell forward over her face . . . 'You bastard,' said Bond through his teeth" (218–219). In *Moonraker* (1955), the henchperson Kreb begins to undress Gala Brand, who is feigning unconsciousness while bound to a chair. The book conveys the impression that Brand faces not only physical danger (as Krebs specializes in torture) but also sexual danger through the threat of rape. In both cases, the forceful removal of clothing is framed not only as an act of sexual violence against the woman but also as an act of aggression toward Bond; the violation appears to be more abhorrent because it is happening to "Bond's girl" (i.e., the Bond Girl) and challenges the phallocentric claim of the white male hero (to the white woman).

Sexual assault plays a more formative role in shaping the back-stories of women to explain their "colder" dispositions and distrust of men, positioning them as greater sexual challenges/conquests for Bond. In *Diamonds Are Forever* (1956), Felix Leiter reveals that Tiffany Case was gang-raped as a teenager and "won't have anything to do with men since then" (69). The impact of this trauma is evident when Bond kisses Case, who "suddenly stiffened and fought her way free" from his embrace (78). Bond is set up in the narrative as a good man who eventually wins her trust and is contrasted with the violent men who violated her years before. *Goldfinger* (1959) takes this approach one step further and offers a deeply troubling explanation for why Pussy Galore is not sexually interested in Bond. She is characterized as a lesbian and her sexuality is framed as a by-product of the trauma she experienced as a child. Galore tells Bond, "I come from the South. You know the definition of a virgin down here? Well, it's a girl who can run faster than her brother. In my case I couldn't run as fast as my uncle. I was twelve" (279). This con-versation is followed up by the pair engaging in some "TLC" as they recover from a plane crash. Thus, Bond is depicted as "the only man" who could "rescue" Galore from sexual and social "deviance," especially since homosexuality was a criminal offense in the United Kingdom at the time (Black 107). Moreover, the novel relays the problematic message that lesbianism is not a true identity but rather a temporary phase that can/must be "resolved" through a "proper" heterosexual encounter. It ends with the restoration of phallocentric order through the validation and successful performance of Bond's heteronormative masculinity.

Sexual assault—be it actual, suggested, or threatened—is frequently used in fiction to convey physical vulnerability in even the strongest of women characters. They are presented with a "visible fragility" that renders them more conventionally feminine and thus appealing to men in the audience (McRobbie 79). At times, these women are given the opportunity to avenge their attack (e.g., rape revenge films of the 1970s) and sexual assault is (problematically) used as a justification for women to (temporarily) enact violence on men. This approach is taken in *Dr. No* (1958) to emphasize the vulnerability of Honeychile Rider, described by Fleming as headstrong, independent, and self-taught. Midway through the novel, Rider relays to Bond that she was raped as a teenager and sought revenge by placing a black widow spider in her attacker's bed (122–123). Bond is sympathetic and accepts her reasoning for enacting violence while instructing her not to make a habit of killing men. Importantly, when Rider is sexually threatened later on by local men (of color), Bond steps in and protects her. Thus, the backstory of Rider not only provides a "crack" in the veneer of one of the strongest women in the novel series but also opens up space for Bond to save the vulnerable white woman from hostile men of color, subsequently reaffirming one of the oldest themes in white culture: resistance to miscegenation.

In the novels, Bond also develops close friendships with white men who engage in intimate partner violence by inflicting physical, emotional, and/or physiological abuse on their partner/spouse. In *From Russia with Love* (1957), Kerim Bey claims that "all women . . . long to be slung over a man's shoulder and taken into a cave and raped" (140) before describing the "little Bessarabian hell-cat" he "won" in Istanbul: "So I got her to my place and took away all her clothes and kept her chained naked under the table. When I ate, I used to throw scraps to her under the table, like a dog. She had to learn who was master" (141). When his mother tried to return the woman to her home, she refused to leave Bey's side, and he describes their "encounter" as "an interesting lesson in female psychology" (141–142). A similar backstory is conveyed by Bond's (future) father-in-law, Marc-Ange Draco, in *On Her Majesty's Secret Service* (1963). He describes his "relations" with an English governess who had "a subconscious desire to be raped . . . she found me in the mountains and she was raped—by me. The police were after me for a time. . . . But for some reason she refused to leave me" (43). This "encounter" resulted in the birth of his daughter, Tracy, whom Bond later marries. In both instances these acts are justified by presenting the victims—whose names and personal experiences are not relayed—remaining with their attackers as to suggest that the violence was ultimately acceptable. Rather than condemning these actions, Bond relays his growing affection for both white men, drawing attention to their increasing kinship that extends to Bond's treatment of women.

In the novels, many of Bond's sexual encounters are similarly coded with the language of sexual violence. In *Casino Royale* (1953), Fleming writes that Bond's "conquest" of Vesper Lynd's body "would each time have the sweet tang of rape" (156). In *Thunderball* (1961), Bond "could almost see the proud, sensual mouth bare away from the even white teeth in a snarl of desire and then, afterwards, soften into a half-pout of loving slavery" (117). In *The Spy Who Loved Me* (1962), Fleming writes, through the third-person perspective of Vivienne Michel, his narrator, that "All women love semi-rape. They love to be taken. It was his sweet brutality against my bruised body that made his act of love so piercingly wonderful" (139). In *On Her Majesty's Secret Service* (1963), Bond's future wife Tracy tells Bond, "Make love to me . . . Do anything you like. And tell me what you like and what you would like from me. Be rough with me. Treat me like the lowest whore in creation" (31–32). The regular use of violent imagery, often requested by women (and thus "justified"), to describe the sexual encounters of Bond relays problematic messages about gender and power in the novels. As such, it contributes to the sexism and misogyny that define the literary world of Bond.

In his analysis of female characterization in the Bond novels, James Chapman argues that Fleming forwards a troublesome fantasy of men about the sexuality of women that would "leave some readers apoplectic with rage" (14). The Bond novels not only convey the *Playboy* ethos in their depiction of guilt-free sexual relationships and positioning of women of erotic objects of desire (13) but also trivialize sexual consent by almost negating its existence. By forwarding the idea that all women *want* to be raped and/or sexually dominated, the novels remove personal agency by claiming that women do not need to consent to sex. Throughout his novels, Fleming projects a fantasy of men's desire and relays a patri-archal worldview in which the sexual needs of certain (white British) men (through the figure of Bond) take precedence over the objections of women. And it is these novels, with their problematic sexual and gender politics, that serve as the source texts for the James Bond films.

Rape as Backstory and Trope

The Connery-era Bond films (1962–1971) are adaptations of Fleming's literary series. The novels have not been adapted in order and they range in terms of their fidelity to their literary sources. The inaugural *Dr. No* (Young 1962) is an adaptation of the sixth novel and introduces the character of Bond as well as other elements that have come to define the cinematic brand, such as the Bond theme composed by Monty Norman. While the film remains faithful to its literary source, a few key elements have been added, effectively shaping the character of Honey Ryder who is considered by many to be the quintessential Bond Girl.

Ryder is best known for her iconic introduction into the film, which emphasizes her beauty and attractiveness; she is framed as an object of desire via the "male gaze" (see Mulvey). Midway through the film, Bond awakens on the beach to the sound of a woman singing "Underneath the Mango Tree." As noted by Anna Piotrowska, the lyrics confirm the sexual availability of the woman "by positioning her as a prospective bride dreaming of getting married, making 'boolooloop' and having children" (175). As I have argued elsewhere, "the arresting image of [a bikini-clad] Ryder not only attracts and holds the attention of Bond but also distracts him from his colonizing mission on the island. When Honey Ryder asks Bond if he is looking for shells on the beach, Bond replies that he is simply interested in "just looking" at her body ("I Know" 467). The film cuts to his point of view, and the audience is encouraged to share his gaze. This moment of scopophilia is replicated when Bond's helper, Quarrel, runs down the beach to inform him of an incoming ship. He stops and stares at Ryder. Once again, the camera shares a man's point of view, but Bond interrupts his line of sight by running toward Quarrel/the camera asking, "What's the matter?," effectively claiming/controlling the gaze and returning attention to the mission at hand while stopping any potential for miscegenation. From the outset of the film/series, the white Bond Girl is explicitly set up as an object of desire for (the white man) Bond and her body is arguably framed as being "for his eyes only."

Much like her novel counterpart, Ryder relays her backstory, which provides an explanation as to why she mistrusts all men, including Bond. As she recounts the details of her rape and how she killed her attacker, Ryder is wearing a (dry) white shirt over her bikini, completely covering her body. This helps to focus the attention of Bond (and the audience) on the details of her account rather than on her body. In this scene, which works in opposition to the "male gaze" (or at the very least deflects it), rape is presented as an unacceptable form of sexual violence perpetrated by evil men. Bond appears sympathetic and understanding, and the film positions him as the man who will safeguard Ryder from evil forces; armed with a "license to kill," Bond (and not Ryder) is framed as the one who should be utilizing deadly force for a just cause.

Following the trajectory of the novel, Bond and Ryder are subsequently captured by Dr. No and imprisoned at his facility on Crab Key.

In the novel, Ryder is presented as being in constant danger from sexual assault from the (hench)people of color working there. Fleming writes:

> His eyes were alight with cruelty. He looked past Bond at the girl. The eyes became mouths that licked their lips. He wiped his hands down the sides of his trousers. The tip of his tongue showed pinkly between the purple lips. He turned to the other three. "What say, fellers?" The three men were also looking at the girl. They nodded dumbly, like children in front of a Christmas tree. (139)

The film, however, is more subtle in depicting this threat. While at dinner, Ryder is costumed in a short white/light pink kimono shirt/dress paired with pink trousers. When she is rescued by Bond in the final moments of the film, her pants have been removed; she is found lying on her back chained to the ground with her legs spread apart and hands tied above her head. While there are always minor continuity issues in film with respect to costuming, an actor missing their pants is a glaring error. It is my argument that this imagery is suggestive of sexual assault as Ryder has been rendered physically vulnerable to sexual attack (via costuming) and unable to protect herself (via restraints) from the licentious men of color in the narrative.

Most films do not feature rape sequences because they are violent, difficult to watch, and have a significant impact on the tone of a film. Instead, filmmakers typically position women in scenarios that suggest rape, as the threat alone is powerful enough to convey. But in the case of *Dr. No*, the film does not address the possible assault so as not to impact the tone of the film's denouement: Bond has just killed the villain, is saving his "girl," and will be rewarded for his actions with sex on the rowboat. Audiences who have picked up on the visual cues might feel unconformable with this ending given Ryder's recent (re)victimization, but the film skirts the issue by having her initiate the final sexual encounter. The film ends with the pair kissing as the song "Underneath the Mango Tree" plays to stress that their lovemaking is consensual and warranted.

Much like its novel counterpart, *Dr. No* relies on a backstory of rape to introduce Ryder, emphasize her vulnerability, and position Bond as her rightful protector. However, the acknowledgment of Ryder's victimization does not extend to her potential violation on Crab Key and the film presents an inconsistent message about the severity and impact of sexual violence. As a result, rape in *Dr. No* appears to be less about the trauma(s) of Ryder and more about what her assault(s) means for her suitor/boyfriend Bond. She is *his* Bond Girl and, as relayed through the problematic term itself, she is not necessarily conceptualized as a stand-alone figure but rather is inextricably dependent on Bond for definition. As a result, *Dr. No* establishes a relationship between gender, sex, and power that influences how subsequent and predominantly white women are conceptualized and treated in the film series.

Myth of Corrective Rape

Although *Goldfinger* (Hamilton 1964) is the third film in the series, it is considered by many to be the one that established the Bond brand: it is the first that looks and feels like a "true" Bond film. While *Goldfinger* set a new standard through its combination of "style, setting, and technology" (Black 117), it also relays some troubling messages about women, particularly in relation to sexuality and affirmative consent. Although some of these ideas may have been in circulation when the film was made, they are deeply problematic and work against heroic development by marring the reputation of Bond who is defined by his libidinal masculinity.

In many early Bond films, women are given a double entendre for their name that usually contains a sexual innuendo. This works to trivialize women and reduce their narrative importance as they are being essentialized according to their sexuality and/or sex characteristics. The name Pussy Galore is one of the few that appears in the novel series along with its film adaptation. In the novel, Galore is explicitly characterized as lesbian, and her name indicates both sexual interest in and access to other women. In the film, however, Galore's sexual orientation is suggested rather than explicitly relayed. Audiences unfamiliar with the source novel might not pick up on these undertones leading to multiple readings of her encounters with Bond. This might shift the focus of sexual innuendo in her name from the women pilots in her squad (i.e., her desire for them) to James Bond (i.e., his desire for her). In the process, the sexual agency of Galore begins to be undermined.

From the outset of the film, Galore makes it clear that she is not interested in Bond. Unlike her novel counterpart, the filmic Galore does not disclose her sexual orientation or sexual history and is not presented with a backstory of sexual assault. Galore does not provide a reason for her disinterest in Bond, nor does she signal that her feelings toward Bond have changed, but this does not stop him from propositioning her in the barn. When Galore refuses to betray the villain, Bond pulls her close and a startled Galore responds by trying to push him away. When Bond refuses to let go, she flips him onto his back. The soundtrack codes this action as playful, as well as the subsequent arm twist Bond uses to flip Galore onto her back. When Bond climbs onto her with the intention of having sex, Galore places her hands around Bond's neck and tries to push him off. As Bond gradually overpowers her and leans in for a kiss, Galore continues to resist and even turns her face away from him. When Bond finally kisses her, she keeps resisting for seven seconds before eventually giving in/up. The music accompanying this scene, and particularly the use of the harp to signify her "eventual consent," codes this sequence as being romantic.

On the surface, this predatory encounter appears to validate Bond's libidinal masculinity. Galore is a high value target whose allegiance plays a critical role in the success of his mission. After her (forced) sexual encounter with Bond, she appears to fall in love and switches sides. The film (re)enforces the impression that Bond *needs* to sleep with women—through seduction or by force—in order to turn them into assets. Thus, Bond's libidinal and arguably imperial white masculinity is presented as playing a vital role in mission success.

Upon deeper consideration, the barn scene does not confirm but rather draws into question Bond's sexual magnetism. Galore does not provide affirmative consent, and Bond responds to her rejection of him with violence. Although Bond is a popular culture icon known for his serial seduction of women, the image of Bond forcing himself on Galore undermines his libidinal masculinity and detracts from his heroism. Moreover, the film ends with Bond and Galore together as a couple. This is reminiscent of the backstories of Kerim Bey and Marc-Ange Draco in their respective novels that validated intimate partner violence. Regardless of how the film tries to code the encounter—via a narrative justification, playful soundtrack, eventual "consent," and relationship status—nothing justifies, validates, or negates Bond's use of sexual violence. Although Bond possesses a "00" license that permits him to kill without legal censure, he does not have a license to sexually assault women.

The sexual orientation of Galore further problematizes this scene. If Galore is conceptualized as a lesbian in the film, then her sexual assault takes on additional meaning. As noted by Roderick Brown,

> The term "corrective rape" stems from the prevalence of
> the crime in South Africa, where it is used to describe rape
> perpetrated by straight men against lesbian women in order
> to "correct" or "cure" their "unnatural" sexual orientation.
> The problem is not unique to South Africa . . . The term
> is beginning to be used more broadly to include the rape of
> any member of a sexual minority in an effort to "correct"
> them. (2012, 45–46)

The attack in the barn denies not only Galore's bodily autonomy but
also her sexual identity as a lesbian. Both the novel and film convey
the impression that lesbianism is a phase and not a true sexual identity.
Where they differ is how sexual assault factors into their explanation:
while it serves as a catalyst for "sexual dysfunction" in the novel, it is
utilized as a perverse "conversion therapy" in the film. While both are
deeply problematic, the latter is greater cause for concern given the
popularity of the film, its standing in the Bond film canon, and its
widespread circulation. Years after its release, *Goldfinger* continues to
relay troubling impressions of sexual consent and identities.

Sexual Coercion in Spy Culture

The Connery-era films introduce the character of Bond and key elements
that have come to define the cinematic brand. They also highlight the
centrality of sex in spy culture. Bond is expected to do "whatever it
takes" to defend Queen and country. This often means sleeping with
women with the goal of persuading them to support his mission. While
Bond seems to enjoy this "delightful duty," as Rosa Klebb describes it in
From Russia with Love (Young 1963), not all of the women he encounters
are as enthusiastic. Some are expected to sleep with Bond, and many
fear (violent) repercussions from Bond and/or the villain if they refuse.
A consideration of these encounters draws into question the sexiness of
spy culture as relayed through the world of Bond.

In the first two Bond films, women spies are tasked with sleeping
with Bond to render him vulnerable for attack. In *Dr. No*, Miss Taro is
set up as a sexual lure. As I have argued elsewhere, Taro is characterized
as a Dragon Lady, a racial stereotype for Asian women, and is presented
as being cunning, alluring, and capable of seducing the white man away
from his colonizing mission. The film emphasizes the desirability of

Taro when she lays on her bed in a silk robe and heels while speaking to Bond on the phone. She sets a trap and expects Bond to be killed on his drive over. When Bond arrives at her place, after evading the attackers, Taro appears surprised and "uses her sexuality to distract him while her counterparts organize another attack" (Funnell, "Objects" 81)

What is missing from my original analysis is a recognition of how fearful Taro looks when Bond enters her apartment. She has just showered and is wearing only a towel. When Bond makes sexual advances, Taro is noticeably uncomfortable, and her facial expressions and body language suggest that she does not want to have sex with him. Even though her reluctance registers with Bond, he continues his sexual pursuit and she eventually complies. The film conveys the impression that Bond is justified in this sexual conquest given the actions and affiliation of Taro. What is overlooked is the role that coercion plays as Taro would likely face violent repercussions for her refusal from either her boss, Dr. No, who does not tolerate failure, or Bond himself, who is armed with a "license to kill."

Sex is presented in a similar way in *From Russia with Love*. While Tatiana Romanova is aware of her role as a sexual lure, she is operating under false pretenses; she believes she is working for her homeland when really she is unwittingly serving as an agent of SPECTRE. Importantly, she does not volunteer for this assignment but instead is threatened with violence if she does not comply:

> ROSA KLEBB: "You are not here to ask questions! You forget to whom you are speaking!
>
> . . . From now on you will do anything [Bond] says."
>
> ROMANOVA: "And if I refuse?"
>
> KLEBB: "Then will not leave this room alive."

Romanova is visibly startled by these threats, especially when Klebb smacks her cane against the chair, exclaiming, "You will be *shot!*" From the outset, Romanova is coerced into having sex with Bond under the threat of violence from her superior.

The initial sexual encounter between Romanova and Bond is further complicated by the fact that it is being taped without, at the very least,

Bond's consent. While the creation of a secret sex tape is presented as "standard practice" in spy culture, it is both a sexual violation and a crime: unlawful surveillance. While Bond can be blackmailed, so too can Romanova, who was coerced into this assignment in the first place. Thus, in the initial Bond films, "sexpionage" is presented as obligatory, relying strongly on sexual coercion and drawing into question the bodily autonomy of the woman spy. Moreover, it is the employer (individual, institution, state) that trades in the bodies/sexualities of women for access to power and resources. Women are seemingly disposable agents in the world of Bond, and many do not experience the "delights" from their coerced "duties."

Unlike the novels, the libidinal masculinity of Bond in the Connery era is defined by his sexual interactions with multiple women in each film. They typically feature at least one "Secondary Girl"—a minor character who may or may not be named, spends limited time on screen, and has little impact on the storyline or mission success. Instead, she is there to confirm Bond's virility by serving as an "object of desire" that he gazes at and oftentimes sleeps with before committing to his Bond Girl by the end of the film. Charles Burnetts likens these women to " 'fluffers' in the porn industry, [as] they keep the male 'agent' aroused until the primary sexual object, the Bond Girl, arrives at which point they disappear off-screen" (60). Bond conveys a sense of entitlement when it comes to accessing the bodies of "secondary girls," many of whom are civilians, thus revealing the misogyny that often underlines his libido-based masculinity.

Thunderball (Young 1965) features a deeply troublesome sequence in which Bond sexually harasses a nurse at the health clinic Shrublands. During his visit, Bond propositions Patricia Fearing verbally and physically. Fearing is clearly uncomfortable with Bond's advances, especially when he traps her in an embrace and forcefully kisses her. When she finally pushes him away, she looks disheveled and exasperated as Bond's sexual harassment escalates into assault. Later, after Bond is attacked by a fellow patient while laying on a motorized traction table, Fearing apologizes, believing the incident was the result of her neglect. Instead of correcting Fearing, Bond capitalizes on her vulnerability and agrees not to issue a formal complaint for "a price." He follows her into a Turkish bath as she states "Oh, no no no" while wagging her finger at him. She can be seen leaning against the frosted glass as Bond takes off her uniform. The film seemingly applauds Bond for his persistence and frames his "payoff" in a playful manner.

Like other Bond women, Patricia Fearing has a double entendre for a name, but the sexually suggestive secondary meaning highlights her trepidation of Bond on personal and professional levels. Moreover, her name challenges the coding of their encounter as consensual. As explained by Susan Leahy, "Where an individual submits to sexual activity because of a threat that a secret will otherwise be revealed, this cannot be said to be an autonomous choice" (312). This scene challenges the libidinal masculinity of Bond and his positioning as a hero given his reliance on deception, intimidation, and violence to accomplish his goal—something that a villain like Rosa Klebb would do. In both the novel and film adaptation of *From Russia with Love*, Klebb's sexual harassment of Romanova is deemed inappropriate given her position of authority as well as broader notions of sexual deviancy associated with lesbianism at the time. By comparison, *Thunderball* attempts to code Bond's sexual harassment as harmless fun. Since the exchange takes place outside of an official mission, his actions are personal rather than professional. In other words, his sexual misconduct cannot be explained away as a field tactic and he thus comes across as predatory.

Bond also has disturbing encounters with a series of "golden" "secondary girls" in the opening scenes of *Goldfinger*. First, Bond dismisses his companion Dink to order to engage in "man talk" with Felix Leiter. He tells her to "say goodbye," but before she can verbally respond, Bond spins her around and slaps her butt to shoo her away. The sexual silencing of another woman occurs a few scenes later after Bond seduces Jill Masterson, the kept woman of the villain. Bond awakens to find her naked and dead in their bed, her body covered in gold paint. Both encounters take place within ten minutes of the opening title sequence, which features close-up shots of a woman painted in gold. As noted by Sabine Planka,

> the gold color stylizes the [female] body into a luxurious object that one can possess or collect. The title sequence both foreshadows and commemorates the violence that is to come through the symbolic and aesthetic rendering of the golden female body. And it is this element—a female body marked symbolically and aesthetically by violence—that draws the viewers into the diegesis. (143)

Thus the objectification and silencing of golden women in the opening scenes of *Goldfinger* establishes a dangerous precedent of sexualized violence that culminates in Bond's assault on Pussy Galore later in the film (see analysis above).

This imagery appears again in *Diamonds Are Forever* (Hamilton 1971), the final film in the Connery era. The film opens with Bond tracking down the elusive Blofeld and questioning his accomplices. Bond eventually approaches Marie, who is sunbathing face down in a gold bikini—an image that recalls the death of Masterson and thus anticipates the disposability of Marie. When she asks if she can do anything for him, Bond reaches around her body, unclips her bikini top, and wraps it around her neck, briefly exposing her breasts to the viewer in the process. As Bond tightens the makeshift noose, the topless woman gasps for air and the film cuts to her frightened face in a close-up shot. When the woman does not respond to his questions (since she cannot talk), Bond quips, "Speak up darling, I can't hear you." The film cuts away from this scene without addressing her fate.

This thirty-second scene not only presents a startling image of gender-based violence but also has little influence on the plot. The film tries to downplay the violence by having Marie moan in a sexually suggestive way during the attack, but the camera is focused on Bond when this happens. Given the frequency of voice dubbing throughout the Connery era (see Funnell 2008), this response may have been added in post-production to adjust the tone of the scene. And yet, this moan does not negate the violence endured by Marie or the lack of consent she expresses through her body (since she clearly cannot speak). With no further mention of Marie, we are left with the violent image of Bond stripping a woman of her clothing, agency, and voice. *Diamonds Are Forever* closes out the Connery era by demonstrating that once again Bond is not opposed to sexually harassing, assaulting, and silencing women operating both inside *and* outside of the service.

Post-Craig Era

The Connery era establishes many of the conventions that have come to define the Bond film franchise. In the inaugural *Dr. No*, Honey Ryder explains to Bond that she was raped; the film relays the importance of affirmative consent by framing sexual assault as a deplorable act. Yet, across the Connery era, Bond continually enacts sexual violence on women and disregards their bodily autonomy. While this should render him a villain or at the very least frame him as being less than heroic, Connery's Bond, with this white libidinal masculinity, has become a cultural icon and one of the most popular iterations of the character. His attitudes toward women are reflective of the time (but were never okay) and exemplify some of the reasons why second-wave feminists challenged the patriarchal ideologies governing social structures and interactions. By raising awareness about sexual harassment, assault, and rape, they began to draw attention to the importance of physical safety and psychological security in all spheres of life, including the workplace and relationships.

As the series progresses, Bond's attitude toward and treatment of women begins to be adjusted. While a detailed consideration of the next four decades is beyond the scope of this study, it is important to note that misogyny and sexual violence have not been expunged from the series. The Craig-era film *Quantum of Solace* (2008) features an homage to the death of Jill Masterson in *Goldfinger* as Strawberry Fields is discovered lying face down in bed with her naked body covered in crude oil. *Skyfall* (2012) features an uncomfortable sex scene between Severine and Bond behind frosted/steamed glass reminiscent of *Thunderball*. Bond walks in on Severine showering after she has just relayed her backstory of sexual exploitation (i.e., she is a kept woman and sex worker) and she is subsequently murdered by her captor Silva for her (sexual) betrayal. In *Spectre* (2015), although Dr. Madeleine Swann does not experience sexual violence, she is a composite figure of various Bond Girls across the series (Funnell, "Reworking" 19), such as Honey Ryder, who have been the victims of such violence. Moreover, her decision to walk away from Bond is not respected; she is "stripped of her agency" by the villain Blofeld who kidnaps her, effectively transforming her into the "princess in the castle" who requires saving from Bond (20).

These scenes draw into question the *necessity* of sexual violence and conquest in the contemporary franchise, especially in light of the recent #TimesUp and #MeToo movements. Given the connection between the Connery- and Craig-era films, will the franchise continue to employ sexually exploitative strategies in future films that effectively feed into a (spy) culture of misogyny and white imperialist masculinity that justifies the infliction of sexual violence on women? Or will they (begin to) respect the bodily autonomy and sexual identities of women within the world of Bond? Only time will tell.

Works Cited

Black, Jeremy. *The Politics of James Bond: From Fleming's Novels to the Big Screen.* Lincoln: University of Nebraska Press, 2005.

Brown, Roderick. "Corrective Rape in South Africa: A Continuing Plight Despite an International Human Rights Response." *Annual Survey of International & Comparative Law* 18, no. 1 (2012): 45–66.

Burnetts, Charles. "Bond's Bit on the Side: Race, Exoticism, and the Bond 'Fluffer' Character." In *For His Eyes Only: The Women of James Bond*, ed. Lisa Funnell. London: Wallflower, 2015. 60–69.

Chapman, James. "'Women Were for Recreation': The Gender Politics of Ian Fleming's James Bond." In *For His Eyes Only: The Women of James Bond*, ed. Lisa Funnell. London: Wallflower, 2015. 7–17.

Fleming, Ian. *Casino Royale.* 1953. Penguin Classics ed. London: Penguin, 2004.

———. *Diamonds Are Forever.* 1956. Penguin Classics ed. London: Penguin, 2004.

———. *Dr. No.* 1958. Penguin Classics ed. London: Penguin, 2004.

———. *From Russia, With Love.* 1957. Penguin Classics ed. London: Penguin, 2004.

———. *Goldfinger.* 1959. Penguin Classics ed. London: Penguin, 2004.

———. *Live and Let Die.* 1954. Penguin Classics ed. London: Penguin, 2004.

———. *Moonraker.* 1955. Penguin Classics ed. London: Penguin, 2004.

———. *On Her Majesty's Secret Service.* 1963. Penguin Classics ed. London: Penguin, 2004.

———. *The Spy Who Loved Me.* 1962. Penguin Classics ed. London: Penguin, 2004.

———. *Thunderball.* 1961. Penguin Classics ed. London: Penguin, 2004.

Funnell, Lisa. "From English Partner to American Action Hero: The Heroic Identity and Transnational Appeal of the Bond Girl." In *Heroines and Heroes: Symbolism, Embodiment, Narratives, and Identity*, ed. Christopher Hart. Kingswinford, UK: Midrash, 2008. 61–80.

———. "I Know Where You Keep Your Gun": Daniel Craig as the Bond-Bond Girl Hybrid in *Casino Royale.*" *Journal of Popular Culture* 44, no. 3 (2011): 455–472.

———. "Objects of White Male Desire: (D)Evolving Representations of Asian Women in Bond Films." In *For His Eyes Only: The Women of James Bond*, ed. Lisa Funnell. London: Wallflower, 2015. 79–87.

———. "Reworking the Bond Girl Concept in the Craig Era." *Journal of Popular Film and Television* 46, no. 1 (2018): 11–21.

Funnell, Lisa, and Klaus Dodds. *Geographies, Genders and Geopolitics of James Bond.* London: Palgrave Macmillan, 2017.

Hawkins, Harriet. *Classics and Trash: Traditions and Taboos in High Literature and Popular Modern Genres.* Toronto: University of Toronto Press, 1990.

Leahy, Susan. "'No Means No,' but Where's the Force? Addressing the Challenges of Formally Recognizing Non-Violent Sexual Coercion as a Serious Criminal Offence." *Journal of Criminal Law* 79 (2014): 309–325.

McRobbie, Angela. *The Aftermath of Feminism: Gender, Culture and Social Change*. London: Sage, 2008.

Mulvey, Laura. "Visual Pleasure and Narrative Cinema." In *Film Theory and Criticism: Introductory Readings*, ed. Leo Braudy and Marshall Cohen. New York: Oxford University Press, 1999. 833–844.

Piotrowska, Anna. "Female Voice and Bond Films." In *For His Eyes Only: The Women of James Bond*, ed. Lisa Funnell. London: Wallflower, 2015. 167–175.

Planka, Sabine. "Female Bodies in the James Bond Title Sequences." In *For His Eyes Only: The Women of James Bond*, ed. Lisa Funnell. London: Wallflower, 2015. 139–147.

Wood, Julia T., *Gendered Lives: Communication, Gender, & Culture*. 10th edition. Boston: Wadsworth Cengage Learning, 2013.

CHAPTER 2

Before #MeToo

Maria Schneider and the Cultural Politics of Victimhood

Sabrina Moro

Throughout her life, French actor Maria Schneider (1952–2011) was vocal against sexism in the film industry. She vehemently criticized director Bernardo Bertolucci for the emotional and psychological exploitation she endured on the set of *Last Tango in Paris* (1972). In a 1976 interview with Delphine Seyrig, Schneider denounced her systematic exclusion from the creative and executive decision process by Bertolucci and her co-star Marlon Brando. She revealed the extent of Bertolucci's abuse in 2007, detailing how the infamous rape scene was written and filmed without her consent (Das). However, it was only in December 2016 that Bertolucci's abuse of Schneider drew public outrage in the entertainment industry, when a clip from a 2013 press tour resurfaced in which he admitted that the filming of the scene was nonconsensual. The clip is an excerpt from an interview with Bertolucci at the Cinémathèque Française, edited and published by a Spanish nonprofit on the 25th of November in recognition of the International Day for the Elimination of Violence Against Women. The story was picked up by *Elle* magazine in an article titled "Bertolucci Admits He Conspired to Shoot a Non-Consensual Rape Scene in *Last Tango in Paris*" (Khan). The article prompted several

Hollywood celebrities to publicly condemn the filmmaker and reconsider the place of *Last of Tango in Paris* within the film canon.

The story raises important questions pertaining to the cultural and social transformations in U.S. society's attitudes toward sexual violence. Why wasn't Schneider's testimony heard for nearly four decades? Why did it take so long for Bertolucci's abuse to be condemned by the film industry? According to the media coverage, it is because sexual assault was less taboo in 2016 than it was in 1973. For instance, the *Elle* article includes hyperlinks to Schneider's 2007 *Daily Mail* interview and Bertolucci's 2013 panel discussion at the Cinémathèque Française to imply that the evidence needed to believe Schneider's testimony was already accessible, but recent cultural shifts made it legible. Similarly, a *Washington Post* article situates renewed interest in Schneider's testimony within a news cycle increasingly concerned with the treatment of women in the entertainment industry, citing for instance the highly publicized 2014 Bill Cosby sexual assault cases (Izadi). Other media outlets highlight the role of celebrities in galvanizing the public outcry against Bertolucci. For instance, a *Guardian* article cites tweets by Ava DuVernay, Jessica Chastain, and Anna Kendrick, who have all since been outspoken against sexual harassment in the film industry[1] (Summers).

This rewriting of Schneider's testimony as celebrity news fits neatly into a linear narrative of social change that would explain the #MeToo and #TimesUp era as a revolution led by famous women who finally found the courage to speak out. The present chapter explores why Schneider's sexual assault testimony remained unintelligible for more than forty years yet complicates the claims that Schneider's sexual assault testimony became legible solely because it was caught in the wind of change that brought about moments of mass disclosure culminating in #MeToo and #TimesUp.

I draw on celebrity studies and feminist media scholarship to interrogate the political potential of celebrity sexual assault narratives. Specifically, I am interested in the ways in which the claim of a new era for believing women who speak out against powerful men obscures gendered hierarchies of fame still in place. Similarly, I nuance the sudden interest in Schneider's testimony, and indeed a news cycle invested in prominent women's indictment of sexism, as also being symptomatic of a convergence of celebrity culture and confessional media cultures. The aim of this chapter is thus to interrogate the complex visibility of sexual assault narratives in the public sphere. I undertake a close reading of interviews in which Schneider exposed the abuse she experienced on the set of *Last Tango in Paris*, asking what they reveal about the ways in which celebrity culture reconfigures victimhood and feminist politics. I argue that the contested reception of Schneider's account of sexual assault reveals the contours of a form of agency that troubles dominant construction of victimhood.

The *Last Tango in Paris* Controversy

The film *Last Tango in Paris* focuses on an encounter between Paul (Marlon Brando), an American businessman in his forties distraught by his wife's recent suicide, and Jeanne (Maria Schneider), a young French woman in her twenties engaged to a documentary filmmaker. They meet in an apartment in Paris they are both interested in renting and immediately start a sexual relationship. On Paul's insistence, they agree to remain anonymous and keep their affair secret. The film revolves around a series of similar sexual encounters that become increasingly degrading and violent as Paul becomes more controlling. This abusive pattern culminates with the infamous rape scene in which Paul pins Jeanne on the floor of the apartment and uses butter as a lubricant to anally rape Jeanne. Paul's abusive behavior continues in the following encounters as he suddenly demands they share with each other intimate stories, revealing his wife's tragic death and other personal details. Jeanne eventually ends her relationship with Paul. Unable to let her go, Paul follows her home, tells her he loves her, and asks what her name is. Jeanne reveals her name before fatally shooting him.

The film was controversial for its multiple scenes of female nudity, graphic portrayal of sexual violence, and themes. Whilst some critics acclaimed Bertolucci for challenging society's conformism and exploring the dark side of the sexual revolution, others deemed the explicit sexual content gratuitous and pornographic. In France and in the United States, the film got the adult-only 18+ or X rating, while it was censored in other countries, including Bertolucci's native Italy where he was prosecuted for obscenity (Schneider 60). These regulations were framed by critics as a selling point, inviting moviegoers to decide for themselves whether the film's multiple sex scenes "shocked, titillated, disgusted, fascinated, delighted or angered [them]" ("Self-Portrait of an Angel and Monster"). The virulent debates surrounding the film attest to the profound sociocultural changes of the early 1970s, in the aftermath of May '68, the sexual liberation, and the rise of feminist movements (Schneider 65; Nuytten and July). They also contributed to the film's commercial success by exploiting its treatment of sexuality as scandalous.

This was particularly salient in interviews with Brando and Schneider where questions about their relationship on- and off-set fed into the clamour. For instance, a *Time* magazine article picked up on rumors: "there were whispers that [Brando] was more than a daddy [to Schneider], that the intense sexual encounters in the film were not all simulated" ("Self-Portrait of an Angel and Monster"). The article then proceeded to draw parallels between Brando's personal life and his character's arc, leveling Brando's tumultuous love life with Paul's emotional and sexual intensity. Similarly, a *New York Times* interview with Schneider used the speculations on the sex scenes to reveal intimate details about the actor, including her bisexuality, portraying her as a precocious and promiscuous girl (Klemesrud). The actors' sexuality thus became an additional source of scandal to promote the film. These interviews cemented Brando's and Schneider's star images within the scandalous reputation of the *Last Tango in Paris*.

Celebrity Agency and the Conditions of Speaking Out

Interviews with film stars constitute an example of what Sean Redmond has termed celebrity confessional texts—that is, moments of revelation and affective display that allow a celebrity to consolidate their public persona (152). According to Redmond, the celebrity confessional operates on three elements: meditations on fame, self-criticism, and a performance of intimacy. These self-reflexive moments produce a paradoxical narrative: the celebrity may be critical of the demands put on them by the manufacture of publicity, yet they owe the industry this discursive space to voice their criticism. Consequently, it is important to consider both the content and the context of enunciation of celebrity sexual assault testimonies. Indeed, the changing legibility of Schneider's story exemplifies the ways in which celebrity first-person accounts of sexual assault are either silenced or amplified, depending on the cultural configurations in which they are shared.

Lorraine York's conceptualization of celebrity agency is helpful to interrogate the legibility of Schneider's testimony. York defines celebrity

agency as a "web of relational, contextual agendas" (1341) that structures and constrains the industry of fame, rather than an idiosyncratic
quality that individual celebrities possess or loose. For York, celebrity is
conceptualized as "a sum of industrial relations of power" (1340), and
celebrity agency is one of the many forces at play in celebrity culture.
To understand celebrity agency in terms of industrial interactions enables
an analysis of celebrity sexual assault testimony attuned to the complex
operations of public visibility. Celebrity agency is thus a concept that
allows us to consider famous women's intervention in the public sphere
stemming from their inner strength *and* a window of opportunity in
celebrity culture.

Schneider's sexual assault testimony can be retrieved through a
textual analysis of a range of interviews with the actor in Francophone
and Anglophone media, spanning over four decades. In addition to these
various media appearances, the (auto)biography published posthumously
by her cousin and confidant Vanessa Schneider, which they had originally planned on writing together, provides invaluable archival material.
This corpus of celebrity confessional texts addresses the evolutions of
the actor's star image as she gained international recognition. It also
makes tangible the industrial forces shaping opportunities for high-profile
women to denounce sexism in Hollywood.

I situate my discussion within media studies scholarship on confessional media cultures (Nunn and Biressi 2010), testimonial cultures
(Ahmed and Stacey 2001), and the commodification of therapeutic
biographies (Illouz 2007). This body of work shows that the demands
for a performance of authenticity and intimacy made upon celebrities are
imbricated within a larger ideology of intimacy predicated on the cultural
imperative to perform a range of emotions in public. My analysis thus
weaves through this bilingual corpus to retrieve some of the nuances of
Schneider's testimony that would help contextualize her fraught celebrity
agency. In each section, I explore similarities and differences in the ways
in which French and U.S. media construct Schneider's celebrity persona.

The Gendered Hierarchies of Fame

Schneider's celebrity agency depends on gendered hierarchies at play
within celebrity culture. Chris Rojek's classification of celebrity is useful in
showing how certain modes of visibility are privileged over others. Rojek

identifies three types of fame: achieved celebrities are famous because of their personal talent and accomplishment in a particular field; ascribed celebrities owe their media visibility to their lineage; attributed celebrities are noteworthy because of the sheer amount of media attention they galvanize (19). This typology posits achieved celebrity as more legitimate than ascribed and attributed celebrity. Indeed, achieved celebrity reifies an active subject whose cultural worth is realized through their actions. In contrast, ascribed and attributed celebrity are relegated to the realm of representation and undeserving publicity.

As Su Holmes and Diane Negra argue, this typology of celebrity culture upholds gendered assumptions around work, status, and the legitimacy of fame. This is further demonstrated by Brenda Weber, who notes that "fame marks aspiration; celebrity brands ambition. Fame indicates valour; celebrity stains scandal" (18). It casts achieved celebrity as inherently male and attributed celebrity as female, thus reinforcing longstanding anxieties over women's presence in the public sphere. Consequently, managing the transition from attributed celebrity to achieved celebrity is particularly decisive for female celebrities. As Melanie Kennedy notes, this demand is even more pronounced for young female celebrities. Her work locates the tween celebrity as the ideal postfeminist and neoliberal subject (4). The postfeminist ethos of self-discipline is framed as the aspirational ideal the rising star should strive toward, and the figure of the trainwreck celebrity is construed as a warning sign.

Maria Schneider's celebrity persona crystallizes most of the anxieties around female tween celebrity victims. She is first introduced by the French media as the illegitimate teenage daughter of famous actor Daniel Gélin, which casts her into the realm of ascribed celebrity. This narrative of underserved fame is further developed in the media coverage of the *Last Tango in Paris* release. The public outrage around the film's release stains Schneider's ascent to fame and circumscribes her public image to attributed celebrity. For instance, a 1978 *Paris Match* article "Maria Schneider: cinema's lost child" summarizes Schneider's career as "the scandal, but also the fabulous success of *Last Tango in Paris*"[2] (Chateauneu, my translation). Schneider's fame is attributed to the scandalous success of the film, which capitalizes on the actor's sexualized physical appearance, rather than her acting skills. She is described as a "cover-girl" who possesses the "eroticism of an unripe fruit" and is admired by the "gray-haired men who fancy Lolita"[3] (Chateauneu, my translation). The emphasis on Schneider's lineage and physical attributes infantilizes the actor and frames her career within the realm of ascribed and attributed celebrity.

Schneider herself criticized the impact this type of media discourse had on her personal life in a 2007 interview with the *Daily Mail*: "I was treated like a sex symbol—I wanted to be recognized as an actor and the whole scandal and aftermath of the film turned me a little crazy and I had a breakdown" (Das). This downward spiral is central in the discursive construction of Schneider as a trainwreck celebrity who failed to manage the transition into achieved celebrity. For instance, the *Paris Match* article details gossips pertaining to Schneider's drug use and mental health history as further evidence of her professional missteps. Schneider's bisexuality is evoked as further evidence of her scandalous reputation and as a way to legitimize these intrusions into the actor's intimate life. As Chateauneu writes, "the price of fame is heavy when one has captivated millions of eyes with one's body and moves"[4] (my translation). Not only does this excerpt reify rape myths framing bisexual women as promiscuous (Johnson ad Grove 440), it also upholds gendered hierarchies of fame by positing female stardom and sexual violence as mutually constitutive.

The double standard of celebrity culture is most salient when considering the ways in which Schneider's sexuality is used as a rationale to construct her trainwreck persona, whereas Bertolucci's sexual history sustains his *auteur* persona. Indeed, Bertolucci was praised for the graphic depictions of sex in *The Last Tango in Paris*, which, according to critics, challenges social norms. For example, Joan Mellen writes that the film "is an indictment of the bourgeois family which dominates culture and society" (10). Bertolucci claims the rape scene was meant to be political. However, its political potential is limited by its inability to aesthetically challenge the "male gaze" (Mulvey) and fundamentally alter the gendered power relations at play in the film industry (Beattie). The centrality of the heteronormative male gaze in the film for which Bertolucci was praised is all the more relevant to consider given how Schneider's bisexuality was used to discredit the actor (see Chateauneu; Klemesrud). While Bertolucci received accolades such as an Academy Award nomination for his rebellious reputation and went on to have a successful career, Schneider's celebrity image is forever tainted by the infamous *Last Tango in Paris*. The willingness to separate the man from the artist while holding women accountable for their sexuality is symptomatic of a widespread double standard at play in the film industry.

In addition, the figure of the male *auteur* further sustains this gendered hierarchy, which authorizes the emotional and physical exploitation of the actor in the name of art.

According to Schneider, Bertolucci mined her and Brando's personal life for inspiration. In a 2004 *Paris Match* interview, Schneider says that she and her co-star felt used by the director, who submitted them to intensive improvisation sessions, forcing them to share childhood memories. For Schneider, this emotional exploitation "proved to be more indecent than nudity scenes"[5] (Schneider 181, my translation). Yet, this self-referential practice is one-sided, and the *auteur* draws the line at their private lives. For instance, Bertolucci explains that he edited out a shot of Brando's genitalia because he strongly identified with the actor: "I cut it out of shame for myself. To show him naked would have been like showing myself naked." (Mellen 13). Bertolucci's willingness to exploit the personal life of his actors into his creative work is thus gendered. In addition, this rhetoric of emotional and sexual exploitation in the name of art sustains *auteur* apologism, a standard practice that calls for the separation of the art from the artist persona and is often used as a defence to excuse criminal acts of iconic male artists (Marghitu 492).

Schneider's testimony further sheds light on the depth and pervasiveness of sexism in the entertainment industry. In the *Daily Mail* interview, Schneider explains how the assault was set up by her colleagues:

> That scene wasn't in the original script. The truth is it was Marlon who came up with the idea. [. . .] [Bertolucci and Marlon] only told me about it before we had to film the scene and I was so angry. I should have called my agent or had my lawyer come to the set because you can't force someone to do something that isn't in the script, but at the time, I didn't know that. (Das)

Not only does her account denounce one of many instances where the lead actor and filmmaker abused their directorial authority, but it also places the on-camera assaults on a continuum of sexist violence entrenched in Hollywood in which some agents of celebrification, such as directors and producers, can also be perpetrators.

Gendered assumptions around labor and legitimacy of fame cast Schneider as a trainwreck celebrity and Bertolucci as a celebrated artist. This value system bolsters the practices of disbelief that presents

Schneider as a "tainted witness" (Serisier 200), thus making her sexual assault testimony illegible. Moreover, the celebrity confessional itself reinforces cultural configurations that give more weight and credibility to male voices. Indeed, Schneider's story was not sufficient to garner media attention or belief on its own; Bertolucci's own admission was needed to validate her testimony. This example best illustrates the gendered double standard of the celebrity confessional: Bertolucci's word was needed to support Schneider's allegations against him. It also points to the ways in which first-person accounts of sexual violence are dismissed.

However, the fact that Bertolucci's 2013 confession was not admitted as evidence of abuse until 2016 complicates the ways in which authority and agency operate within the celebrity confessional. Bertolucci's confessions are shaped by the same industrial forces that delineate the credibility of Schneider's account. The correlation between social status and the amount of support powerful men accused of sexual assault receive (Boyle 114) explains the different responses to Bertolucci's confession. In 2016, Bertolucci was no longer at the height of his fame and power[6] and thus didn't benefit from "himpathy" (Boyle 109). Bertolucci faced backlash not when he admitted the abuse but when his revelation could easily be rewritten as an anomaly that would not directly take on the sexist premises of celebrity culture.

The Cultural Politics of Victimhood

Schneider's resistance to being victimized explicitly challenges the industrial structures that configure her agency, which explains why her testimony was illegible for so long. The cultural hierarchy of fame I discussed earlier supports a specific testimonial genre that relies on the postfeminist neoliberal subject to overcome the passivity of victimhood to become an active survivor (Serisier 15). The figure of the trainwreck celebrity is once more invoked as a caveat to the celebrity role model; it represents the postfeminist victim's failure to deal with the impact of both stardom and sexual violence. The production of Schneider's trainwreck persona makes explicit the convergence of cultural anxieties around the "appropriate" transition from girl to woman, attributed to achieved celebrity, and victim to survivor. This triple demand made upon young female celebrities highlights the double bind in which famous women are caught: "their success depends on their sexualization, yet their sexualization undermines the seriousness with which they are judged not only as artists but also [. . .] as victim/survivors of sexual exploitation and abuse" (Boyle 81).

Schneider speaks to the transformative potential and challenges of public narratives of sexual violence. Her testimony exemplifies, yet complicates, a narrative in which the victim becomes a survivor. For example, in an interview for the *Cinéma Cinémas* series, Maria Schneider resists being defined by the *Last Tango in Paris* controversy ("Interview Maria Schneider," my translation):

> MARIA SCHNEIDER: No. I don't want to talk about the *Tango*. [Silence]

> JOURNALIST: You are not able to separate the film's strength from what you experienced.

> MARIA SCHNEIDER: [Sigh] It's a film, that's all. [. . .] I do not want to be forever associated with it. Everywhere, the *Tango* is always with me. Well. [Silence] *Basta*. [Silence]. Besides, I prefer to talk about *The Passenger*, which is a film closer to me. If we are to talk about me, let's talk about this one.[7]

The journalist's statement suggests that Schneider's refusal to discuss *Last Tango in Paris* amounts to a rejection of the very media event that made her famous. It implies that Schneider's celebrity persona is inextricable from the film because it contributed to her fame and, as such, will always be a feature of her celebrity confessional. Consequently, Schneider's refusal to be victimized attests to the oppressive media surveillance she experienced as a young female celebrity. Furthermore, the actor's reference to *The Passenger*, filmed two years after *Last Tango in Paris*, reorients the conversation toward her ongoing professional and personal development. It illustrates the ways in which the discourse around sexual violence relies on an imperative of "moving on." However, I also read Schneider's resistance throughout the interview as an attempt to challenge the cultural expectations that would cast her as a survivor and role model. This becomes salient through the media coverage of Schneider's drug use and mental health history.

Schneider's struggles with drug use and addiction are recounted in the biography written by her cousin Vanessa Schneider. The book weaves a personal account of the actor's life with a reflection on the impact her career and fame had on her and her family. Through this hybridization of two genres—biography and memoir—Vanessa Schneider reveals her enduring childhood fascination for the actor seventeen years her senior, but also the emotional toll supporting her cousin through numerous drug-related hospitalizations during her teenage years. Vanessa presents Maria as her personal hero; her story contrasts her uneventful daily routine with descriptions from afar of her cousin's extraordinary life. Vanessa's (auto)biography offers a compassionate account of her cousin's struggles, as well as a critique of rampant sexism within the film industry. It nonetheless reasserts Maria's failure—or perhaps refusal—to become a role model, thus rejecting the expected survivor narrative.

The book, like most media coverage of Schneider's career, draws on the metaphor of the rising star hindered in her ascent by misfortune. These narratives revolve around the assumption that an immediate fame is unsustainable. For example, an article published seven years after the *Last Tango in Paris* describes the then twenty-year-old actor as "a child unknown the day before, who brutally took off to the peak of her glory with her acid charm and her halo of depraved *ingénue*" (Chateauneu, my translation).[8] The analogy of the fleeting fame is supported by the figure of the woman-child, forever caught between childhood and womanhood, between attributed and achieved celebrity. The eulogy Brigitte Bardot wrote for Schneider's funeral relies on a similar trope and describes the late actor's career as both sudden and short-lived:

> With her eternal woman-child face and her wild little cat-like character, she conquered the world with the dazzling speed of a burning meteorite, pulverising everything in its wake! Blazing yet ephemeral trajectory, offering her velvet body to Marlon Brando at the pinnacle of his glory, she shocked, her impudence scandalised, but her insolence marked forever an era she now personifies. (Schneider 41, my translation)[9]

Whilst celebrating Schneider's achievement and praising her irreverence toward an industry that thrives on the exploitation of young female bodies, Bardot's tribute also reifies Schneider's debauched *ingénue* on- and off-screen star image.

Schneider's wrecked *ingénue* persona overshadows her resistance to the exploitative regime of celebrity culture. In 1975, *Elle* magazine published the transcript of an interview in which Schneider opposes the codes of the celebrity confessional:

CATHERINE LAPORTE: Do you like your job as an actor?

MARIA SCHNEIDER: It's not really work.

CL: What do you do when you are not filming?

MS: I hang about.

CL: And when you are filming?

MS: I also hang about. [. . .]

CL: Are you a politically engaged actor?

MS: I am nothing.

CL: Are you uncomfortable in your own skin?

MS: What do you think . . .

CL: You don't like interviews?

MS: No, I have nothing to say. (Schneider 76–77, my translation)[10]

While Schneider's disavowal of acting as "work" was mostly commented upon by the media as symptomatic of the "whirlwind [of drugs and sexual "provocations] in which she almost lost herself"[11] (Chateauneu, my translation), I argue that this interview gestures toward the actor's sustained critique of the film industry.

Indeed, Schneider's impassivity not only challenges the journalist's intrusive questions, it also subverts the economic value of celebrity performance of intimacy. Through a display of utter indifference, Schneider effectively resists the ways in which the media take advantage of the affective spectacle of tween stardom. In dismissing acting as work, Schneider also responds with irony to the "realism" defense voiced by directors such as Bertolucci, Sam Peckinpah, and Alejandro Jodorowsky to justify their unsafe rape choreography (Wolfe). In arguing that not discussing sexual assault scenes with actors beforehand leads to more realistic representations, the filmmakers imply a distrust in the actors' professional skills.

Schneider clarifies her critique of the sexist premise of female stardom the following year in an interview with Seyrig (1976) and develops her position in subsequent interviews. She attributes the lack of interesting female roles and the on-set exploitation of young female actors to an overwhelmingly masculine workforce—from casting directors to technicians to directors to film critics. She repeatedly points out the great age discrepancy between male and female leads and its consequences for early career actors. For instance, speaking up against Bertolucci's manipulative practices, she states: "Brando felt cheated, violated, abused. Me too. But he was fifty and I was twenty"[12] (Schneider 227, my translation). Schneider's resistance to being victimized is thus supported by an eloquent critique of the ways that the exploitation and sexualization of young girls and celebrity culture are mutually constitutive.

However, her feminist analysis of the film industry is obfuscated by the very gendered hierarchies of fame she denounces. She gained international recognition through the media coverage of the controversy surrounding the release of *Last Tango in Paris* that cast her as a sexual icon of the 1970s. Schneider's activism is erased because her celebrity status derives from the sexist and heteronormative structures that permeate film stardom. As a publicly out bisexual woman, Schneider challenges the heteronormativity that stems from the misogyny at play in the film industry. Yet, her sexual orientation is noticeably absent from accounts of her sexual assault. It is evoked only in articles that portray her as a downfallen *ingénue*. This association of bisexuality with sexual and celebrity provocations is symptomatic of broader power dynamics. Indeed, bisexual women occupy a liminal position in the media: they are both hypervisible as a male sexual fantasy and invisible for their potential to unthink heterosexuality (San Filippo 16). In addition, the hypersexualization of bisexual women upholds rape myths centred on disbelief and victim blaming (Johnson and Grove 443). Schneider's status as a (bi)sexual icon rendered her illegible as a sexual assault victim until Bertolucci corroborated her claims.

The political dimension of her sexual assault testimony remains unintelligible for the most part until after her death because her critique of the film industry resists the demands of the celebrity confessional.

The hostility she expresses in interviews are coded as a failure to comply with the codes of therapeutic culture centered on public displays of vulnerability and redemption narratives. In addition, her challenge to the celebrity confessional troubles the meritocratic myth of hard work that maintains hierarchies of fame. For instance, her struggles with drug addiction are incompatible with the neoliberal self-care governmentality and don't fit within the dominant cultural politics of victimhood. Similarly, her resistance to being victimized is in direct opposition with the cultural imperative that sexual assault survivors move on as part of a broader neoliberal ethos of self-management.

Schneider's critique of the film industry's sexism and heteronormativity is mostly absent from U.S.-based news outlets. Accounts of her sexual assault testimony published by Anglophone media in 2016 only briefly allude to her mental health and struggles with drug use, yet entirely leave out her bisexuality or resistance to being victimized. Her testimony is thus polished in a way that makes it more suitable for the dominant narrative of victimhood at play in therapeutic cultures prevalent in the U.S. mediascape. The omission of her activism and sexual orientation is central to the posthumous reconstruction of Schneider's celebrity image into a symbol of tragic victimization. This explains how her story gained sudden traction in the recent discursive conjecture leading to moments of mass disclosure like #MeToo and #TimesUp.

Conclusion

In this chapter, I argued that Schneider's refusal to be victimized constitutes an act of resistance to the scrutinizing public gaze that objectifies young female celebrities. At the same time, her noncompliance with the cultural imperative to "move on" renders her critique of stardom and sexual violence illegible. Taken together, these two readings of Schneider explain why her sexual assault remained unintelligible for more than forty years. An analytical framework that ignores the celebrity agency and the conditions of speaking out runs the risk of reproducing a linear narrative of social change and glossing over a long history of women's activism within and beyond Hollywood.

Schneider's story sheds lights on the complex operations of fame and the cultural politics of victimhood. It helps better understand which celebrity #MeToo stories will be shared, and which ones will be sidelined. My analysis shows how Schneider's gender, mental health struggles, and bisexuality were used to discredit her. Yet Schneider's posthumous consecration into a tragic sexual assault icon is a powerful reminder that dominant narratives of victimhood are centred on whiteness and Western celebrities. This chapter has explored in detail the interplay of sexism, biphobia, and ableism in rendering sexual assault illegible. Further studies on the intersection of white supremacy, public disclosures of sexual violence, and celebrity culture are warranted.

Hollywood's spectacular recuperation of Schneider's sexual assault narrative is a cautionary tale: whilst the #MeToo and #TimesUp movements have successfully raised awareness on a pervasive continuum of violence in the entertainment industry and beyond, a feminist politics solely based on publicly sharing sexual assault testimonies is inherently limited. As I have demonstrated, the political scope of celebrity confessional texts can be undermined by industrial forces. In Schneider's own words, "in the film industry, like everywhere, men have the power"[13] ("Interview Maria Schneider," my translation). Consequently, what is needed are radical shifts in the gendered power imbalance within the film industry and beyond.

Notes

1. Ava DuVernay and Jessica Chastain signed the open letter that founded the Time's Up foundation and that was published in the *New York Times* on January 1, 2018. Anna Kendrick has supported Time's Up at various red-carpet events.

2. "Maria Schneider, ce fut le scandale mais aussi le fabuleux succès du *Dernier Tango à Paris*."

3. "Elle est alors une sorte de Brigitte Bardot pour temps de contestation générale, seins encore enfantins sous la courte tunique, un érotisme de fruit vert, longues jambes de pensionnaires moulées dans les hautes bottes que chérissent les grisonnants amateurs de Lolita."

4. "Il est lourd le prix à payer, quand on a fasciné avec son corps, ses gestes, des millions de regards."

5. "Nous avons été mal dans notre peau [Brando] et moi lorsque nous avons vu le film pour la première fois. [. . .] Pas tant par les scènes physiques que par ce que nous y disions. Bertolucci nous avait fait faire un gros travail d'improvisation, nous obligeant à livrer des souvenirs de nos enfances respectives. *Cela s'est révélé être plus impudique que les nudités.* Marlon en a été très irrité. Il a eu le sentiment d'être trahi" (emphasis added).

6. Bertolucci's last film was released in 2012. He died in 2018.
7. Maria Schneider: Non. Je ne veux pas parler du *Tango*. [Silence]

Journaliste: Tu n'es pas capable de faire la part de la force du film et de ce que tu as vécu toi.

Maria Schneider: [Soupir] C'est un film, c'est tout. . . . Je ne veux pas qu'on me rattache toujours à ça. Partout, j'ai toujours le *Tango* avec moi. Bon. [Silence] Basta. [Silence] Et d'autre part, je préfère qu'on parle de *Profession : reporter*, qui est un film plus près de moi. Si on veut parler de moi, qu'on parle de celui-là."

8. "une gamine inconnue la veille et qui brutalement s'envolait au sommet de la gloire, avec son charme acide et son auréole de perversité ingénue."
9. "Avec sa bouille d'éternelle femme-enfant et son caractère de petit chat sauvage, elle a conquis le monde avec la fulgurance d'une météorite enflammée qui pulvérisa tout sur son passage! Passage éclatant mais éphémère où, offrant son corps de velours à un Marlon Brando au faîte de sa gloire, elle choqua, scandalisa par son impudeur, mais marqua à jamais par son insolence une époque qu'elle a désormais personnifiée" (Schneider 2018, 41).
10. "Catherine Laporte: Vous aimez votre métier d'actrice?

Maria Schneider: Ce n'est pas vraiment du travail.

CL: Que faites-vous quand vous ne tournez pas?

MS: Je traîne.

CL: Et quand vous tournez?

MS: Je traîne aussi. . . .

CL: Êtes-vous une actrice engagée?

MS: Je ne suis rien.

CL: Êtes-vous bien dans votre peau?

MS: À votre avis . . .

CL: Vous n'aimez pas les interviews?

MS: Non, je n'ai rien à dire."

11. "ce tourbillon [de drogues et provocations sexuelles] où elle a fail se perdre."

12. "Brando s'est senti grugé, violé, abusé. Moi aussi. Mais il avait cinquante ans et j'en avais vingt."

13. "dans le cinéma, comme partout, les hommes ont le pouvoir."

Works Cited

Ahmed, Sara, and Jackie Stacey. "Testimonial Cultures: An Introduction." *Cultural Values* 5, no. 1 (2001): 1–6.

Beattie, Debra. "The Potential for Excess in the Toxic Nature of Gendered Power in the Production of Cinema." *Hecate: An Interdisciplinary Journal of Women's Liberation* 42, no. 2 (2016): 128–139.

Bertolucci, Bernardo, director. *Last Tango in Paris*. Produzioni Europee Associati, Les Productions Artistes Associés, 1972.

Bertolucci, Bernardo. "Bertolucci par Bertolucci : une Leçon de Cinéma." *Cinémathèque Française*, September 14, 2013. www.cinematheque.fr/video/323.html

Boyle, Karen. *#MeToo, Weinstein and Feminism*. London: Palgrave MacMillan, 2019.

Chateauneu, Roger. "Maria Schneider l'enfant perdue du cinéma." *Paris Match*, February 3, 2011 [June 1978]. www.parismatch.com/Culture/Cinema/Disparition-de-Maria-Schneider-l-enfant-perdue-du-cinema-146744

"Interview Maria Schneider." *Cinéma Cinémas*. Antenne 2, Ina.fr, February 2, 1983. www.ina.fr/video/I11034288

Das, Lina. "I Felt Raped by Brando." *Daily Mail*, July 19, 2007. www.dailymail.co.uk/tvshowbiz/article-469646/I-felt-raped-Brando.html

Holmes, Su, and Diane Negra. *In the Limelight and Under the Microscope: Forms and Functions of Female Celebrity*. London: Bloomsbury Academic, 2011.

Illouz, Eva. *Cold Intimacies: The Making of Emotional Capitalism*. Boston: Polity, 2007.

Izadi, Elahe. "Why the *Last Tango in Paris* Rape Scene is Generating Such an Outcry Now." *Washington Post*, December 5, 2016. www.washingtonpost.com/news/arts-and-entertainment/wp/2016/12/05/why-the-last-tango-in-paris-rape-scene-is-generating-such-an-outcry-now

Johnson, Nicole L., and MaryBeth Grove. "Why Us? Toward and Understanding of Bisexual Women's Vulnerability for and Negative Consequences of Sexual Violence." *Journal of Bisexuality* 17, no. 4 (2017): 435–450.

Kennedy, Melanie. "Hannah Montana and Miley Cyrus: 'Becoming' a Woman, 'Becoming' a Star." *Celebrity Studies* 5, no. 3 (2014): 225–241.

Kennedy, Melanie. *Tweenhood. Femininity and Celebrity in Tween Popular Culture*. London: IB Tauris, 2018.

Khan, Mattie. "Bertolucci Admits He Conspired to Shoot a Non-Consensual Rape Scene in *Last Tango in Paris*." *Elle*, December 3, 2016. www.elle.com/

culture/movies-tv/news/a41202/bertolucci-last-tango-in-paris-rape-scene-non-consensual

Klemesrud, Judy. "Maria Says Her 'Tango' Is Not Blue." *New York Times*, February 4, 1973. www.nytimes.com/1973/02/04/archives/maria-says-her-tango-is-not-movies.html

Marghitu, Stefania. "'It's just art': *Auteur* Apologism in the Post-Weinstein era." *Feminist Media Studies* 18, no. 3 (2018): 491–494.

Mellen, Joan. "Sexual Politics and Last Tango in Paris." *Film Quarterly* 26, no. 3 (1973): 9–19.

Mulvey, Laura. *Visual and Other Pleasures*. London: Palgrave, 1989.

Munt, Sally. "*Argumentum and Misericordiam*: The Cultural Politics of Victim Media" *Feminist Media Studies* 17, no. 5 (2017): 866–883.

Nunn, Heather, and Anita Biressi. "'A trust betrayed': Celebrity and the Work of Emotion." *Celebrity Studies* 1, no. 1 (2010): 49–64.

Nuytten, Bruno and Serge July, directors. *Il était une fois . . . Le Dernier Tango à Paris*. Folamour Productions, 2004.

Redmond, Sean. "Pieces of Me: Celebrity Confessional Carnality." *Social Semiotics* 18, no. 2 (2018): 46–161.

Rojek, Chris. *Celebrity*. London: Reaktion Books, 2001.

San Filippo, Maria. *The B Word: Bisexuality in Contemporary Film and Television*. Bloomington: Indiana University Press, 2013.

Schneider, Vanessa. *Tu t'appelais Maria Schneider*. Grasset, 2018.

Serisier, Tanya. "A New Age of Believing Women? Judging Rape Narratives Online." In *Rape Narratives in Motion*, ed. Ulrika Andersson et al. London: Palgrave Macmillan, 2019. 199–222.

Serisier, Tanya. *Speaking Out: Feminism, Rape and Narrative Politics*. London: Palgrave Macmillan, 2018.

Seyrig, Delphine, director. *Sois belle et tais-toi!* Centre Audiovisuel Simone de Beauvoir, 1976.

Summers, Hannah. "Actors Voice Disgust over *Last Tango in Paris* Rape Scene Confession." *The Guardian*, December 4, 2016. www.theguardian.com/film/2016/dec/04/actors-disgust-last-tango-paris-rape-scene-confession-bertolucci

"Self-Portrait of an Angel and Monster." *Time*, January 22, 1973. www.uk.news.yahoo.com/self-portrait-angel-monster-201952426

Weber, Brenda. *Women and Literary Celebrity in the Nineteeth Century: The Transatlantic Production of Fame and Gender*. Farnham, UK: Ashgate, 2012.

Wolfe, April. "Rape Choreography Makes Films Safer, But Still Takes a Toll on Cast and Crew." *LA Weekly*, July 11, 2017. www.laweekly.com/rape-choreography-makes-films-safer-but-still-takes-a-toll-on-cast-and-crew

York, Lorraine. "Star Turn: The Challenges of Theorizing Celebrity Agency." *Journal of Popular Culture* 46, no. 6 (2013): 1330–1347.

CHAPTER 3

A Rapist in My Apartment

Class, Rape, and *Saturday Night Fever*

Katherine Karlin

The #MeToo movement and the drive to incorporate greater represen-tation of women, especially as directors, in the film industry give critics a tool for reappraising the past. This assessment calls into question not only the work of individual directors but the cultural context of the films themselves. It is difficult to watch the intergenerational romance in Woody Allen's *Manhattan* (1979), for example, without reading it as a preemptive excuse for suspect behavior. Nor can we see tropes of sexual seduction—plying a woman with alcohol, perhaps, or physically overpow-ering her because nice girls say no when they mean yes—as innocent rites of courtship. The language of sexual conquest is inextricable from the gendered power dynamics that give it momentum.

This reappraisal is complicated by the critical afterlife a film accretes due to its social or aesthetic relevance. Some movies with an unremarkable theatrical opening found a cult status on video or on streaming services. Sam Mendes's *American Beauty* (1999) and Paul Haggis's *Crash* (2004) in particular have since become punchlines with their initial favorable reception a source of puzzlement. And other movies, *Saturday Night Fever* among them, have become so deeply associated with a particular cultural moment they will always emit a whiff of nostalgia, even to later generations.

Saturday Night Fever, released in 1977 and directed by John Badham, had a marketing campaign that immediately provoked anticipation for an upbeat, youthful musical that captured the style and optimism of the disco era, even though the movie itself is grim. Audiences who went to screenings of *Saturday Night Fever* hoping to catch some of the excitement of the disco scene were not disappointed, however, were they willing to overlook the plot and focus on the songs, the appeal of its young star, and the exuberant dance scenes? Today, the collective memory of this movie may be less about its content and more about its poster, featuring John Travolta as Tony Manero, in white pocketless trousers, pointing to the heavens as he danced; in the original poster, Tony's dance partner, Stephanie Mangano (Karen Lynn Gorney) can be seen flailing in the background, and in later versions she was cropped out of the picture. This memory is also shaped by the phenomenally successful soundtrack album—the best-selling soundtrack for fifteen years before being toppled by Whitney Houston's *The Bodyguard*. The album, mostly songs written and performed by the Australian group the Bee Gees, is credited with igniting the disco craze, although it might be more accurate to say it is the album that took disco out of gay dance venues and Black clubs (Frank 284) and made it popular among straight, young white men, in turn making the Bee Gees and *Saturday Night Fever's* producer, Robert Stigwood, very wealthy. "Because they were white and presented an image of heterosexuality, the Bee Gees and Travolta made disco safe for white, straight, male, young, and middle-class Americans and were crucial to disco successfully crossing over to this new audience" (Frank 288). Many versions of *Saturday Night Fever* circulated for years on broadcast television and in video stores, some bowdlerized.

The long history of *Saturday Night Fever* paraphernalia—the album, the poster, the videocassettes, and even the less-successful sequel, *Staying Alive* (Stallone 1983), obscure the fact that the movie is not simply a cheery musical keyed to take advantage of the disco craze. It is also a desolate, kitchen-sink drama about a working-class kid. It is about violence, racism, and alienation, and, most strikingly, it is about rape. The movie's final act includes not one but two sexual assaults—Tony's attempted rape of his dance partner, Stephanie, and his friends' gang rape of Annette, the girl who pines for him.

The sexual violence central to *Saturday Night Fever* may have been forgotten in part because the movie's feel-good image has outlasted its more brutal content, but also because the film appeared at a moment when the cultural definition of rape was undergoing rapid transformation. Indeed, when Stephanie, after much persuasion via intercom, lets Tony into her home in the final scene, saying, "This is the first time I let a known rapist in my apartment," her indictment was jarring to audiences at the time. Sure, Tony got a little rough. But a *rapist*? After all, it was something of a trope in '70s films that women said no when they really meant yes: look at how easily Susan Anspach's character surrendered to Jack Nicholson's in *Five Easy Pieces* (Rafelson 1970), for example, even after she asked him to leave. As they rehearse for their dance contest, share meals, and walk around Brooklyn, Stephanie repeatedly stresses she is not romantically interested in Tony; keeping their relationship platonic is a condition of her agreeing to partner with him. Yet their bodies have chemistry on the dance floor, and in a tender moment Stephanie rests her head on his shoulder. In their final dance they share a brief kiss. Audiences at the time were primed to detect the disparity between a woman's verbal refusals and carnal desires, and to read the denials as a necessary feint in foreplay. The disparity between Stephanie's words and the audience's interpretation of her body language also reflects the difference between the screenplay and the direction.

The fact that Stephanie calls Tony a rapist, but nonetheless admits him to her apartment, reflects the instability of the social definition of rape at the very moment of the movie's release. Only four years after the passage of Roe v. Wade, as second-wave feminism was ascendant and still struggling to define its contours, 1977 marked a moment when rape was being dragged out of the shadows and discussed as a social problem. The notion that rape was not necessarily the act of a stranger, but could be committed by a friend or family member, was gaining currency in some feminist circles, as it was being dismissed in other discourses. Indeed, the same year *Saturday Night Fever* hit the movie theaters, Duke Law School's journal *Law and Contemporary Problems* published an article on federal sentencing that trivialized the idea of date rape with scare quotes: "Current federal rape legislation does not differentiate between savage attacks by strangers and so-called 'date rape,' that is, intercourse between voluntary companions which may indeed have been forced but only following tolerated sexual foreplay" (Schwartz 4). In the year of the movie's release, Oregon was the first state to end spousal immunity for rape charges; when the law was tested a year later, a jury, swayed by a defense that presented the victim as promiscuous, vengeful, and untrustworthy (Eskow 693), acquitted John Rideout of raping his wife,

Greta (Ledbetter). Although, by 1993, every state had laws allowing prosecution for spousal rape, in the late 1970s the concept was still in play, with the character of the victim under scrutiny.

The confusion on what is and isn't rape that characterized the year is mirrored by the confusing subtexts of the movie, a confusion that to some degree lingers today as men claim they are unable to read consent. *Saturday Night Fever* catches, mid-flight, the moment of '70s zeitgeist that accommodated various—and conflicting—definitions of rape. Molly Haskell wrote during this period that "the closer women come to claiming their rights and achieving independence in real life, the more loudly and stridently films tell us it's a man's world" (213). As an example, she cites the famous end of *The Godfather* (Coppola 1972). When Michael Corleone shuts the door on Kay, it's as if filmmakers were shutting women out of films for the decade. *Saturday Night Fever* reveals both the feminist impulse and the backlash. It features a strong and assertive female character, and then it has its hero assault her. Stephanie's decision to open her door to her assailant at the movie's close may say even more about the ambivalent role of women in '70s film than Kay's isolation.

The ambivalence about rape gestures also to the split personality of the movie as a whole. On the one hand, the exuberant dance scenes, culminating in a much-anticipated contest, constitute the movie we tend to remember: a feel-good romance about striving and succeeding. But *Saturday Night Fever* is also a spare, sometimes brutal, look at working-class life in pre-gentrified Brooklyn, a realist drama that shares more in common with the films of Martin Scorsese than those of Vincente Minnelli. The tug-of-war represents the conflicting visions of two men. On the one hand was Robert Stigwood, an Australian music producer and agent who longed to get into the film industry. Stigwood was a genius of promotion, and he made two key decisions. One was to cast young John Travolta, whose breakout role on the TV sitcom *Welcome Back, Kotter* (1975) had made him something of a teen idol. The other was to corral his clients, the Australian brother act the Bee Gees, best known for pop ballads, into the studio to write and record some disco songs. All the Bee Gees music, some of which is nondiegetic and some of which plays in the club where Tony dances, was dropped into the film post-production, often replacing the Black artists to whose music the dancers were synchronizing their moves (Kashner). The only mention of music in the screenplay is when Tony and Stephanie agree that the

Cape Verdean-American R&B act Tavares is "a good band." But to a large extent the irony of Tony and his racist friends grooving to Black music is undermined by Stigwood's insistence on the Bee Gees.

The other creator was Norman Wexler, a cranky leftist screenwriter known for socially conscious urban dramas like John G. Avildsen's *Joe* (1970) and Sidney Lumet's *Serpico* (1973). Wexler's screenplay brings to light the less savory aspects of Tony's milieu: the exploitative sex, dead-end jobs, bitter racism, and threats of gay-bashing. The dreariness of Tony's life is at odds with the light-as-spun-sugar Bee Gees vocals, intersecting only when the opening-credits song "Staying Alive" trails off with the line, "I'm going nowhere, somebody help me."[1]

Saturday Night Fever is the story of a nineteen-year-old Italian American who clerks in a paint store. His father is a laid-off construction worker, his mother is querulous and depressed, and their relationship is punctuated with a volley of mutual slaps and insults. Their despair deepens when Tony's favored brother quits the priesthood. Tony finds relief only on the weekends, when he and his buddies—Joey, Double J, Gus, and the unhappy Bobby C—dress up and hit the local disco, a shabby affair with the aspirational name 2001 Odyssey. They are "the faces," the kings of the disco floor, especially Tony. Gearing up for a lucrative dance contest, Tony discards Annette, the neighborhood girl who loves him, in favor of the ambitious and elusive Stephanie.

Race is central to the frustration of Tony's gang, who feel they've gotten a raw deal. In the disco scenes, the camera, as if imitating the angry glare of the locals, lingers on 2001 Odyssey's one Black regular. Tony first notices Stephanie because she and her partner are the only dancers who don't leave the floor when the DJ plays a salsa record. The Italian Americans feel their claim to their Bay Ridge neighborhood is under attack by Black and Puerto Rican trespassers. When Gus is hospitalized after a street fight, the gang, acting on little evidence, viciously attack a Puerto Rican social club. These disco kings, appropriating the music and dance from Black, queer, and Puerto Rican spaces, use their rage to uphold their illusion of white superiority.

The movie touches briefly on the hostility Tony and his friends harbor toward gay men, as well. As they strut through a park in midday, the gang encounters a male couple who are thrown into a panic, outnumbered by this dominant, tough-looking and straight-acting pack of youths. The camera cuts to the couple's point of view, and we see Tony and his friends as they appear to anyone in their path: glaring and menacing. It is the only moment in the movie that we switch to a distinctive point of view other than that of Tony, and the shot implies sympathy with the male couple. The scene also firmly establishes the Italian Americans' heterosexual bona fides, in spite of their devotion to disco, which had been, earlier in the decade, a celebratory queer genre. Indeed, the group dancing, the performative nature of their sex acts (Tony's friends watch each other having sex with women outside the disco), and the fastidious grooming rituals demonstrate, as Frank points out, how disco "undermined gender differences and, by implication, heterosexuality" (Frank 296). Conversely, the liminal space of the disco underscores Tony's anxiety about sexuality. Frank makes clear that the anti-disco backlash of the '70s, culminating in the rabid "Disco Demolition Night" in Chicago's Comiskey Park on July 12, 1979, was a violent reaction to the growing visibility and confidence of gay culture. Tony's compatibility with aspects of gay culture feed his resentment.

Indeed, it is Tony's confusion about race and identity that sparks his rage at the film's climax, and, eventually, his assault of Stephanie. On the night of the big dance contest, a Black couple and a Puerto Rican couple outdance the home team (although Tony—and by extension the movie—recognizes the superior talent of the Puerto Rican and not the Black dancers), eliciting a hostile reaction from the 2001 crowd. When the prize money unsurprisingly goes to Tony and Stephanie, Tony is furious, and hands both trophy and prize money to the Puerto Rican couple. "You deserve it," he says.

This is an extraordinary moment of self-awareness. Tony, we would say today, has become cognizant of his own (relative) white privilege,[2] and he refuses to cooperate with the system that grants it. But it is at this very moment that Tony orders Stephanie into Bobby C's car and tries to rape her. Tony's sexual aggression is fueled by his rage against the system—represented by the cronyism of his white neighborhood—and the growing realization that his life is circumscribed by conditions beyond his control. His sexual assault comes directly from his social frustration, and, with his parents' behavior as an example, he naturally transfers this frustration into anti-woman violence.

The belief that a correlation exists between working-class status and violent behavior gained currency in the decades following World War II, largely due to University of Pennsylvania criminologist Marvin Wolfgang, whose writing on the "subcultures of violence" moved criminal science from the realm of medicine and psychology to the aegis of sociology. Whereas earlier studies of criminality focused on the criminal mind, Wolfgang's studies led him to the crime-fostering social structures. His data convinced him that violent criminals tended to come from socioeconomic circles that tended to reinforce problem resolution through the use of fists rather than language.

The prototype of the inarticulate slum youth acting out his frustrations was a staple of postwar movies like *Knock on Any Door* (Ray 1949), or *The Blackboard Jungle* (Brooks 1955). These films presented the juvenile delinquent as a basically good kid whose penurious circumstances and lackadaisical upbringing have pushed him over the edge into mildly violent crime. The juvenile delinquent is perhaps most memorably etched in our culture by Stephen Sondheim's lyrics for "Officer Krupke" from *West Side Story* (Wise and Robbins 1961). The mischievous gang members, the Jets, demonstrate how they can manipulate authority figures—a cop, a judge, a psychiatrist, and a social worker—by invoking the moral failings of their indigent homes. As sung in the verse of "Gee, Officer Krupke," "My sister wears a mustache, my brother wears a dress. Leaping lizards, that's why I'm a mess."

Tony Manero and his gang, like the denizens of Scorsese's mean streets, are the descendants of these juvenile delinquents. A brief, miserable scene at the Manero dinner table shows us how Tony learns to communicate, as a petty family argument spirals into a slap-fest. Tony has an inner life; we know this from the discipline he applies to his dancing and from his encyclopedic knowledge of the Verrazzano-Narrows Bridge, which he sees as his path out of Brooklyn. His hunger to know a larger world is revealed when he ditches his previous dance partner, the love-starved, conventional Annette, for the ambitious, career-minded Stephanie. "You only talked about your married sister," he complains to Annette about their one date. "And your other married sister. And your third married sister. I felt that you just wanted to be a married sister." Stephanie, on the other hand, has a job in a Manhattan talent agency, and drops names like Cat Stevens and Laurence Olivier. "Maybe you can't handle hearing about a kind of life that's so different from yours," Stephanie taunts. But Tony accepts the challenge and Stephanie, the girl who works in the city, becomes his Verrazzano-Narrows personified. Stephanie challenges him, even though he detects her pretensions. But in order to grow, Tony's reflective side must overcome the petty violence of the streets from which he sprang. Dance may serve as an alternative outlet for his aggression.

In addition to Wolfgang, another writer influenced the discussions registered in the movie. Two years before the movie's release, Simon and Schuster released Susan Brownmiller's groundbreaking 1975 study, *Against Our Will: Men, Women, and Rape*. It's hard to say if Wexler would have read Susan Brownmiller. But *Against Our Will* was one of those books whose reach extended far beyond its readership, and its influence in general discourse can be felt in *Saturday Night Fever*. Building on work begun by Susan Griffin in her 1970 Ramparts article, "The All-American Crime," *Against Our Will* is generally credited as the first attempt to examine a history of rape, and to discuss it as an assertion of power rather than sexuality. Its importance cannot be overstated, and Brownmiller's battle cry—that the threat of rape is the means by which *all* men oppress *all* women—resonated powerfully.

However, the book has some wild weaknesses, particularly on issues of class and race. Brownmiller is widely quoted as saying, "The typical American rapist might be the boy next door." But reviews often omit the following sentence: "Especially . . . if the neighborhood you live in happens to fit the socioeonomic description of lower class or bears the appellation of ghetto."

Brownmiller has no qualms about equating arrest reports with actual violations, even though she admits elsewhere in the book that rape is rarely reported and even more rarely ends in conviction; it never occurs to her that arrests and convictions might be disproportionately meted out against Black and working-class men. In her tautological method, the fact that Black men are disproportionately convicted of rape only proves that they come from violent backgrounds. "There is no getting around the fact that most of those who engage in antisocial, criminal violence . . . come from the lower socioeconomic classes; come from the lower socioeconomic classes; and . . . the majority of black people contribute to crimes of violence in numbers disproportionate to their population" (Brownmiller 181). Any bias, either on her own part or on the part of law enforcement, is discounted.

Convinced that Black and working-class men have a cultural propensity for violence, she sees threats of sexual assault wherever they congregate. In one passage she recalls watching a bunch of young boys bash a vending machine on a subway platform, mining for loose change, and her imagination escalates their minor vandalism to rape. "That could be my body," she asserts (Brownmiller 193–194). Even more disturbing is her passage on Emmett Till, whose savage murder at the hands of racists, never punished, launched the mid-century civil rights movement. While conceding that the murder of Till, who was a child, was disproportionate to his alleged action, Brownmiller contends that Till's act of whistling at a white woman was a typical violation of a woman's autonomy. "Emmett Till was going to show his black buddies that he, and by inference they, could get a white woman" (Brownmiller, 247). Her language condemns Till and his "black buddies" for his innocent act, attributing to them violent intentions on the grounds of her demographic statistics.

Brownmiller's data came from *Patterns of Forcible Rape*, a statistical analysis published by Menachem Amir, who had studied with Marvin Wolfgang at the University of Pennsylvania, and, like Amir, Brownmiller adheres to Wolfgang's analysis of the "Subculture of Violence." She describes it thus:

> Within the dominant value system of our culture there exists a subculture formed of those from the lower classes, the poor, the disenfranchised, the black, whose values often run counter to those of the dominant culture, the people in charge. The dominant culture can operate within the laws of civility because it has little need to resort to violence to get what it wants. The subculture, thwarted, inarticulate and angry, is quick to resort to violence; indeed, violence and physical aggression become a common way of life. Particularly for young males. (Brownmiller 180–181)

Interestingly, by the time Brownmiller published *Against Our Will*, Wolfgang himself had begun to distance himself from some of the uses of his own methods. A traditional liberal, Wolfgang hoped that programs like public housing, school lunches, and Head Start might disrupt the patterns of violence he studied in Philadelphia. He adamantly opposed the death penalty and regretted that his work was cited as a rationale for stiffer prison sentences. One of his admirers, sociologist James Q. Wilson, who wrote an appreciation upon Wolfgang's death for *The New York Times Magazine*, is the author of the "broken windows" theory that served as the underpinning for Rudolph Giuliani's "stop and frisk" police operation in New York City. "I no longer have much interest in crime causation," Wolfgang resignedly told an interviewer in 1971. "I'm still interested in looking for patterns . . . I'm still interested in statistically analyzing the behavioral consequences of exposure to a social system. . .

But I have never allowed myself to be caught in the kind of dogmatism and absolutism" (Snodgrass 47). The leap from studying sociological statistics of crime to predicting criminal behavior based on class was not one Wolfgang was about to take.

If the Wolfgangian analysis of "subcultures of violence" was already in decline among progressives in 1976, Brownmiller clung to it. And, for all its cultural cache, *Against Our Will* provoked backlash from both the right and left. A Marxist group, the Sojourner Truth Organization, issued a pamphlet, "Rape, Racism, and the White Women's Movement," that declared that Brownmiller's work "is a dangerous book. It is a law-and-order book that is picking up liberal support because in the case of rape, the victims of crime are members of an oppressed group" (Edwards 1). Writing in the feminist academic journal *Signs*, Edward Shorter, sticking to the Freudian model, maintains that, given the rise and fall of incidents of rape (again, he is working on the notion that rapes are reported equally across classes), " 'sexual frustration' works better as a primary explanation than 'politics' " (Shorter 473). Brownmiller's defenders, on the other hand, point to her passages on how rape was used as a means of oppression under slavery, and that if Black men are disproportionately prone to rape, it means that Black women are disproportionately victims. In the radical feminist newspaper *off our backs*, Janis Kelly says, "Another interesting aspect to the criticism of [Brownmiller's] treatment of black rapists is the number of critics who think she is talking about black men raping white women. Rape is overwhelmingly an intra-racial phenomenon, and Brownmiller says so repeatedly. I think this particular misreading of her book is an example of the double burden of racism and sexism black women are subjected to: only someone to whom black women are invisible could make such a mistake" (Kelly 17).

But what ignited the cultural imagination, and the reason *Against Our Will* remains influential, was the move away from the Freudian. The rapist was no longer the "deviant," the loner. He could be a date, a boyfriend, or a husband. Rape, Brownmiller contends, is commonplace, often encouraged through homosocial activity. The overlap of this new feminist definition of rape with the old Wolfgangian predictions of violence probably appealed to screenwriter Wexler, who saw rape as one more way disaffected youths might lash out. Indeed, we see the same predilection in *West Side Story*'s Jets, whose attempted rape of Anita expresses racist hostility rather than sexual frustration. (And again the Jets, in true Wolfgangian form, blame the system; when the kindly Doc interrupts the rape-in-progress, he scolds, "When do you kids stop? You make this world lousy," one of the gang replies, "We didn't make it, Doc.")

The two sexual assaults in *Saturday Night Fever* are very different and shed light on the range of contemporaneous discussions on rape. Both take place in the backseat of Bobby C's car, the usual trysting spot for Tony's gang and their pickups. They also occur within minutes of each other. After conceding his victory in the dance contest to the Puerto Rican couple, Tony hustles Stephanie out to the car. She is angry. She has a right to be; she won the dance contest, too, and Tony, as generous as his concession might have been, never consulted her. "Everybody's gotta dump on somebody, *of course*," Tony complains. "My pa goes to work and gets dumped on, so he comes home and dumps on my mother, *of course*. And the spics they gotta dump on us so we gotta dump on the spics, *of course*." That Tony gives this speech just before assaulting Stephanie completes the Wolfgangian circle. Tony has to dump on Stephanie. "Even the humping is dumping," he realizes. Of course.

Yet, a bit of the Freudian notion of sexual frustration creeps into the depiction of Tony's assault. He calls Stephanie a "cock-teaser," who had deliberately excited him to the point of force. Minutes earlier, in the excitement of the dance contest, Stephanie had kissed Tony for the first time, after weeks of insisting that they were only friends and dance partners. Tony takes the kiss as a signal, but when Stephanie beats him off, he demands to know why she hangs out with him. "You know why?" she says angrily. "I've been dumping my bullshit on you. Selling my act on you. Making you think I love you. It's all bullshit."

Stephanie's response may seem to make her less sympathetic. Had she "provoked" Tony by using him, trying out her act? As Wexler writes her, Stephanie is certainly the most interesting character in the movie. She is a real striver, trying to lose her Brooklyn accent, ordering tea instead of coffee because she sees the professional women in her office doing so, growing out her haircut for a more sophisticated look. She reads books; she practices her dance with balletic precision. We also learn the great cost to her of keeping up appearances; she sleeps with her boss to keep her job and routinely feels humiliated in the office. When she meets Tony, she sees someone who admires her. Whereas at work she's just a Brooklyn girl, in Brooklyn she's the woman with a job in the city. Why wouldn't she try out her act, consolidate her new persona?

Many of the reviews of *Saturday Night Fever* criticized Karen Lynn Gorney's performance as Stephanie. She simply cannot match Travolta's charisma, and even on the dance floor she seems to disappear in his aura. It is tempting to wonder what a tough New York actress of Gorney's generation—Lorraine Bracco, say, or Ellen Barkin—might have done with the role, perhaps grabbing some of Tony's spotlight for herself. But it is also true that, although Wexler wrote Stephanie as a resilient, conflicted, ultimately compassionate woman, *Saturday Night Fever* centers Tony's story while marginalizing that of Stephanie; essentially, the women in the film serve mainly as paths to Tony's enlightenment.

The casting of Gorney as Stephanie, as well as her confession that she used Tony to "try out [her] act," may underscore anxiety about upwardly mobile women like her. It is, after all, Stephanie who has the skills to work in Manhattan, whereas Tony has none, a discrepancy between them that anticipates the opportunities for women in a postindustrial economy. But her success at work is tainted by her affair with her boss, which, she admits, she embarked on so she could keep her job. Stephanie is depicted as a scrapper, rather than a victim—unlike the more domestic-minded Annette—but her ability to strive comes at a great psychological cost. The implication here is that she uses Tony in the way she has been used. Whether all upwardly mobile women are similarly damaged is left to the viewer.

Stephanie's secondary status is further complicated by the glossy touches of Robert Stigwood's post-production decisions. Stephanie successfully fights off Tony and escapes him, but after the film's climax, at which Bobby C throws himself off the Verrazzano-Narrows Bridge, Tony has the inclination to slouch to her new Manhattan apartment for solace. He must wait for dawn, however, and in the ensuing hours he rides the subway disconsolately, as the soundtrack plays the Bee Gees' "How Deep Is Your Love?" The choice of nondiegetic music reframes Tony's search for Stephanie. He is not a rapist seeking absolution, but a mixed-up kid looking for love. The question "How Deep Is Your Love?" is posed to Stephanie, not Tony. Does she love Tony enough to open her door to him after he tries to rape her?

Ultimately, she does, and in the quiet last minutes of the movie they have a frank talk about Tony's future. She will help him get out of Brooklyn, even though, she bluntly points out, he has no skills. As far as their relationship, she confirms they will never be more than friends. "Do you think you could be friends with a girl? Do you think you could stand that?" Tony admits he's not sure, but he will try. Stephanie is tough enough to embrace him, and she can help Tony be a better person, although it is fairly clear that it is the trauma of Bobby C's death, not his attempted rape of her, that has initiated his reform. It is Stephanie's responsibility to forgive, to make Tony whole. Tony bears no responsibility for healing the wound in Stephanie, whose resilience is assumed.

If Gorney cannot quite rise to the complexity of Wexler's screenplay, Donna Pescow's radiant performance as Annette expands the underwritten role. Annette is written to be complacent, beset by low self-esteem and eager for love. But Pescow endows Annette with an aching longing. When Tony refuses—he doesn't want to get Annette pregnant and find himself in the same bind that Bobby C is in—Annette goes out and buys condoms, an act that the film frames as a mark of desperation rather than initiative. On the night of the big dance contest, she drinks and takes pills to cope with the hurt of watching Tony dance with Stephanie, and as she descends into a stupor she flirts with his friends. "Annette's giving everybody snatch pie!" they crow as she piles into Bobby C's backseat with Joey. When Tony half-heartedly tries to stop his friends from the gang bang, Joey says to him, not untruthfully, "You don't give a shit about her." Tony drives the gang around, peeking at the gang-rape of Annette via the rearview mirror. First with Joey, Annette is flirtatious and giggling, but when Double J takes his turn, she grows resistant. "No, don't, no, no," she says. "I don't want to do it." "Shit," Double J complains, "with me she cries."

As the assault of Stephanie raises controversial questions about what constitutes rape (Is it rape when it's a friend? Did she encourage him by kissing him?), the rape of Annette delves even deeper. Is it rape when she is stoned out of her mind? Is it rape when she freely climbed into the car, knowing full well what was to happen? Does her previous purchase of condoms signal her consent? Is it rape when, mid-coitus, *she changes her mind*? These questions may seem settled today, but at the time the discussion was just beginning. As late as 1983, sociologists Lance R. Shotland and Lynne Goodstein were still arguing whether engaging in consensual foreplay precluded the possibility of legal rape. In *Social Psychology Quarterly*, they wrote, "Several authors suggest that it is commonly accepted for a woman to conceal her genuine interest in sexual contact and merely suggest her intentions in subtle or symbolic ways. . . Some people agree that a woman's presence in a man's apartment or her willing involvement in the early stages of sexual foreplay imply her consent to have sexual intercourse" (Shotland 221).

Just as Tony's class frustration manifests Wolfgang's theory about subcultures of violence, Joey and Double J's gang rape confirms it, as well as Brownmiller's assertion of rape often being a social activity, reinforced by mutual encouragement. Wexler provides the viewer with two examples of rape that are, strictly speaking, out of the textbook. He also, problematically, presents two very different victims. Stephanie, smart and independent, fights off her attacker. Annette, who is inebriated and submissive, merely says "no," which is insufficient to prevent her rape. The film suggests the victim, if only through weak character, is somewhat to blame, and this victim-blaming is articulated by Tony's harsh condemnation of Annette after she is raped. "Are you proud of yourself, Annette? Is that what you wanted? Good, now you're a cunt."

Stephanie's capacity to forgive Tony may be offered as proof of her high-mindedness, but we see something even more disturbing when Annette, after seeing Bobby C's plunge into the New York Harbor, finds relief in Joey's arms, minutes after he raped her. Once the police question them, they go off together, apparently as a couple. Although Joey is accorded no inner life (he is marginally kinder to Annette than Double J), he too seems chastened by Bobby C's death, and finds the maturity, perhaps, to enter a relationship with the woman he raped. For both Tony and Joey, rape is a rite of passage, a terrible milestone, like the death of a friend, that they must endure on the way to adulthood. While this notion falls far short of Brownmiller's feminism, it does conform to Wolfgangian liberalism. Far from being a sign of sexual or psychological deviation, rape, for men, is a social condition that they can work hard to overcome. But the effect of sexual violence on women is unexamined.

If *Saturday Night Fever* is confusing, it is because it teeters on the moment when postwar liberalism was fading, and second-wave feminism was regrouping. Its claims about working-class men have aged poorly. In her defense of Brownmiller in *off our backs*, Janis Kelly says, "Brownmiller's conclusions about rapists may be entirely class-biased, but I don't think so. In the first place, she is talking about violent, forcible rape. Middle-class and upper-class men show up less in cases of forcible rape because they have access to other kinds of power over women, like money. They needn't bother with violence so often. Men with fewer options use the ones they have" (Kelly 17). In the age of Epstein and Weinstein, this passage appears willfully blind to implicit class bias. It would be difficult to argue today that rape festers more in the working class than in the monied class. While fraternity boys like Brock Turner may still get light sentences, the debate over whether "acquaintance rape" is a legal crime is in our past.

Saturday Night Fever may be written off as light entertainment, or as needlessly exploitative. However, this movie demands to be studied not only as an example of conflicting artistic visions that combine to make a lasting entertainment but as a cultural artifact that comes out of a turbulent moment as competing ideologies clamored for the public imagination.

Notes

1. If any question remains about the conflict between Stigwood and Wexler, the proof is in Wexler's own script. The movie's oiliest character, Stephanie's boss and lover, is "an arranger, a record producer. He wants to do films. He's moving to a more expensive apartment." The description fits Stigwood perfectly.

2. At the beginning of the twentieth century, Italian immigrants were not considerd to be (entirely) white. Over time, they have gradually been assimilated into this category (see Barrett and Roediger 1997).

Works Cited

Barrett, James, and David Roediger. "Inbetween Peoples: Race, Nationality and the New Immigrant Working Class." *American Exceptionalism?* Ed. Rick Halpern and Jonathan Morris. London: Palgrave Macmillan, 1997. 181–120.

Brownmiller, Susan. *Against Our Will: Men, Women, and Rape.* New York: Simon and Schuster, 1975.

Edwards, Alison. "Rape, Racism, and the White Women's Movement." Chicago: Sojourner Truth Organization, 1979.

Eskow, Lisa R. "The Ultimate Weapon? Demythologizing Spousal Rape and Reconceptualizing Its Prosecution." *Stanford Law Review* 48, no. 3 (1996): 677–709. www.jstor.org/stable/1229280

Frank, Gillian. "Discophobia: Antigay Prejudice and the 1979 Backlash Against Disco." *Journal of the History of Sexuality* 16, no. 2 (May 2007): 276–306. www.jstor.org/stable/30114235

Haskell, Molly. *From Reverence to Rape: The Treatment of Women in the Movie.* Chicago: University of Chicago Press, 2016.

Kashner, Sam. "Fever Pitch." *Vanity Fair.* December 2007. www.vanityfair.com/news/2007/12/saturday-night-fever

Kelly, Janis. "Review: Against Our Will." *off our backs* 6, no. 3 (1976): 17.

Ledbetter, Les. "Oregon Man Found Not Guilty on a Charge of Raping His Wife." *New York Times*, December 28, 1978, p. A1.

Saturday Night Fever. Directed by John Badham, screenplay by Norman Wexler, produced by Robert Stigwood, performance by John Travolta, Paramount Pictures, 1977.

Schwartz, Louis B. "Reform of the Federal Criminal Laws: Issues, Tactics, and Prospects." *Law and Contemporary Problems*, 41, no. 1 (1977): 1–62. www. jstor.org/stable/1191230

Shorter, Edward. "On Writing the History of Rape." *Signs* 3, no. 2 (1977): 471–482.

Shotland, R. Lance, and Lynne Goodstein. "Just Because She Doesn't Want to Doesn't Mean It's Rape: An Experimentally Based Causal Model of the Perception of Rape in a Dating Situation." *Social Psychology Quarterly* 46, no. 3 (1983): 220–232. www.jstor.org/stable/3033793

Snodgrass, Jon, and Marvin Wolfgang. "Dialogue with Marvin Wolfgang." *Issues in Criminology* 7, no. 1 (Winter 1972): 37–58. www.jstor.org/stable/42909649

West Side Story. Directed by Robert Wise and Jerome Robbins, screenplay by Ernest Lehman based on a book by Arthur Laurents, lyrics by Stephen Sondheim, performances by Natalie Wood and Richard Beymer, United Artists, 1961.

CHAPTER 4

Deny the Beast

The Howling (1981) and Rape Culture

Brian Brems

In an essay published in 1980, feminist social critic Robin Morgan pithily summed up a rapidly developing resistance to a then-proliferating societal phenomenon: "Pornography is the theory, and rape the practice" (139). This oft-quoted maxim can sound too much like a bumper sticker divorced from its context, but Morgan's argument suggests that "rape is the perfected act of male sexuality in a patriarchal culture—it is the ultimate metaphor for domination, violence, subjugation, and possession" (134). In Morgan's view, pornography's inherently patriarchal characteristics pave the way for men to commit rape, creating a visual permission structure that trains men how to violate women by showing them what it looks like. During the 1970s, porn went mainstream with the release of films like *Deep Throat* (1972, Dir. Gerard Damiano), and several other high-profile adult films that drew patrons from cities and suburbs alike, made curious by the forbidden. At the same time, New York City's Times Square area became ground zero for pornography, with adult bookstores lining 42nd Street, along with live peep shows and private booths where coin-depositing voyeurs could watch one-reel pornographic films. Similar strips popped up in cities around the country. In 1981, just one year after Morgan's quotable indictment of pornography, Joe Dante's werewolf movie *The Howling* begins with a sequence set in Los Angeles' red light district

63

that culminates in a violent confrontation inside a private, coin-operated booth while images of sexual torture flicker on the wall.

It was a good year for werewolves. In addition to *The Howling*, John Landis's *An American Werewolf in London* set a new bar for on-screen special effects with its jaw-dropping transformation scene. Michael Wadleigh's *Wolfen* fared less well at the box office but was propelled by its social conscience, taking on issues of gentrification and Native American heritage amid New York City's financial crisis. *The Howling* falls somewhere in between, a product of the different creative impulses of director Dante, the drive-in aficionado and showman, and screenwriter John Sayles, whose work as a writer and director is grounded in political ideology. Werewolves are salient metaphors and carry different meanings in the hands of individual storytellers; for Sayles and Dante in *The Howling*, the werewolf takes on psychosexual importance. Its transformation scenes play like aggressively heterosexual white male posturing, and its central character, Los Angeles television reporter Karen White (Dee Wallace), is portrayed as a victim of trauma that parallels the experiences of sexual assault survivors. Over the course of the film, Karen suffers a trauma, struggles to articulate it in therapy, is threatened with total destruction, and then forces others to confront the truth of what happened to her in a public confession in the film's final scene. Though the film predates the revelations of the #MeToo movement by nearly forty years, it strikingly anticipates the trajectory of many women's stories that gained traction in the news media beginning in the fall of 2017. Its sensitivity to Karen's trauma and insightful critique of its white male werewolves make *The Howling* a powerful example of genre cinema that relies on both deep empathy and trenchant social commentary.

The film's story follows Karen in her efforts to recover from a traumatic experience that takes place in the film's opening sequence, during which she serves as bait to catch a serial killer—as a white, heterosexual male, he fits the profile—Eddie Quist (Robert Picardo). She meets Eddie in the private viewing booth in an adult bookstore, but he is shot to death by the police before he is able to kill her. In the aftermath of the attack, Karen struggles to connect sexually with her husband Bill (Christopher Stone), so a pop psychologist named Dr. Waggner (Patrick Macnee) who is treating Karen suggests that the two of them decamp to Waggner's upstate retreat, The Colony, located on the California coast. When Karen and Bill arrive, they are unnerved by some of the other patients and hear strange howling sounds in the woods at night. While

Karen undergoes therapy, the sexually frustrated Bill becomes attracted to a leather-clad seductress named Marsha (Elisabeth Brooks), an interest intensified and then consummated after Bill is attacked and bitten by a werewolf in the woods one night. Karen is further alienated from Bill and calls on her friend and co-worker Terry (Belinda Balaski) to join her at The Colony. Terry interrupts her investigation into Eddie's killings that she has been conducting with her boyfriend Chris (Dennis Dugan), even though Eddie's body has disappeared from the city morgue. Upon arriving at The Colony, Terry continues her pursuit of the truth and discovers that Eddie must have been a visitor to the retreat; she is attacked and killed by a werewolf while she attempts to solicit Chris's help over the phone. Chris buys a box of silver bullets from an occult bookstore and travels up the coast. While he is on the way, Karen discovers Terry's body and confronts the werewolf who killed her—Eddie—who transforms in front of her in an animalistic display of his masculine power. After escaping Eddie's clutches with the help of some well-thrown hydrochloric acid, Karen makes a shocking discovery: all the patients at The Colony are werewolves, and they want to turn her. Chris arrives at the last moment, kills Eddie with a silver bullet, and then rescues Karen from the barn where the wolves have taken her, trapping the beasts inside and setting it ablaze. During their frenzied escape, a werewolf bites Karen, but she kills it with a silver bullet. When the wolf transforms back into its human form after death, she realizes it is her husband, Bill. She and Chris resolve to warn Los Angeles on television; behind the news desk, Karen transforms as a way of revealing the existence of werewolves, and before she can do any harm, Chris shoots her with a silver bullet. The film ends with a humorous, self-aware discussion at a bar when the patrons dismiss Karen's television transformation as the product of Hollywood special effects, but continues the threat when it reveals that Marsha has survived the fire at The Colony and is sitting at the end of the bar, ordering a hamburger cooked rare.

The Howling's political consciousness is likely attributable to screenwriter Sayles whose subsequent work as a writer and director demonstrates an interest in social issues that include economics and racial divisions and often filters those ideas through female characters of substance. Sayles's preceding screenplay for Lewis Teague's Alligator (1980), according to Robin Wood, contains "feminist promise" that it ultimately fails to achieve; if Sayles had also been behind the camera, it might possibly have followed through on its initial approach ("Art and

Alligators," 203). Much of Sayles's film work shows "shrewd underlying awareness of the political implications of his material" (Smith xiv). In both *Alligator* and Sayles's screenplay for *Piranha* (1978, Dir. Joe Dante), businessmen and authority figures are portrayed with a critical eye, fore-shadowing the more overtly political work he would take on when he began directing. In 1983, Sayles would direct the quiet drama *Lianna*, "an implicit critique of gender inequality" that "portrays a lesbian protagonist sympathetically and realistically" (Shumway 27, 28). In his next film, *Baby, It's You* (1983), Sayles took on "new gender relations represented from a woman's perspective" (Shumway 29). Thus, when crafting the screenplay for *The Howling*, which deviates significantly from the book by Gary Brandner upon which it is ostensibly based, Sayles leaned on psychological ideas that reveal his sensitivity to the rich possibilities of the metaphor, arguing that being a werewolf would be akin to having a mental illness or addiction. He says, "If you were a werewolf, you would want to cope. This is a kind of behavior you have to control" (*Sayles on Sayles* 39). He deftly introduces the themes of the film in the opening sequence, when Dr. Waggner is appearing on television at Karen's station, intercut with her participation in the police's trapping of Eddie: "All the psychological stuff the Patrick Macnee character is saying is what the movie is about" (40–41). That "psychological stuff" includes lines like Waggner's assertion that "Repression is the father of neuroses. Of self-hatred" and the concept of "Animal magnetism, the natural man," culminating in his warning that "We should never try to deny the beast, the animal within us." Sayles uses psychological motivations to explore ideas that carry important political implications, including the repression of sexual desire and the impact of male sexual violence on women, to which his screenplay devotes considerable attention. The film's male werewolves are repeatedly aligned with images that suggest rape, and its sympathies lie entirely with Karen, who becomes the victim of sex-ual trauma in the opening sequence. His sensitivity to Karen's trauma encourages the audience to identify with her, filtering the experience of a violent attack through a more conventional horror premise. Sayles's social consciousness also shaped how he crafted the ending, in which Karen commits a kind of ritualistic suicide following the revelation of her trauma. In Sayles's view, the on-air suicide is done "in a way that will bring some attention," which achieves a feminist goal—to make the repressed pain of women who have survived sexual violence visible and impossible to ignore (41).

While Sayles's feminist approach to the material provides the foundation, Dante's direction expands upon his work through its representation of Karen's initial assault and her resulting post-traumatic stress response. The film's opening sequence, the sting operation against Eddie, follows Karen's walk along the streets of Los Angeles' red light district; the environment confronts her with countless images of sexual commodification, with blinking advertisements promising "HARDCORE" and "GIRLS" just inside the shop doors. Eddie calls the phone booth where Karen has agreed to be, and purrs into the receiver, "Are you wearing what I asked you to?" while Dante cuts to a close-up of his mouth, and he licks his lips. She is wearing a wire, communicating her presence to the police, but connections are shaky and the officers monitoring her lose the signal when Karen steps into a store's private booth that promises "Satisfaction Guaranteed," bearing the happy face sticker that serves as Eddie's signature. Eddie appears behind her, dropping a coin into the peep show machine; the projector whirrs to life, and Eddie forces Karen to watch the film reel, a scene of sexual torture in which a nude woman is held down on a bed by a group of white men wearing gloves, screaming and struggling to break free. Eddie reproduces the act of bondage with his own hands, pressing down on Karen's shoulders, his face darkened by the shadowy booth. "I'm going to light up your whole body, Karen," he tells her, and then begins to growl. "Turn around now, Karen." In the flickering light of the projector, Karen sees something horrifying that is withheld from the audience by the chiaroscuro of the booth; when the police officers trailing Karen suddenly arrive and the younger cop blasts Eddie, Karen retreats in fear against the wall, the images of the sadistic sexual torture playing out all over her terrified face. It literalizes the lingering effect of the sexual violence, which will remain with Karen through the rest of the narrative, as a manifestation of her trauma. The interaction with Eddie is loaded with the suggestion of rape, and when Karen is escorted out of the peep show by Bill and the officers, she exhibits typical trauma symptoms, claiming no memory of the event and operating as though she were in a kind of trance with subdued mannerisms and lilting speech. The moment is designed deliberately to suggest that Karen has suffered sexual violence inside the booth, an association confirmed when she relives the attack in flashes during a nightmare the following day. The flashes return later when Karen and Bill are in bed together; he attempts to initiate sex, but she refuses, the first of such interactions between the couple post-attack.

A number of scholars have examined the implications of peep shows for gender and cinematic discourse. The peep show would seem to literalize to almost comic degree Laura Mulvey's influential thesis about the male gaze: "the woman displayed has functioned on two levels: as erotic object for the characters within the screen story, and as erotic object for the spectator within the auditorium, with a shifting tension between the looks on either side of the screen" (33). In an essay focusing specifically on peep show arcades, Amy Herzog argues that "the apparatus of the peep show subjects the body of the patron to a highly individ-ualized and intimate mode of address, compelling in return an active and equally intimate corporeal response" (29). In luring Karen into the booth, Eddie has exerted his control over her; this is reinforced by him placing his hands firmly on her shoulders and forcing her to look at the images of sexual torture playing out on screen. By entering the booth at all, Karen has transgressed into traditionally male space. Herzog's survey of a number of studies of peep show arcades demonstrates that "women were not permitted to enter the arcades at any of the venues observed," making this a private world for men only, a norm common to many spaces of sexual voyeurism, including so-called "gentlemen's clubs" where women may not enter unless accompanied by a man (33). In her estimation, during the act of watching, "The body of the viewer hovers in a suspended existence between the body of the film and the space of the arcade, hyperfocused (at least in the case of certain viewers) on the tactility of the flesh on the screen as well as on the sensations of his own flesh" (35). The sequence in the booth brings together three disparate elements: the visual presence of the on-screen rape, its impact on Eddie's body, and Karen's physical presence. It is hard to imagine a more direct representation of Morgan's famously articulated link between pornography and rape.

For a number of other scholars, however, Morgan's assertion is too simplistic and reductive. Scott MacDonald sees pornography as an outlet "for men to periodically deal with the cultural context which mitigates against their full acceptance of themselves as sexual beings" (15). He does not dismiss Morgan's thesis outright, however, conceding that "porn and rape are part of the same general problem, though I've always felt it more likely that porn offers an outlet for some of the anger engendered by men's feelings of sensual/aesthetic inferiority, than that it serves as a fuel for further anger" (16). Film scholar Linda Williams, however, is much more antagonistic, criticizing Morgan's credo in her book *Hard*

Core as overly simplistic: "A problem arises when we consider the difference between actual abusive sexual practices and their representation in pornographic fantasy. Robin Morgan's slogan obscures this distinction by stressing the connection between a male supremacist ideology—viewed as the content of pornography—and specific abusive practices—viewed as its effects" (17). For Williams, Morgan offers "a woefully inadequate explanation of the causes of sexual violence against women" (275). Across Williams's studies of both pornography and sex on screen, she takes a more positive stance toward visual representation than Morgan. In *Screening Sex*, Williams argues that spectators "learn to appreciate and enjoy certain sexual ways of being, certain forms of (mild or powerful) arousal by watching the mediated sexual contacts of others, whether smoldering glances, kisses, more overt forms of friction or complex scenarios of power, abjection, and need" (6). In Williams's view, on-screen sex can affect spectators in positive ways, and does not necessarily serve as an instruction manual for men to commit sexual assault.

Williams's work on the relationship between pornography and horror sheds light on *The Howling*. In an influential essay called "Film Bodies: Genre, Gender, and Excess," Williams argues that "pornography and horror films are two such systems of excess. Pornography is the lowest in cultural esteem, gross-out horror is next to lowest" (604). In both film genres, "The body spectacle is featured more sensationally in pornography's portrayal of orgasm, in horror's portrayal of violence and terror" (604). In werewolf movies, these ecstatic moments come during the special-effects bonanzas that make up its transformation scenes. Throughout *The Howling*, the practical devices used to make the werewolves transform from men into wolves and wolves into men are pure "body spectacle." This approach takes center stage in the middle of the movie when Karen's husband Bill, having been bitten by a werewolf, is lured into the woods at night by unquenchable sexual desire. Leaving the bed he shares with Karen, Bill finds Marsha waiting for him beside a roaring fire. She strips off her black leather outfit, standing nude before him, and he tosses his robe aside. The flames dance in the foreground of the image while they embrace beyond them. As Marsha and Bill consummate their sexual attraction, the entire forest seems to come alive with the sounds of howling werewolves. Passion ensues, along with romantic scoring and tender dissolves, but these traditional markers of movie sex turn monstrous with a crash of an organ and a smash cut to Bill, whose sexual desire has awakened the beast within. His teeth have become razor-sharp canines; Marsha is changing, too, but the cut back to Bill shows an animal look in his eyes as a sickening glob of saliva drips out of his mouth. The first on-screen transformation in the film comes in the middle of an illicit sexual encounter between these two eager participants, deepening the association between sexuality and animal desire that is established in the peep show booth where Eddie assaults Karen. This encounter between Bill and Marsha is consensual, but both are now werewolves; Karen, still human at this point in the film, is left alone in the marital bed, fighting against the nightmares that reanimate her trauma.

The special effects continue to sexualize the werewolf as a manifestation of animalistic desire throughout the film. During a chase sequence late in the film, the snooping Terry discovers Eddie's lair at the colony—identifiable by the happy face sticker—which is decorated with his drawings of wolves and magazine cutouts of pornography, further aligning sexuality with werewolves. She is suddenly attacked by a werewolf, and she slices off its arm with a hatchet. The practical effects work dramatizes the transition from werewolf arm to human arm as a kind of castration. The wolf flees in pain, leaving its severed paw behind, while on the ground the arm transforms from stiff, erect werewolf appendage, covered in hair and glistening with moisture, to a flaccid, weak human hand, its fingers wagging impotently. Throughout, Dante cuts between individual effects shots and Terry's horrified expressions; such editing patterns serve a practical function, allowing the effects team to create multiple stages of the arm's transformation, but also to emphasize Terry's spectatorship. When another wet, hairy werewolf later confronts Terry in the doctor's office, the attack plays like an assault; the wolf does not maul her but lifts her well off her feet, choking the life out of her until her suspended feet stop kicking. It presses its snout against her dead face, a gesture of shocking violation, and then Dante cuts to an overhead angle of a pile of papers on the floor, waiting for Terry's blood to trickle onto the ground. When Karen discovers Terry's body, her throat has been ripped open, blood collecting around her neck in an image that cannot help but suggest extreme rape. Eddie lies in wait for Karen in the doctor's office, human for the moment.

In *The Howling*, Sayles's writing and Dante's direction especially link sexuality and male violence during the centerpiece transformation sequence, as Eddie changes from man into a wolf in front of Karen.

The sequence is a restaging of the opening scene inside the peep show booth, where Eddie's transformation was interrupted, and his violent assault on Karen went unconsummated. As in many werewolf films, the transformation is pure exhibition, a showcase for the film's special-effects wizards to do their thing, but in *The Howling*, Dante effectively portrays the transformation as a spectacle performed for the female character as a show of masculine heterosexual virility. According to Steven Shaviro, pornography and horror are intrinsic "to any account of cinematic experience. In the realm of visual fascination, sex and violence have much more intense and disturbing an impact than they do in literature or any other medium; they affect the viewer in a shockingly direct way. Violent and pornographic films literally anchor desire and perception in the agitated and fragmented body" (55). *The Howling*'s transformation scene makes the white male body, becoming a wolf body, into a fetish object; the film's narrative more or less grinds to a halt to allow the special effects to take over. Karen is transfixed while Eddie changes, unable to leave the room during each fragmented series of close-ups on his transforming body.

In Williams's book *Hard Core*, she devotes an extended portion of her analysis to so-called "money-shots" that privilege a visual record of male ejaculation. In the werewolf horror film, the spectacle of bodily transformation—man becomes wolf—serves a similar function for spectators seeking visual stimulation through the wet, sweaty, panting release of werewolf special effects. In pornography, "money shots" that capture male ejaculation demonstrate visual proof of male orgasm. According to Williams, "the visual spectacle of external penile ejaculation is a tacit acknowledgment that such real-live sex acts can be communicated to viewers only through certain visual and aural conventions of representation" (121). In *The Howling*, most of the transformation's special effects obviously evoke the male erection. Eddie's skin crackles and glistens with perspiration. His fingernails lengthen first, and then his fingers themselves stretch out. His snout extends, pushing forward away from his face toward Karen. The bladders controlling his body cavity engorge and ripple, filling with sudden life. It is a performance in which Eddie shows off his ability to grow and show his masculine prowess to Karen. It is a reminder of her trauma, as Eddie seeks to complete the ritualized transformation that was interrupted by the police inside the peep show booth; in reverse shots of Karen, she watches in horror, the reminder of the trauma suddenly made flesh right in front of her. The intended effect on the spectator is much the same. In Shaviro's words, pornography and horror

> short-circuit the mechanism of fantasy altogether: they are not content to leave me with vague, disembodied imaginings, but excitedly seek to incise those imaginings in my very flesh. They focus obsessively upon the physical reactions of bodies on screen, the better to assault and agitate the bodies of the audience. This is precisely why porn and horror films epitomize "bad taste." They do not bring me gratified fulfillment or satiation, but insidiously exacerbate and exasperate my least socially acceptable desires. (101)

A number of werewolf transformation scenes, including those in Universal Studios' original effort *The Wolf Man* (1941, Dir. George Waggner) and *An American Werewolf in London*, take place in private and focus on the shape-shifter's individual horror or pain during the change. The presence of a spectator in *The Howling*'s transformation scene foregrounds Eddie's body in both its human and wolf form, but also threatens Karen's body, a clear evocation of sexual assault.

The Howling is overtly concerned with spectatorship, as its opening peep show attack and later transformation scene illustrate. Eddie has developed an obsessive relationship with Karen from afar after watching her in her role as an anchor on the local evening news program; he spends his time looking at her, and the transformation scenes force her to look back. These sequences establish a link between pornography and Eddie's transformation, as both are charged with aggressive eroticism. In the film's expository scenes, it reveals that Eddie is a serial killer who specifically targets women; as his true identity is revealed, it becomes clear that his killings occur when he is filled with the sexual energy that propels him as a werewolf. The film is also concerned with its depiction of Karen's response to the coded sexual assault she experiences in the booth at the start of the film. Dante renders Karen's trauma through images, emphasizing the character's recalled spectatorship in her memories of the attack. When Karen returns to the nightly news, Dante brings back the image of the rape scene from the peep show booth, which Karen sees reflected in the camera's lens, followed by the image of the silhouetted Eddie advancing toward her. In a session with Doctor

Waggner, she tries to explain her gaps in memory but describes what she can remember as "weird little pieces in my dreams." They continue to trouble her on the way to The Colony, when Karen tells Bill, "I don't know if I want to remember" what happened in the booth. Later, she wakens from another nightmare made up of images that remind her of the assault while she lies in bed next to Bill. During a group therapy session with other patients at The Colony, Karen tries to recall the traumatic encounter with Eddie. She breathlessly recounts what happened, the sound drifting over the images first, and then Dante cuts to a shot inside of the booth, the same silhouette of Eddie as before. In one later dream sequence, Karen has taken the place of the bound woman in the film reel, a gag in her mouth. In this particular dream, Karen gets her clearest view of Eddie as a wolf yet, a sight that will only be revealed to her during the transformation scene.

The film's final sequence is especially resonant with the film's exploration of trauma. It also anticipates the revelations of the #MeToo movement with startling prescience. After Karen has been bitten by the werewolf Bill during her escape with Chris, the two have decided to confront the problem by exposing it on live television; during the broadcast, Karen will transform into a wolf so that viewers can see the truth. "We have to warn people, Chris. We have to make them believe," she says. Karen's desire to reveal her secret is an effort to force news viewers to empathize with her trauma. The bite she has suffered that has turned her into a wolf has completed the sexual assault that Eddie began in the private booth at the start of the film and attempted to finish during the transformation scene; his work has been carried on by her husband Bill, brothers in white patriarchy. The station manager Fred Francis (Kevin McCarthy) is nervous about Karen going back on the air; he was quick to pull the plug during her first appearance after the encounter with Eddie, when a post-traumatic memory sent her into a trance while the cameras were rolling. He insists he will cut her off again, ordering the program's technical director to go to commercial "if she shows any signs of freezing like the last time." Francis has no interest in offering Karen a forum to express her trauma and is irate when she reads from a prepared script of her own instead of the agreed-upon teleprompter copy.

It is worth quoting Karen's final monologue at length to demonstrate its resonance with #MeToo stories. Addressing the television camera, she says,

Good evening. From the day we're born, there is a battle we must fight. A struggle between what is kind and peaceful in our natures and what is cruel and violent. That choice is our birthright as human beings and the real gift that differentiates us from the animals. It is as natural to us as the air we breathe and all of us take it for granted. But now, for some of us, that choice has been taken away. A secret society exists and is living among all of us. They are neither people nor animals but something in between. Monstrous mutations whose violent natures must be satisfied. I know what you're thinking because I've been where you are, and it's impossible to imagine, but I have proof. And tonight, I'm going to show you something to make you believe.

She concludes her editorial with a primal scream, but throughout the latter part of the monologue, her voice quivers with emotion as she struggles to suppress the transformation, the manifestation of her trauma. Dante neatly reverses the spectatorial gaze, as the station's men—Francis, Karen's fellow anchor, and Chris—are forced to watch her transformation, just as Eddie made her watch his. Her transformation, however, is different—it is less exhibitionist, for one thing, as a result of the production running out of money in its final shooting days, but the reserved approach has another effect, infusing the moment with sadness. A close-up of Karen's partially transformed face, with a small amount of sprouting hair and sharp fangs, has devastating emotional impact when a tear rolls down her cheek; the emphasis is on her pathos, not the thrill of living as a monster, as the other werewolves do. In this moment, Karen has risked everything to share the evidence of her trauma with the viewing public. Though Karen is not physically threatened by violence in this scene, as she was during Eddie's transformation, "the terror of the female victim shares the spectacle along with the monster" (Williams 606). Karen's terror surfaces through recognition of her trauma; it is not immediate, but its memory can return at any moment to remind her of the attack. The assault has extracted a terrible cost, which rises only when Chris dutifully goes through with the plan's final act and fires the silver bullet, killing Karen live on the air. She is made a martyr; some part of her died in that booth, a little more during Eddie's transformation, and finally she sacrifices her own privacy on live television so that others might know the truth about her trauma. The revelation, though somewhat cathartic, is also a kind of new trauma; it is yet another violation that prolongs the experience of the attack into the everyday position she occupies as a news anchor.

Karen's on-air revelation has resonance with Barbara Creed's idea of the "monstrous-feminine," in which the female monster is "defined in terms of her sexuality" (3). Her confrontational approach ("make you believe") surfaces trauma by showing its monstrous effect on her; she has been irrevocably changed by the assault she has experienced, and in *The Howling*'s conclusion, her testimonial commands society—especially its white heterosexual men—to see the impact of sexual assault on women. According to Creed, "Through the figure of the monstrous-feminine, the horror film plays on [male] fears of menstrual blood, incorporation, domination, castration and death" (155). By revealing her monstrosity, Karen weaponizes male fears of female sexuality through forcing patriarchal society to reckon with its mistreatment of her. The film's conclusion carries with it another overlap with pornography, especially because the presence of the television cameras recalls the rape film that played in the private booth during the film's opening. In pornography's casual misogyny, "the fantasy is in punishing resistant women for their revulsion. Of course, the punishments—usually one form of rape or another—often end with the fantasy woman's discovery of an insatiable hunger for whatever has been done to her" (16). In *The Howling*, Karen's inner wolf does not lead to insatiable sexual desire, as defined Eddie, but instead signifies a traumatic assault. She is not exhilarated by her ability to transform, shot through with sexual energy, but psychologically wounded by it. In transforming into a werewolf on live television, Karen forces viewers to feel her pain, not stand in awe of her power. In author Cynthia Freeland's terms, moments like this exhibit a common horror film tendency: "The woman's flesh, the reality behind the surface appearance, is made visible, and horror shows the 'wound' that we are revolted to look upon" (629).

Horror films have long been studied for their ability to engage with cultural ideas in unexpected ways. Critic Robin Wood's assertion that "seemingly innocuous genre movies can be far more radical and fundamentally undermining than works of conscious social criticism" seems perfectly applicable to *The Howling* ("An Introduction . . ." 83). Dante's film, guided by Sayles's screenplay, reveals a legacy of sexual assault lurking beneath the surface of society; Karen's invocation of the werewolves' ability to hide amongst people, concealing their monstrosity, resonates with surprising revelations about high-profile men abusing their power to sexually terrorize women. In Wood's formulation of horror films' exploration of "the return of the repressed," he argues that "the true subject of the horror genre is the struggle for recognition of all that our civilization represses or oppresses, its reemergence dramatized, as in our nightmares, as an object of horror, a matter for terror, and the happy ending (when it exists) typically signifying the restoration of repression" (79). It is hard to read the end of The Howling as "happy," when the sympathetic protagonist is shot on live television after revealing the marker of her experience of sexual assault, but Karen's death paves the way for the film's retreat to cynicism. It is unclear that her sacrifice will mean anything at all. The patrons in the bar who watched her transformation on television are indifferent or skeptical of its veracity, and Marsha's presence in the final moments is a standard horror-movie conclusion, reminding spectators that the threat has not been fully extinguished. That Marsha has survived the fire at the barn, while Eddie and a number of other male werewolves are dead, represents the film's ambivalence. Dangerous sexuality now walks the streets of Los Angeles, but it is no longer male—Marsha is Creed's "monstrous-feminine" made flesh. The more ubiquitous threat, however, is the audience's unwillingness to believe Karen's transformation. Like many rape victims, Karen has sacrificed in order to make others listen to her story of sexual trauma, but the world meets her painful confession with little more than a shrug. Karen's trauma, revelation, and eventual death continues the perpetual cycle that repeatedly victimizes her. That the television audience is largely indifferent to her story ensures that the cycle of victimization will continue for other women in Karen's position.

The Howling occupies an interesting place in the history of Holly-wood cinema and is something of a transitional work between the New Hollywood era and the blockbuster films that would come to dominate the 1980s. According to author David Greven, films of the New Holly-wood period, notably Taxi Driver (1976, Dir. Martin Scorsese), "represent pornography as an expression of the deadening of male psyches, which has grim consequences for those who wield as well as fall under the male gaze, and results, in part, from a phenomenon we can call por-nographication: the compulsory submission to pornographic sexuality that defines our long cultural moment from the 1960s to the present" (106). In an analysis of William Friedkin's queer slasher film Cruising (1980), Greven argues, "In the New Hollywood cinema, pornography emerges as an allegory for the deadening of all emotions related to sexuality, and, at the same time, as one of the forces behind this deadening" (199). In her book *From Reverence to Rape*, Molly Haskell calls the 1970s "The Age of Ambivalence," which saw a series of cultural arguments over inner conflicts among American women's vision of themselves, when "Hollywood hadn't ignored us." (392). Both Greven and Haskell wrestle with the complicated place of women in New Hollywood cinema, with Haskell focused on their relative erasure and Greven on men's inability to relate to them meaningfully. Haskell sees a change in the following decade, "In the two-steps-forward-one-step-back rhythm of social change, women began making their way back into movies in the eighties, with a subtly new consciousness. However opposed—or indifferent—anyone might be to the themes of feminism, they were there nonetheless, as often in the absence of women as in their presence" (395–396). *The Howling* typifies this change; it is a female-driven horror film that engages deeply with issues of sexual assault and the lingering trauma, with much to say about the necessity of confronting the problem. It does not accomplish this goal in spite of being a horror film, but because it is a horror film. *The Howling* illustrates Steven Shaviro's belief in "film's radical potential to subvert social hierarchies and decompose relations of power lies in its extreme capacity for seduction and violence" (65). Its focus on bodies—the engorged, aroused male werewolf and the threatened female victim—makes horror visceral, condemning male sexual violence and validating the experiences of traumatized female survivors.

Works Cited

Creed, Barbara. *The Monstrous-Feminine: Film, Feminism, Psychoanalysis*. New York: Routledge, 1993.

Greven, David. *Psycho-Sexual: Male Desire in Hitchcock, De Palma, Scorsese, and Friedkin*. Austin: University of Texas Press, 2013.

Freeland, Cynthia A. "Feminist Frameworks for Horror Films." *Film Theory and Criticism*, 7th edition, edited by Leo Braudy and Marshall Cohen. New York: Oxford University Press, 2009. 627–648.

Haskell, Molly. *From Reverence to Rape: The Treatment of Women in the Movies*, 2nd edition. Chicago: University of Chicago Press, 1987.

Herzog, Amy. "In the Flesh: Space and Embodiment in the Pornographic Peep Show Arcade." *Velvet Light Trap: A Critical Journal of Film & Television*, no. 62 (Fall 2008): 29–43. doi:10.1353/vlt.0.0001

MacDonald, Scott. "Confessions of a Feminist Porn Watcher." *Film Quarterly* 36, no. 3 (1983): 10–17. doi:10.2307/3697346

Morgan, Robin. "Theory and Practice: Pornography and Rape." *Take Back the Night: Women on Pornography*, edited by Laura Lederer. New York: William Morrow and Company, Inc., 1980. 134–140.

Mulvey, Laura. "Visual Pleasure and Narrative Cinema." *Issues in Feminist Film Criticism*, edited by Patricia Erens. Bloomington: Indiana University Press, 1990. 28–40.

Sayles on Sayles, edited by Gavin Smith. New York: Faber and Faber, 1998.

Shaviro, Steven. *The Cinematic Body*. Minneapolis: University of Minnesota Press, 1993.

Shumway, David R. *John Sayles*. Urbana: University of Illinois Press, 2012.

Smith, Gavin. "Introduction." *Sayles on Sayles*, edited by Gavin Smith. New York: Faber and Faber, 1998. ix–xvii.

Williams, Linda. "Film Bodies: Gender, Genre, and Excess." *Film Theory and Criticism*, 7th edition, edited by Leo Braudy and Marshall Cohen. Oxford University Press, 2009. 602–616.

———. *Hard Core: Power, Pleasure, and the "Frenzy of the Visible."* Expanded paperback edition. Berkeley: University of California Press, 1999.

———. *Screening Sex*. Durham, NC: Duke University Press, 2008.

Wood, Robin. "An Introduction to the American Horror Film." *Robin Wood on the Horror Film: Collected Essays and Reviews*, edited by Barry Keith Grant. Detroit: Wayne State University Press, 2018. 73–110.

———. "Art and Alligators." *Robin Wood on the Horror Film: Collected Essays and Reviews*, edited by Barry Keith Grant. Detroit: Wayne State University Press, 2018. 201–205.

CHAPTER 5

A Woman of Obvious Power

Witchcraft and the Case against Marital Rape in 1980s America

Emily Naser-Hall

We start with the eternal question: "Are you a good witch, or a bad witch?" In *The Wizard of Oz* (Fleming 1939), Glinda the Good Witch of the North poses this basic form of introduction to a newly arrived Dorothy Gale not merely out of innocent curiosity. Rather, she asks to assess whether this new arrival poses a direct threat to the oppressed Munchkins and their steadfastly protected way of life. Of course, the entire concept of a "good witch" sounds ludicrous to Dorothy, whose sole point of reference for these powerful and magical women seems to be the "old and ugly" version. However, feminist theorists like Silvia Federici (*Caliban and the Witch* 2004; *Witches, Witch-Hunting, and Women* 2018), Lindy West (*The Witches are Coming* 2019), and Starhawk (*The Spiral Dance* 2011), as well as activists such as Sarah Lyons (*Revolutionary Witchcraft* 2019), Brujas in the Bronx, Women's International Terrorist Conspiracy from Hell (WITCH), and the post-2016 uprising of "resistance witches" have worked to reclaim and reappropriate the witch as a wise woman whose supernatural abilities signify a form of oppositional knowledge that resists patriarchal logic and masculinist power structures.

The return of the witch as a source of resistant epistemologies in mid-twentieth-century feminist theory coincided with calls for reforms to a longstanding legal concept that depended, for its perpetuation, on the unquestionability of patriarchal logic on female subordination, sexual subjugation to men, and gendered power dynamics within marriage: the marital rape exemption, which excluded from prosecution for sexual assault husbands who committed acts of physical violation against their wives. The witch, then, acquired renewed relevance in the late 1970s and early 1980s, both as a figure of castrating female threat to the patriarchal order and as a feminist figure of sexual agency and opposition to institutionalized patriarchy. By considering historicist and feminist lenses alongside the complex legal arguments and social conceptions of traditional gender roles that became bound up in the debates concerning reforms to marital rape exemptions, depictions of witches in popular American films engage with previously unseen relationships between legal history and the figure of the witch in the cultural imaginary. Two representative examples of American witchcraft films from the late 1980s and early 1990s—*The Witches of Eastwick* (Miller 1987) and *The Witches* (Roeg 1990)—reveal the tension between increasing female power and sexual agency in the criminal justice system and the cultural backlash that such agency met from deeply embedded patriarchal attitudes of male sexual license and domination.

The Foundational Marital Rape Exemption and Its Links to Witchcraft Mythology

As is often the case in United States common law, the marital or spousal rape exemption, which excludes from statutes criminalizing nonconsensual sexual activity cases where the perpetrator of the assault is the victim's spouse, originated in seventeenth-century England and traveled alongside pilgrims and colonizers across the ocean to be transplanted wholesale into the burgeoning legal system of the new territories. Legal systems are notoriously slow to respond to shifts in popular cultural thought, and such responses, whether in the form of legislation or case law, typically concretize those shifts in public opinion only after extensive exercises in speech and debate. The marital rape exemption, however, appears to have emerged into English jurisprudence fully formed from the writings of Sir Matthew Hale and persisted almost entirely unchanged for nearly two hundred years. In his posthumously published *Historia Placitorum Coronae* (*The History of the Pleas of the Crown*) (1736), Hale states the common law position that "a husband cannot be found guilty of a rape committed by himself upon his lawful wife, for by their mutual matrimonial consent and contract the wife hath given herself up in this kind to her husband which she cannot retract" (Martin, Taft, and Resick 330). Hale cites no case law and no preexisting statutes to justify his position. Instead, he relies on an amalgamation of traditional conceptions of female bodies as property, first of their fathers and then of their husbands, legally subject to sanctionable violation only when assaulted by someone who is not their father or husband. Fathers and husbands, then, retained possessory rights over their daughters and wives and could exercise those rights through acts of sexual violence. Indeed, the origin of the word "rape" lies in the Latin word "*rapere*," meaning "to seize," highlighting the crime's initial and longstanding classification as a property crime rather than a crime against a body.

Judeo-Christian influences, particularly the Biblical elaboration of the "conjugal debt" a wife owes her husband and the unities doctrine in which the husband's and wife's bodies become singular (and therefore inviolable by each other) found in 1 Corinthians 7: 3–5, infiltrated both the Hale Doctrine and Blackstone's later elaboration of the unities theory in his *Commentaries on the Laws of England* (1765), which argues that "the legal existence of the wife is suspended during marriage" (Bennice and Resick 229). Since a wife was presumed to be the property of her husband, it was inferred that marital rape could not exist because a man could not steal his own property or commit an act of sexual violation against himself (Wiehe and Richards 59). However, Hale articulates none of this and his source material and rationale have been left to be inferred by legal scholars. Diana E.H. Russell, for example, states, "Though Hale offered no legal authority in support of his opinion, case law in the United States indicates an unquestioning acceptance of the Hale *dictum*, almost as if the courts were incapable of conceiving other resolutions of the issue" (Russell 17). The Massachusetts Supreme Judicial Court officially incorporated the Hale doctrine into US law in *Commonwealth v. Fogerty* in 1857, when the court relied solely on Hale's writings to hold that a man cannot commit a rape against his own wife. The Hale doctrine remained unchallenged until the early 1970s, when founder of the National Clearinghouse on Marital and Date Rape Laura X started a campaign to criminalize marital rape in California (Martin, Taft, and Resick 331). The Hale doctrine reemerged over one hundred years after its initial mention in U.S. case law in the 1976 murder trial of Judy

Hartwell, in which a Wayne County, Michigan, jury acquitted Hartwell of the fatal stabbing of her husband on the grounds that she acted in self-defense when he attempted to rape her (Cohen 3). Circuit Judge Victor Baum articulated the first judicial challenge to Hale's prevailing doctrine in his jury instructions: "A married woman has the right to forcibly resist unwanted sexual advances by her husband" (Cohen 3).

Besides casually penning the doctrine of marital rape exemptions that survived well into the twentieth century, Hale also made a name for himself as a consultant and presider at the 1662 Bury St. Edmunds witch trials, a series of cases conducted intermittently between 1599 and 1694 in Suffolk. Many scholars view Hale's role in witchcraft trials as a bruise to his legal ethos. David Finkelhor and Kersti Yllo, for example, claim, "It is now generally acknowledged that Hale, for all his legal erudition, was a rabid woman-hater who made his mark among his contemporaries by burning women at the stake as witches" (163). However, it is precisely Hale's active participation in early witchcraft trials and his articulation of the legal basis for such proceedings that granted his writings on marital rape their authority.

The language used to describe accused witches, from at least the 1448 publication of *Malleus Maleficarum* (*The Witch's Hammer*) to contemporary representations of witches in popular culture, hinges on the demonization of women who, in a variety of ways, defy patriarchal authority or threaten, sometimes by their mere existence, the stability and unquestionability of male-dominated power structures. The marital rape exemption similarly depends upon the acceptance of the conjugal debt and male ownership of the female body as property, both in legal doctrines that reinforce the maintenance of masculine control over political and social structures. The language employed in legal, historical, and critical writings on witchcraft relies on the same themes of power and control and the subjugation of women. From the early English marital rape doctrine and seventeenth-century witchcraft trials to texts produced during the major marital rape reform movements in the 1970s and 1980s, we can identify the tensions between shifting conceptions of women as property to women as individuals possessing bodily autonomy.

The gendered hostility associated with witchcraft charges, which G. Geis rather understatedly identifies as "a useful method for men to keep women inferior and in fear'" (39), manifests in similar ways in all cases of rape, including marital rape. Working from an intersectional perspective that acknowledged the interlocking oppressions of racism and sexism,

Black feminists began organizing around the issue of sexual violence as early as the 1940s. Esther Cooper and Rosa Parks aided Recy Taylor, the victim of a violent gang rape, in bringing her rapists to justice in 1944 (McGuire 47). Five years later, Mary Church Terrell participated in efforts to acquit Rosa Lee Ingram and overturn the death sentence she received from an all-white, all-male jury for the murder of a white sharecropper who had repeatedly sexually and physically assaulted her (Biondi 198–199). Much of the radical feminist criticism and activism of the time period focused on power relations within the family, fostering an emergent movement against legal reforms to sexual assault laws and coverture specifically. Estelle B. Freedman cites early nineteenth-century feminists such as Elizabeth Cady Stanton and Emma Goldman as inspirations for 1970s and 1980s feminist activists who called for sexual self-sovereignty for women within and outside of marriage (281). Critics of the family unit and of traditional gender dynamics called into question those assumptions about the naturalness of marriage, particularly its construction as both legally and socially giving men the right to sex with their wives at any time. As such, they interrogated the narrative of female subjugation, often manifested through physical violence, as a natural and therefore desirable and unchangeable phenomenon, creating an opening for the dismantling of deeply instilled patriarchal logics about female chastity, the conjugal debt, and inherent masculine superiority over women.

Landmark Marital Rape Case Law in the United States

This language of egalitarian relationships, the inherent power dynamics of heterosexual sex, and violence as a tool of masculinist domination formed the basis for feminist legal activism to eliminate marital rape exemptions in the United States in the late 1960s and 1970s. The late 1970s saw the first real victories in efforts to criminalize marital rape, both through a number of well-publicized cases and through legislative reform at the state level. In 1978, a state's marital rape exemption directly came under scrutiny in *Oregon v. Rideout*, the first case in the United States in which a man was prosecuted for raping his current wife. The news coverage of Rideout's prosecution provides significant insight into the ways in which questions of female bodily autonomy and independent subjectivity became inextricably bound in the issue of marital rape. An article published in 1979 with the title "I Kept Thinking I Could Help Him" details the violent emotional and sexual dynamics of the Rideout marriage, along with Greta Rideout's economic dependence on her abusive husband for the financial support of their young daughter. The article notes that Greta ultimately "quit submitting to [John's] desires," but that "her husband's sexual aggression became so violent she could label it nothing less than rape" (Celarier). Although the Oregon jury acquitted John of the charge of first-degree rape, Greta's comments to the press during the trial reveal the struggles of a habitually abused woman both to confront her abuser and to re-establish a sense of self. Notably, Greta's commentary directly ties John's sexual aggression to his violent hatred of women's displays of strength—a theme that reappeared in 2017, when John was convicted of sexually assaulting two other women. On refusing to have sex with her husband, Greta said, "'Before this point I had submitted. Now I was swimming to the surface to get out of the gutter, and he knew it. He saw the strength rising in me . . .'" (Celarier). Upon hearing his guilty verdict at his 2017 trial, John faced his accusers and stated, "I'm proud of these two ladies. They stood up to me" (Selsky).

As the first prosecution of a husband for allegedly raping his cohabiting wife, the Rideout case garnered national attention and brought to the surface the previously hidden or erased dialogues concerning the inherent power dynamics at play in cases of marital rape. News media coverage indicates how late-1970s American society viewed male violence against women and growing legal recognition of female bodily autonomy. Les Ledbetter of the *New York Times* highlighted witness testimony that claimed Greta had "taunted her husband with Oregon's revised rape law" and threatened him with malicious prosecution (Ledbetter A16). Perhaps no individual piece of commentary on the Rideout case better captures the underlying assumption of women's subjugation within the marital relationship than the off-the-cuff statement of California Senator Bob Wilson in 1979: "But if you can't rape your wife, who can you rape?" (Bazhaw 4, quoting O'Reilly 23).

Following the initial legislative and judicial moves to limit or eliminate the marital rape exemption, significant conservative backlash sought to preserve the patriarchal values underscoring such exemptions. While a number of states removed their exemptions entirely, others maintained protections for men in cohabiting couples or adopted new "voluntary social companion" exemptions, which gave partial immunity to men who had been permitted previous sexual contact with the accusing woman (Finkelhor and Yllo 148–149). These insidious strands of opposition to legal reforms engaged in more blatantly misogynist rhetoric. As Finkelhor and Yllo claim, "Probably the most passionately held 'new argument' against defining marital rape as a crime is that it will lead to frivolous complaints by vindictive women" (169). Such an argument was hardly new to the early 1980s; Matthew Hale and his contemporaries articulated the same concern in the seventeenth century, although the difficulty or impossibility of proving one's innocence hardly seemed to concern Hale at Bury St. Edmunds. Proponents of maintaining marital rape exemptions feared the scorned woman who, angered at her husband for some inconsequential reason, accused her husband of a crime of which he would be helpless to prove his innocence. For example, Alfred Onorato, a member of the Connecticut General Court, was convinced of this peril: "The jails are full of guys because of vengeful wives, and there are a lot of them. . . . And since society is already burdened with these kinds of women, the *last* thing we need is a law making it illegal for a husband to sexually assault his wife" (Finkelhor and Yllo 169).

The leap from angry wife to "evil witch" requires little mental effort. Witches pose a threat not only to the masculinist power balance of dominant man/subordinate woman, but also directly target those agents, always depicted as innocent, upon whom the patriarchy props its innate authority. Victoria L. Godwin notes, "Rhetorical use of the witch has been extremely effective at justifying normative gender roles" (91). Media representations of witches during the 1980s and 1990s, which experienced significant backlash against the previous decades' feminist activism from the Reagan administration and the Family Values movement, portrayed witches as hypersexualized man-haters who used their fearful magical powers for evil and disruption. As such, many witchcraft films disciplined witches either by forcing them into the roles of wives and mothers or by violently punishing them for transgressing patriarchal norms. Marion Gibson echoes Godwin's observations, identifying the ways in which the empty signifier of the witch has been filled with meaning via authorial positioning in the debate between American conservatives and liberals in the area of gender politics (89). The historical moment of the late 1980s and early 1990s saw not only legal withdrawals from or overt resistance to marital rape reform but also more broadly in gender dynamics and the structure of the heteronormative family within American cultural and political discourse. Increasingly public displays of feminine power and sexual autonomy, from growing prominence of Take Back the Night and sex-positive feminism to increasing female participation in corporate America, met brutal resistance during the Reagan administration's prioritization of familialism, Christian bedrock values, and welfare reform that disproportionately affected women. Anne-Marie Bird articulates the myths perpetuated with regard to the powerful "new" woman of the 1980s—embodied most clearly in the figure of the UK's first female Prime Minister, Margaret Thatcher—as influential in increasingly misogynist representations of witches and *femme fatales* in film. As women adopted a more assertive and active role in the public sphere and encroached on what was perceived as the traditionally masculine territory of the workforce, the "sexually aggressive, economically independent, power-dressed, successful career woman, with her own briefcase-carrying, mobile-phone-wielding personal assistant" manifested in cultural narratives as the 1980s power woman or "castrating bitch" (Bird 126). Anti-feminist backlash from Phyllis Schlafly, Katie Roiphe, Nancy Reagan, and others decried liberalization of sexual and reproductive justice, calling instead for a return to "traditional" womanhood and Christian family values.

It is worth noting, however, that mainstream cinematic representations of the witch as a threat, for better or worse, to patriarchal and familial authority relied on white constructions of the figure. From the initial sources of the vengeful pointy-hat-wearing witch stereotype such as *I Married a Witch* (Clair 1942) and *Bell, Book, and Candle* (Quine 1958) to depictions of witches as tamable in *Teen Witch* (Walker 1989), witches have been white and straight, with their powers devoted entirely to manipulating the world of men. Only in the mid-1990s, with films like *The Craft* (Fleming 1996) and *Eve's Bayou* (Lemmons 1997), did Black witches appear onscreen as central and (at least in the case of *Eve's Bayou*) wholly developed characters. Representations of Black witches typically focused on voodoo, depicting the religion with such sensational and hyperbolically horrifying images as animal sacrifices and rarely granting Black witches happy endings. For example, *Ouanga* (Terwilliger 1936) stars Fredi Washington as a Haitian voodoo priestess who curses her white neighbor after he overthrows her in favor of a white woman. Black authors and filmmakers, however, reappropriated the witch with historical specificity and sensitivity to the dual oppressions of sexism and racism that Black practitioners of voodoo and other forms of witchcraft experienced. Kasi Lemmons's *Eve's Bayou* and Maryse Condé's

1992 translation of *I, Tituba, Black Witch of Salem* remedied these prior erasures and flattening of Black witchcraft, reclaiming witchcraft in its specifically Black roots.

"It's Women Who Are the Source": Sex with the Devil in *The Witches of Eastwick* (1987)

Cultural narratives forward a particular vision of women and female sexuality that enables laws to be solidified. Court decisions and legislation codify cultural beliefs and enable them to be further disseminated, with the full disciplining and mandatory authority of the state, and facilitated through recirculation as established political and social norms. As such, a consideration of cultural representations through a historical and legal lens allows us to understand how we arrive at a certain understanding of female sexuality. Female sexuality is a cultural and legal construction, particularly given that human subjectivity itself is a social, and therefore legal, construction. The law is not a mere symptom of cultural attitudes, but a much more important signifier of norm formation that codifies and facilitates larger cultural narratives. It is no surprise, then, that the historical moment in which we identified the simultaneous propagation of discourses on marital rape and female bodily autonomy also saw a proliferation of renewed interest in filmic representations of the witch. Late 1980s and early 1990s iterations of witches reflect many of the narrative tropes of the binary between the male-serving normative wife/mother figure and the "new" sexually autonomous woman that are apparent in writings on marital rape.

George Miller's film adaptation of John Updike's novel *The Witches of Eastwick*, starring Cher, Susan Sarandon, Michelle Pfeiffer, and Jack Nicholson, exemplifies these tropes against the backdrop of a small New England community, a clear allusion to Salem and its famed witch trials. The movie narrates the transformation that three local women—Alexandra, Sukie, and Jane—undergo as they form a polyamorous sexual relationship with the slightly repulsive yet erotically irresistible newcomer Daryl Van Horne, acquire and hone supernatural powers, and, after magically banishing Daryl and his manipulative machinations from Eastwick, establish a matriarchal commune to co-parent their children. The women's discovery of their sexual pleasure and witching abilities, however, ultimately serves only to foreground both their initial subordination to Daryl and their final return to the traditional domestic domain of normative, desexualized maternal womanhood.

Daryl's manipulation extends beyond the purely sexual into discussions of female power as itself a supernatural entity. He commiserates about the lack of respect for women in the workforce into a clear branching of female autonomy, patriarchal desires for sexual domination, and magic: "Their dicks get limp when confronted by a woman of obvious power and what do they do about it? Call them witches." Daryl has thus drawn on the same vocabulary of growing female autonomy and its threat to masculine virility that was used to describe Judy Hartwell, Greta Rideout, and the widows at Bury St. Edmunds, now twisted into the language of demonic seduction. Intention, however, distinguishes this rhetoric coming from Daryl's mouth from the same words originating with Greta Rideout. Rideout testified about John's hatred of her own nascent empowerment in order to highlight the ways in which John's violence results not only from personal failures but also from structural patriarchal attitudes about female power. Daryl merely parrots the language of female autonomy as a seduction tactic while bringing the women further under his control.

Eventually, Alex, Sukie, and Jane acknowledge Daryl's manipulations and appropriation of their magic and respond by denying him his core objective: unlimited access to their sexuality. No longer able to dominate the Eastwick trio sexually or utilize their magical powers for his own purposes, Daryl now considers the women a threat. He initially dismisses the women's magical revenge as the result of "a little trouble at home, a little domestic problem, a little female problem," but ultimately reveals his embedded masculinist logic: "Women: a mistake, or did [God] do it on purpose? Because I really want to know! Because if it's a mistake, maybe we can do something about it!" In essence, Daryl asks whether women are mistakes constructed, and therefore easily dominated, by men, or whether women possess some otherworldly (i.e., not belonging to patriarchal power structures) knowledge and abilities about which men can understand and do nothing.

The film adaptation of The Witches of Eastwick, then, responds conservatively and from a patriarchal perspective to the assertions of female bodily autonomy that the early marital rape trials enacted into legal protections. Daryl's final rant about "do[ing] something about" the "mistake" of women implies this patriarchal perspective as the sole authority for defining the boundaries and margins of "acceptable" female power and sexuality that can be conceded while maintaining masculinist logic. Film critics, narrative scholars, and feminist theorists deride the film's erasure of Updike's original suggestion that witchcraft can exist in all intelligent, independent-minded women and that such power can be unlocked specifically through their frustration with and contempt for men (Welsh 153–154) and its predictable, given the historical moment in which the film was released, conversion from an allegory about witchcraft and feminism into "a special-effects orgy" (Podhoretz 121). *The Witches of Eastwick* film depicts a binary between empowered, supernaturally capable women and submissive mother figures, with a clear preference for the latter given the film's highly maternalized ending, and portrays female sexual autonomy as awakened solely through the machinations of dominant men. As such, the film challenges the narrative of female independence that criminal prosecutions for marital rape attempted to forward and instead falls on the side of continued patriarchal attitudes of male ownership of the female body.

She Never Looks Dangerous: Renewed Misogyny in *The Witches* (1990)

If *The Witches of Eastwick* portrays assimilationist disciplinary approaches to female autonomy, then Nicolas Roeg's 1990 film *The Witches* brutally depicts the necessary violence of disciplining feminine power, which manifests in the form of the castrating woman. Witches pose a threat not only to the masculinist power balance of dominant man/subordinate woman but also directly target those agents, always depicted as innocent, upon whom the patriarchy props its innate authority. *The Witches*, an adaptation of Roald Dahl's 1983 dark fantasy novel, masquerades as a children's movie but more often than not functions as traumatic nightmare fuel not only for its horrifying visual of Anjelica Houston removing her own face but also for its central storyline: a young English boy, whose parents have recently died, discovers while on a seaside vacation with his Norwegian grandmother that a secret society of child-hating witches exists in every country and is planning a mass offensive against their tiny antagonists. Grandmother Helga, as a figure of safe patriarchal femininity and motherhood, teaches her impressionable grandson about the threat of castrating women. In advising Luke to remain constantly vigilant, Helga warns, "What makes her dangerous is the fact that she never looks dangerous." That's right, kids! Real witches can come from anywhere!

Significant critical attention focuses on the film's blatant misogyny, which, as with the shift from feminine power to masculine discipline in the adaptation of *The Witches of Eastwick*, rewrites the central tension between childhood and adulthood in Dahl's original tale into a more sexualized conflict between traditional social values and the 1980s power bitch. Roeg's revisualization of the witches, particularly Grand High Witch Eva Ernst, highlights not only their grotesqueness, but also their carnality; their hands end in long talons, and the camera often lingers on Ernst's pointed, devouring teeth. The focus on eating—Helga's stories about witches eating children, close-up shots of Ernst appearing ready to consume the boys-turned-mice, and the discovery of the witches' plans to open candy stores to lure children to their deaths—draws a connection between Roeg's incarnation of Dahl's witches and the powerful woman as castrating, or "man-eating" (in this case a boy). Bird suggests that these witches invoke the mythic specter of the *vagina dentata*, with their alluring, terrorizing eroticism marking them simultaneously as monstrous and overly sexual (122–123).

If, as Kerry Mallan argues, "the female grotesque refuses the limits imposed on her body" (26), then Ernst, in her true, deformed shape, signifies the monstrosity read on the bodies of the 1980s woman of power. In *The Witches of Eastwick*, Alex, Sukie, and Jane experiment with their burgeoning sexuality but ultimately return to normative roles as nurturing mothers; Ernst embodies such deeply evil resistance to traditional womanhood that rehabilitation cannot occur. Roeg adds a new character and rewrites Dahl's original ending both to highlight the possibility for reassimilating reformed women and to punish, with shocking brutality, the irredeemable witch. Miss Irvine, Ernst's assistant, ultimately escapes her boss's talons and uses her powers to return Luke to his human form, thus indicating her transformation from magical witch to maternal figure. She appears nowhere in Dahl's book but manifests in the film as an indicator that "female power, like the figure of the witch itself, was only a fantasy, a temporary aberration" (Bird 128).

Furthermore, Roeg depicts Ernst's death not as a darkly comic accident but rather as the intentional murder of a woman whose powers have been violently ripped from her. After Luke tricks Ernst into taking her own potion, Ernst literally shrinks into a diminutive version of her grotesque self, speaking in a high-pitched squealing and now rendered entirely nonthreatening. Luke traps Ernst under a glass jug, and the male hotel owner stomps Ernst to death. With his adaptation, and these rhetorical moves specifically, Roeg reasserts the relevance of the witch to give monstrous shape to contemporary society's anxieties about the threat that newly powerful women, with new legal protections supporting them, pose to patriarchal society.

Conclusion

If the question "Are you a good witch or a bad witch" threw Dorothy Gale for a loop, then imagine how wildly unprepared she must have been to consider the nuances of such deceptively simplistic terms as "good," "bad," and "witch" that we have explored. Witchcraft narratives have profoundly shaped the western imagination, and narrative treatment of American witches respond to the cultural politics of their time. What witches always share, however, is their predisposition for challenging consensus; how amenable society is to that challenge of course depends on the specific political, legal, and cultural context of a given historical moment. Considerations of who and why a woman becomes classified as a witch and how and for what purpose the figure of the witch reemerges in the cultural imagination in a particular historical moment would certainly delay Dorothy's journey down the Yellow Brick Road, but for those with sufficient time and inclination they can reveal previously under-investigated trends and attitudes in such apparently divergent arenas as feminist standpoint epistemologies, pop culture, and nationwide legal reforms to a principle that had gone unquestioned for over two hundred years.

Arguments in favor of repealing marital rape exemptions in the 1970s and 1980s faced the monumental challenge of overcoming deeply entrenched patriarchal attitudes about traditional gender roles and accepted power dynamics under the marital contract. Based as it was in an understanding of wives as marital property whose physical bodies became incorporated into their husbands' bodies and as sexual objects obliged under the conjugal debt to provide their husbands with sex at any time, exemptions from prosecution for cases of marital rape grounded themselves on a firm foundation of masculinist logic. Feminists and legal reformers faced the challenge of convincing largely male-dominated judicial and legislative institutions to question their most basic assumptions about gender relations in a patriarchal society. With the figure of the witch, represented in popular films such as *The Witches of Eastwick* and

The Witches, we can establish a bridge between legal reforms to marital rape exemptions and feminist writings on female sexual and intellectual autonomy and consider how popular constructions of women and their sexuality respond to legal and theoretical shifts in the cultural imaginary.

But the witch's work is not done. While marital rape became illegal in all fifty states by 1993, most states continue to differentiate, both in prosecution and in sentencing, between marital and nonmarital rape. Feminist legal activists and women's rights organizations lobbied the federal elimination of marital immunity from sexual assault prosecution. In 1990, Robin West proposed the Married Women's Privacy Act to guarantee protection to every woman against violent sexual assaults, arguing that a federal law would "prohibit irrational discrimination against married women in the making and enforcement of rape laws" and guarantee that "states would not perpetuate or insulate the sexualized social, private, or intimate subordination of women by men" (76). Congress never passed such a law, and many states still treat spousal rape differently from other forms of sexual assault. In seventeen states, a spouse cannot be convicted of raping a partner who was unconscious, drugged, or incapacitated; in thirty-nine states, a spouse cannot be convicted of raping a partner under laws that criminalize statutory rape or sexual contact with people over whom they have a supervisory relationship (AEQuitas 1–2). Furthermore, feminist lobbyists in favor of uniform marital rape criminalization often neglect to address the implicit heterosexism at the heart of spousal rape legislation. Marital rape statutes require that the partners in question be legally married; given that same-sex marriage only became legal in the United States with the 2015 Supreme Court case *Obergefell v. Hodges*, marital rape legislation therefore applied solely to heterosexual couples. Despite activism particularly on college campuses to shed light on the prevalence of acquaintance rape, few legal or social headways have been made to address other forms of intimate violence (Anderson 1512–1513). The issues of ongoing consent, domestic coercion, and trauma that spurred the original feminist efforts to criminalize marital rape are not unique to the marital relationship. Formal neutrality on marital status in rape and sexual assault laws would not only enable states to criminalize marital and nonmarital sexual assault equally but also eliminate the silent heterosexism at the heart of marital rape legislation. Perhaps this is work for the new generation of witches, from *The VVitch*'s (Eggers 2015) Thomasin to the 4,900 members of the #BindTrump movement to the indigenous queer collective FirmeArt.

Works Cited

AEQuitas. "Charging Considerations in the Prosecution of Marital Rape." *Strategies In Brief* 34 (2019): 1–8.

Anderson, Michelle J. "Marital Immunity, Intimate Relationships, and Improper Inferences: A New Law on Sexual Offenses by Intimates." *Hastings Law Journal* 54 (2003): 1463–1572.

Bazhaw, Melissa Anne. *For Better or for Worse? Media Coverage of Marital Rape in the 1978 Rideout Trial.* 2008, Georgia State University, Master of Arts dissertation. *ScholarWorks*, https://scholarworks.gsu.edu/cgi/viewcontent.cgi?referer=?httpsredir=1&article=1034&context=communication_theses

Bennice, Jennifer A., and Patricia A. Resick. "Marital Rape: History, Research, and Practice." *Trauma, Violence, & Abuse* 4, no. 3 (2003): 228–246.

Bird, Anne-Marie. "Women Behaving Badly: Dahl's Witches Meet the Women of the Eighties." *Children's Literature in Education: An International Quarterly* 29, no. 3 (1998): 119–129.

Biondi, Martha. *To Stand and Fight: The Struggle for Civil Rights in Postwar New York City.* Cambridge, MA: Harvard University Press, 2006.

Brownmiller, Susan. *Against Our Will: Men, Women, and Rape.* New York: Simon and Schuster, 1975.

Celarier, Michelle. "I Kept Thinking Maybe I Could Help Him." *In These Times*, January 10–16, 1979.

Commonwealth v. Patrick Fogerty and Others. 74 Mass. 489 (Mass. Sup. J.Ct. 1857).

Davis, Kathe. "The Allure of the Predatory Woman in *Fatal Attraction* and Other Current American Movies." *Journal of Popular Culture* 26, no. 3 (1992): 47–57.

Federici, Silvia. *Witches, Witch-Hunting, and Women.* San Francisco: PM Press, 2018.

Federici, Silvia. *Caliban and the Witch: Women, the Body, and Primitive Accumulation.* Brooklyn: Autonomedia, 2004.

Finkelhor, David, and Kersti Yllo. *License to Rape: Sexual Abuse of Wives.* New York: Holt, Rinehart, and Winston, 1985.

Freedman, Estelle B. *Redefining Rape: Sexual Violence in the Era of Suffrage and Segregation.* Cambridge, MA: Harvard University Press, 2013.

Geis, G. "Lord Hale, Witches, and Rape." *British Journal of Law and Society* 5, no. 1 (1978): 26–44.

Gibson, Marion. "Retelling Salem Stories: Gender Politics and Witches in American Culture." *European Journal of American Culture* 25, no. 2 (2006): 85–107.

Godwin, Victoria L. "Love and Lack: Media, Witchcraft, and Normative Gender Roles." *Media Depictions of Brides, Wives, and Mothers*, edited by Alena Amato Ruggerio. Lanham, MD: Lexington Books, 2012. 91–101.

Ledbetter, Les. "Oregon Man Found Not Guilty on a Charge of Raping His Wife." *The New York Times*, December 28, 1978, p. A1.

Ledbetter, Les. "Woman in Oregon Rape Trial Says Husband Beat Her." *The New York Times*, December 27, 1978, p. A16.

Lyons, Sarah. *Revolutionary Witchcraft: A Guide to Magical Activism*. Philadelphia: Running Press Adult, 2019.

Mallan, Kerry. "Witches, Bitches, and *Femmes Fatales*: Viewing the Female Grotesque in Children's Films." *Papers: Explorations into Children's Literature* 10, no. 1 (2000): 26–35.

Martin, Elaine K., Casey T. Taft, and Patricia A. Resick. "A Review of Marital Rape." *Aggression and Violent Behavior* 12 (2007): 329–347.

McGuire, Danielle. *At the Dark End of the Street: Black Women, Rape, and Resistance—A New History of the Civil Rights Movement*. New York: Random House, 2010.

O'Reilly, Jane. "Wife Beating: The Silent Crime." *Time*, September 5, 1983, pp. 23–26.

Podhoretz, John. "She Lost It at the Movies." *The American Scholar* 58, no. 1 (1989): 117–122.

Russell, Diana E.H. *Rape in Marriage*. Bloomington: Indiana University Press, 1990.

Selsky, Andrew. "Oregon man accused of raping his wife in 1978 gets 16 years in other sex assaults." *The Seattle Times*, March 18, 2017. www.seattletimes.com/seattle-news/oregon-man-accused-of-raping-his-wife-in-1978-gets-16-years-in-other-sex-assaults

Starhawk. *The Spiritual Dance: A Rebirth of the Ancient Religion of the Great Goddess*. Twentieth Anniversary Edition. New York: HarperCollins, 2011.

State v. Rideout, 5 Fam. L. Rep. 2164 (December 27, 1978).

Welsh, J.M. "Bewitched and Bewildered Over *Eastwick*." *Literature/Film Quarterly* 15, no. 3 (1987): 152–154.

West, Lindy. *The Witches are Coming*. New York: Hachette Books, 2019.

West, Robin. "Equality Theory, Marital Rape, and the Promise of the Fourteenth Amendment." *Florida Law Review* 42 (1990): 45–69.

Wiehe, Vernon R., and Ann L. Richards. *Intimate Betrayal: Understanding and Responding to the Trauma of Acquaintance Rape*. London: SAGE Publications, 1995.

The Witches of Eastwick. Directed by George Miller, Warner Brothers Studio, 1987.

The Witches. Directed by Nicholas Roeg, Lorimar Film Entertainment, 1990.

CHAPTER 6

"The Rapiest Film of the 1980s"

Analog "Revenge Porn," Raced and Gendered Surveillance, and *Revenge of the Nerds*

Julia Chan

On September 27, 2018, U.S. Supreme Court nominee Brett Kavanaugh (now a Supreme Court justice) delivered a fiery opening statement to the Senate Judiciary committee decrying the accusation that he sexually assaulted Christine Blasey Ford in 1982 when they were teenagers. Of particular public interest was Kavanaugh's high school yearbook from that time, which appeared to be riddled with in-jokes and references to sex and heavy drinking, and whether the meanings of the in-jokes could shed light on his character and the alleged assault. Strikingly, in his explanation of the yearbook's contents, Kavanaugh cited iconic teen films from that time as culturally and socially influential:

> As high school students, we sometimes did goofy or stupid things. I doubt we are alone in looking back at high school and cringing at some things. For one thing, our yearbook was a disaster. I think some editors and students wanted the yearbook to be some combination of *Animal House*, *Caddy Shack*, and *Fast Times at Ridgemont High*, which were all recent movies at that time. Many of us went along in the yearbook to the point of absurdity. This past week, my friends and I

have cringed when we read about it and talked to each other.
(Kavanaugh)

No doubt Kavanaugh pointed to the influence of these teen films as a
way to indicate the "goofy" youthfulness of their yearbook jokes and,
perhaps, to absolve any personal responsibility for the yearbook's bad
taste by pointing to larger pop-cultural trends of the time.

But in a short piece for the *Guardian*, Steve Rose ruminates on
the significance of the films in terms of their gender politics: "Looking
back, those frat-house movies of the late 1970s/early 80s look less like
a celebration of masculine 'goofiness' and more a dodgy celebration of
rape culture and male entitlement—if not a training manual" (Rose).
Laura Kiesel of *BUST.com* makes a similar observation:

> Many men who, like Brett Kavanaugh, came of age in the
> 1980s are now climbing up or fully claiming the upper levels
> of power in this country. In many ways, the behavior alluded
> to in Kavanaugh's high school yearbook and calendar both
> exposes and embodies the lack of ethics and generally warped
> sexual standards that defined the era that marked his adoles-
> cence and young adulthood. His alleged sexual misconduct in
> high school and college is a reflection and byproduct of the
> decade, but it also existed well before. (Kiesel)

Rose and Kiesel are not the only ones reexamining older comedy "classics" from the vantage point of the contemporary #MeToo[1] moment
and reflecting on the representations of white male power and privilege
that run through them. *Revenge of the Nerds*, directed by Jeff Kanew and
released in 1984, is under similar contemporary scrutiny. *BlastMagazine.
com* listed it in their post entitled "4 coming-of-age classics that celebrate
rape culture" in which writer Melanie Elizabeth Bartlett argues:

> In these films, rape, disrespect, and invasions of privacy are
> mild annoyances at worst and great segues into new relation-
> ships at best. What strikes me as even more sinister is the
> way they present themselves as charmingly nostalgic anecdotes
> about growing up—about young boys being boys. Suddenly the
> horrifying sympathy for the Steubenville rapists in the media
> starts to make a whole lot more sense. (Bartlett)[2]

Similarly, Hadley Freeman in the *Guardian* writes, "In case you ever get asked in a pub quiz what was the rapiest film of the 1980s, [*Revenge of the Nerds*] is the official answer."

Set on a fictional American college campus, *Revenge of the Nerds* follows the struggles of a group of so-called nerds to start their own fraternity and exact revenge on their enemies: the cruel, exclusionary beautiful people who rule the campus. A successful Hollywood comedy, it grossed almost $41 million dollars in U.S. theaters (Roberts) and was followed by three sequels: *Revenge of the Nerds II: Nerds in Paradise* (Roth 1987), *Revenge of the Nerds III: The Next Generation* (Mesa 1992), and *Revenge of the Nerds IV: Nerds in Love* (Zacharias 1994). The *Revenge of the Nerds* series played a key role in constructing the figure of the nerd in the popular imagination (Quail 463; Shary 34). A former studio executive who had a hand in the film's genesis remarks on its influence on the current prominence of geek/nerd culture: "The audience response was startling. 'Nerds,' directed by Jeff Kanew, caught the wave. 'A geek classic,' raved *USA Today*. In heralding the film's Blu-ray re-release, Rotten Tomatoes declares it the film 'perhaps most synonymous with the '80s'" (Bart 18). Indeed, the DVD box's description of the film (the "Panty Raid Edition," released in 2007, which references a sequence in which the main characters perpetrate a "panty raid" on a sorority) bills it as "THE FRAT BOY COMEDY THAT STARTED IT ALL!"

Lesley Speed identifies three distinct eras of the "vulgar teen comedy film": the 1970s, the early '80s, and the late '90s (821). Whereas the 1970s films tend to depict youthful social rebellion, the '80s and '90s films mark "a crisis of male youth privilege" (Speed 822, 827). According to Speed, *Revenge of the Nerds* forms part of a particular film subset that incorporates voyeurism, including *Hot Chili* (Sachs 1985), *American Pie* (Weitz and Weitz 1999), and *Road Trip* (Phillips 2000) (836). Many '80s teen-sex comedy films—including "*Zapped!* (1982), *Getting It On* (1983), *Private School* (1983), *Screwballs* (1983), and *Revenge of the Nerds*"—were inspired by the success of the Canadian-made *Porky's* (1981) and tended to include "plenty of leering at bare-breasted young women through windows and peepholes into girls' bedrooms, locker rooms, and shower rooms, sometimes with the help of strategically placed cameras" (Tropiano 166–167).

Considering the realities of ubiquitous sexual assault on university and college campuses, the increasing awareness of so-called "revenge porn" and other forms of image-based sexual abuse, and the cultural and social reflection taking place in our contemporary #MeToo and #TimesUp moment, it is important to reconsider "classic" films like *Revenge of the Nerds*. In this chapter, I investigate the repertoire of discourses, tropes, and representations of sociocultural practices informing Rose's "training manual" that circulate in and through *Revenge of the Nerds*. In particular, I am interested in its relevance for understanding what is currently called "image-based sexual abuse" (McGlynn, Rackley, and Houghton), or IBSA. Its relevance is not necessarily as the frat boy comedy that started it *all*, as forms of nonconsensual sexualized imaging and surveillance occurred prior to the 1980s (Koskela 49; Calvert 203), but certainly as an important piece of popular and cinematic culture that both reflected and helped shape these forms as we encounter them today. These forms of looking are deeply entangled with what J. Macgregor Wise, among others, has identified as our collective surveillant imaginary: "the collection of stories, images, ideas, practices, and feelings that are associated with surveillance at a particular point in time" (4).

Ultimately, this chapter argues that *Revenge of the Nerds* can be read as an "analog" version of IBSA, with particular similarities to so-called "revenge porn." The narrative employs nonconsensual sexualized images of one of its main characters, Betty, as part of the titular "revenge." Accordingly, the film invests her image with social and economic value. The terms of this value are created in two ways, both of which are themselves circumscribed with raced and gendered notions of privacy. The first is through sociocultural understandings of whiteness that inform how we value bodies. The second is through the use of the surveillance frame/relationship. By "surveillance frame/relationship," I refer to the idea that surveillance as a conceptual frame around the image, or as the relationship between the looker and the looked-at, impacts how we read an image and thus how its value is created (McGrath 31–32; Turner 96–97).

This chapter begins by examining how *Revenge of the Nerds* aligns the establishment of the main characters' (white) masculinity with the procuring of nonconsensual sexualized images. It then argues that the narrative places particular social and economic value on the character of Betty, her body, and nonconsensual images of her naked body because of her social positioning as a white, cisgendered, able-bodied, heterosexual, normatively attractive female. The chapter concludes with the claim that the way the main characters procure images of this body—through sexualized covert surveillance—is a process of sexualized domination that has parallels with contemporary "revenge porn" and other violent expressions of misogyny.

Dominant White Male

The 1980s were a time in which America began a clear political shift to the right (Prince 11). Many films at that time reflected an overall project of reasserting ideals of masculinity both socially and culturally in reaction to the progress of feminism (Traube 19). In specific relation to straight white middle-class teen masculinity, the teen films of the 1980s dramatized this particular subjectivity as more concerned with its entitlement to a good time than with what effects such behavior might have on others, and the larger "crisis" around that subjectivity's access to such "male, middle-class privilege" (Speed 820). As this chapter will show, these questions of masculine entitlement and struggle can be seen in *Revenge of the Nerds* right through to the contemporary moment as it finds myriad expression in campus rape culture, "alt-right" movements, and certain iterations of IBSA, among many others.

Applying apparatus theory reveals the cinematic legacies of gender and race that undergird contemporary iterations of IBSA and the discourses that surround it. For Jean-Louis Baudry, the cinematic experience centers the viewer, merging them with the cinematic apparatus and its point of view—and, crucially, this positioning is ideological (364). Christian Metz adds to this theorization by observing that much of the pleasure of cinematic spectatorship is in its evocation of a voyeuristic experience (60). Finally, Laura Mulvey posited that not only did classical Hollywood cinema depend on the pleasure of voyeurism for its continued success, but that this pleasure is specifically articulated from a Western heterosexual male point of view that makes the female body its focus (838). From this vantage, the ideology of cinematic vision centers not just any spectator, but a presumed (white) heterosexual male spectator, and focuses on not just any "object," but the (white) female body. Some scholars[3] have rightly challenged the emphasis on whiteness and heteronormativity in theories of cinematic spectatorship; in this sense, reading *Revenge of the Nerds* as deploying a cinematic gaze that assumes a white, heterosexual, and male point of view is useful for understanding the social and cultural economies at work in this particular narrative. We might therefore understand how the "centered" (straight, white) male film viewer, receiving voyeuristic pleasure through the cinematic apparatus that allows him an all-seeing access to the white female body, is replicated on the narrative level in *Revenge of the Nerds* through the (mostly white and heterosexual) nerds' pleasurable viewing of female bodies. In a similar approach, Despoina Mantziari explores how creepshots of women's bodies can be understood as an "exten[sion] of such [cinematic] 'pleasures'" (398). Critically, though, this pleasure is informed not just by gender and gendered structures of looking but also by race, racial privilege, and practices of surveillance.

The plot follows the nerds' struggle to form a new fraternity called Lambda Lambda Lambda (or "Tri-Lambs"), at a fictional school called Adams College. The Tri-Lambs, led by the main character Lewis Skolnick, plot to take revenge on the all-male Alpha Beta fraternity and all-female Pi Delta Pi (or "the Pis") sorority—both of which comprise conventionally attractive, mostly white members—that have repeatedly humiliated them. As an exemplary "nerd," Lewis is denied the privileges of more socially accepted forms of masculinity. While the Tri-Lambs' membership includes Lamar, a gay Black man, and Takashi, a Japanese man, the fraternity's two main figures are the white Lewis and his best friend Gilbert. At the same time, Lori Kendall notes that "the film also sometimes codes the white nerds (especially Lewis) as Jewish. Indeed, the authors of the screenplay indicated that they 'tried to write almost [an] anti-Nazi movie' (*People Weekly*, 1984)" (266). Winning Betty, the most desirable Pi woman, is central to Lewis's revenge on the college's perceived beautiful people. Initially, Betty leads Lewis to believe she might be sexually interested in him, but ultimately colludes with her boyfriend Stan (a football player and leader of both the Alpha Betas and the entire Greek council) to harass the Tri-Lambs. When this collusion causes serious damage to the Tri-Lambs' bid to become a full fraternity, Lewis and his friends plot revenge. As Gilbert puts it, "Their action tonight demands an immediate retaliation. And if we don't, we're nothing but the nerds they say we are." Lewis comes up with a two-part plan for revenge: one for the fraternity, and one for the sorority. The Alpha Betas get "liquid heat" rubbed into their jock straps—a simple revenge aimed at injuring a body part clearly associated with the Alpha Betas' masculinity and, perhaps, their sexual access to women like the Pis. The revenge on the Pis, however, is much more involved. One night, under the sound of the *Mission Impossible* theme, the Tri-Lambs invade the sorority house in an apparent panty raid. However, amidst the screams and confusion, two Tri-Lambs secretly infiltrate the attic to install a series of surveillance cameras. The live surveillance feed, beamed straight into the Tri-Lambs' house, allows them unfettered visual access to the naked sorority sisters—including Betty.

The cameras allow the Tri-Lambs to access a voyeuristic power that begins to inscribe them—and particularly Lewis—with an aggressive, heteronormative masculinity (Kendall 269). The film expresses "not simply a subordinated masculinity but one that is violently erupting in an attempt to become dominant, creating a tentative and shifting relationship between dominant and subordinate constructs" (Quail 463). A similar dynamic of masculinity has been observed in studies of so-called "creepshot"[4] sites and communities: "The act of taking a creepshot is [understood as] a performance of one's masculinity," Chrissy Thompson and Mark Wood observe, and those who do not live up to the community's standards may have their masculinity challenged (10–11). Thus, the process of creating nonconsensual sexualized images of the sisters can be read as an important step in the Tri-Lambs' ascension into a position of dominant "masculine" power on the Adams campus, where Lewis begins to perform and embody a particular ideal of masculinity: aggressive and sexually dominating.

Revenge of the Nerds can be located in relation to other teen films released during the same period that explore the "geek" character's particular challenges of masculinity and sexual coming-of-age (Driscoll 49). Geeks and nerds are primarily associated with a white, straight masculinity more broadly (Massanari 332). The preexisting Tri-Lamb fraternity that the nerds attempt to create at Adams is presented as a fraternity for Black men; in this sense, the film aligns the nerds with the civil rights movement while simultaneously "displac[ing] claims of African Americans for civil rights" (Kendall 267, 266). The film thus shifts the subject of oppression and resistance from Black communities to the (mostly) white nerds, even as it apparently denounces the normative masculinity embodied by the Alpha Betas (Kendall 265). In other words, the film's critique of normative masculinity is framed largely in relation to less-advantaged white male subjects (Kendall 267). This narrative move elides the injustices that Black communities and other marginalized groups have historically experienced and resisted by framing the mostly white nerds as an equivalent group (Kendall 265–266) in order to justify the nerds' ultimate "revenge." Indeed, Kom Kunyosying and Carter

Soles observe more generally that "geek" narratives tend to ascribe to geeks a "simulated ethnicity" that signals "a put-upon status equivalent to the markedness of a marginalized identity such as that of a person of color" ("Postmodern"). The nerds' struggle, then, is with a normative, dominating, white masculinity personified by the Alpha Betas, and while the "oppression" of the nerds is associated with social justice movements like civil rights, they attempt to and ultimately succeed in inhabiting the very masculinity the film apparently critiques (Kendall 266).

Echoes of this critique can still be seen today in more virulent, complicated forms in "the manosphere" as explored in Debbie Ging's 2017 study, such as in those who identify as incels—short for involuntary celibates[5]—or PUAs—short for pick-up artists (Ging 3, 12). Still, the "manosphere's" alternative masculinities do not challenge all aspects of the status quo: citing the work of D.Z. Demetriou, Ging notes that "hegemonic masculinity borrows aspects of other masculinities that are strategically useful for continued domination" and thus "the result is not a homogenous pattern of hegemonic masculinity" (5). In other words, like incels and PUAs, the nerds' actions in *Revenge of the Nerds* may seem on their face to critique or resist so-called "alpha male" culture (to use today's parlance). However, the more complicated patchwork of masculinity the film employs still ultimately reifies traditional gender dynamics that rely on masculine domination and relations of violence: the nerds are not terribly interested in equality, only in reversing the existing hierarchy in order to secure the "top" social spot on campus for themselves.

It is presented as important for the nerds—especially Lewis—to assert domination/masculinity to escape their subordinated/feminized position (Kendall 264). Carine Mardorossian argues that all forms of violence—not just the sexual variety—is "sexualized" (5). That is, the perpetrator/victim relationship is culturally and socially understood as a heteronormative binary in which "the dominant masculine position . . . cast[s] the other in the subordinate feminine one" (5). Crucially, anybody of any gender can occupy either position in a violent encounter: Mardorossian is not ascribing essential qualities to violence or to masculinity/femininity. Rather, the aggressive position is socially and culturally constructed as masculine and the victimized position as feminine, inscribing violence with heteronormativity and vice versa. *Revenge of the Nerds* reproduces this gendered binary, even though the film appears on its surface to challenge hegemonic forms of masculinity.

Valuable White Female

In terms of normative female sexual desirability, Betty is presented as the ideal: white (with blond hair and blue eyes), cisgender, heterosexual, middle/upper class, and able-bodied with a thin physique. The film suggests that this particular woman is the most socially and sexually desirable, and effectively creates "a hierarchy of attractiveness which puts white people, particularly blond white people, at the top" (Kendall 268). In addition to her physical desirability, Betty is a prominent figure on campus as a sorority sister and cheerleader. As such, she is the focus of Lewis's sexual attention: to win her affections would grant him access to social currency and elevate him from the socially damning label of "nerd." Betty's social and sexual value, then, is a function of her desirability: the intersection of her race, gender, and class positioning as a normatively attractive white female occupying a particular social status on campus. Kimberle Crenshaw's important notion of intersectionality, developed to explain the layers of discrimination that Black women can experience (Crenshaw 149), demonstrates that one's social position is the result of the confluence of several social factors, including race, gender, class, ability, sexuality, and others. Importantly, then, the value of any *images* of Betty's desirable white female body are likewise indexed to her particular social positioning.

Underpinning this idealization of Betty and the subsequent value of her surveilled naked body (which, later in the film, is transformed into images for distribution) is a gendered and racialized notion of privacy (Osucha 72). The young, white, middle-class, heterosexual female is a figure often associated with victimhood and protection in relation to sexual assault—including IBSA (Karaian 2012, 2014; Chun and Friedland 2015; Hasinoff 2015). In their article on online nude photo leaks, Wendy Hui Kyong Chun and Sarah Friedland argue that cultural discourses around this phenomena are informed by gendered and raced anxieties. Specifically, they draw on the work of Eden Osucha and Eva Cherniavsky to show that "the right to privacy in the United States was juridically defined in relation to a white femininity that was allegedly injured by mass circulation" (Chun and Friedland 3). Osucha demonstrates that the notion of protecting "white femininity" informed the creation of American privacy laws and shaped media discourse on privacy rights at the turn of the twentieth century (69). Samuel Warren and Louis Brandeis's key American legal paper, "The Right to Privacy" (1890),

framed the potential harms of visualizing technology as a particular
concern for white female bodies, "in which the technologized consumer
gaze produced in the mass-mediated public sphere is characterized as an
intrinsically pornographic one" that is trained on an "archetypal violated
object . . . invariably gendered female" (Osucha 70). Osucha contrasts
the nineteenth-century mass-media visualization of white female bodies
and the anxieties of its commodifying effect with the unproblematized
visual stereotyping of female bodies of color, where such stereotyping
facilitates commodification and exploitation (73). For Osucha, this potential transformation into commodity is understood as most "injurious" to
white female bodies above all others.

Chun and Friedland draw upon Cherniavsky and Osucha to focus
their analysis on the notion of a "ruined" white female modesty (9).
However, I am further interested in Cherniavsky's discussions of the
cinematic practice of producing Mitsuhiro Yoshimoto's "commodity-im-
ages" (78) and the place of white female bodies in those practices.
Cherniavsky introduces the concept of "incorporation," which is the
idea that one's full expression as a subject with social and economic
value is bound up with one's raced and gendered body (xv). The body
racialized as non-white loses its individuality more easily—selfhood and
body seen as not fully integrated or "incorporated"—and is thus more
vulnerable to exploitation and "dispersal" (Cherniavsky xv). The white
body, on the other hand, is afforded fuller "incorporation" and is thus
more protected (Cherniavsky 85).

For Chun and Friedland, "Web 2.0's crisis of exposure is being played
out . . . over the young [white] girl who is circulated pornographically"
and thus whose "virtue" is subjected to "ruin" (9). The key harm that
media discourses on nude-photo leaks articulate is "injur[y] by mass [dig-
ital] circulation" that parallels familiar slut-shaming discourses: the "slut"
who gets around and whose reputation is subsequently destroyed (Chun
and Friedland 3). But Osucha's discussion of this injury, which Chun
and Friedland do not take up, further posits the idea of "publicity as
commodification" (82). In other words, the young, white, "incorporated"
(to use Cherniavsky's term) female body that is imaged and subsequently
circulated is a commodifying—and thus injurious—process, because it
strips her of not just her "virtue" but of her *social and economic value*
accrued through bodily privacy. Such privacy may be aligned with (expectations of) sexual chastity, which historically has been understood as a
valuable "commodity" for young white women on the marriage market

(Cocca 11). While Betty is not characterized as particularly "chaste" or virginal, she is positioned as sexually out of reach for men of lower social standing. Thus, the economic value of the white female body is tied to its perceived (sexual/visual) inaccessibility.

The higher valuation of white female bodies and their privacy in relation to female bodies of color is reflected in a number of other cultural phenomena, such as in pornography, where Black women performers are routinely paid less than white women performers (Miller-Young 237); in the cultural privileging of white women's experiences of sexual violence, suggesting the devaluation of female bodies of color (Projansky 158); and in the film narratives that characterize women of color as sexually voracious and thus more accessible than white women (Shohat and Stam 157). These various racialized imaginings assign a higher cultural, social, and economic value to the white female body, its association with privacy, and its perceived ability to withhold sexual consent.

Due to the difficulty of access, then, Betty's body and her sexual consent are highly valued in the narrative's economy of bodies. If Betty's initial ability to withhold her body from Lewis is a function of her higher social status—a status predicated on the valued privacy of her white femininity—then Lewis's sexual surveillance of her reverses this status through the violation of that privacy and the visualization of her naked white body. Prized for her inaccessibility as an idealized white woman, the surveillance images procured of her translate into both social and monetary value for Lewis as they simultaneously devalue Betty.

Surveillance Technologies, Whiteness, and the Value of the Nonconsensual Image

Looking at white female bodies, and especially using media technologies to do so, occurs frequently throughout *Revenge of the Nerds*. Laura Mulvey's work on the male gaze and female screen bodies is taken up by Kelly Oliver (2017), Anne Burns (2018), and Stuart Hargreaves (2018) in their analyses of creepshots. While Hargreaves correctly observes that creepshots "are better understood as new forms of public surveillance, with a particularly gendered bent" (180), race is also critical to consider. In this film, the targeted and observed female body is white, and this fact plays a role both in the value of the *image* and in (re)producing the value of *whiteness*. Surveillance creates (a) a specific frame around the image of the white body that heightens its value even more, and (b) a specific relationship between the (presumed white male) watcher and the watched that is important to the ultimate transformation of Lewis from emasculated nerd to "champion" (in the film's final scene, the Queen song "We Are the Champions" plays to underscore the jock–nerd social status reversal).

The Authenticity and Nonconsent of Surveillance

Images produced through surveillance are believed to be truthful and authentic. Thomas Levin argues that where film narratives once tended to represent photographic imagery as an authentic and trustworthy source of "evidence," since the 1990s they have increasingly turned to "real-time" surveillance imagery instead for their "seemingly unproblematic, reliable referentiality" (585). The Tri-Lambs' surveillance feed allows them to watch the sorority sisters in "real time" without their knowledge, and this watching violates or vitiates consent. The point of this type of surveillance is to guarantee the "authenticity" of the imagery and create a gendered relationship of domination. This type of imagery is an example of what David Bell has called "surveillance porn," which he compares to "other sexual practices which eroticize power dynamics, such as sadomasochism" (205). Bell notes that the covert acquisition and candid nature of hidden camera footage "gives it extra value" (207). Authenticity thus functions to increase the economic and erotic "value" of the sexual surveillance image—a dynamic that clearly plays out in *Revenge of the Nerds*: not only do many of the Tri-Lambs derive sexual pleasure from the eroticism of the surveillance feed's "authenticity," they also eventually profit from that authenticity when they sell Betty's naked image in a fundraising competition (a scene to be discussed shortly).

The nonconsent of this surveillance, meanwhile, serves to establish a gendered relation of domination between the popular sorority women and the unpopular nerds. The surveillance feed can be considered in terms of John McGrath's "performative space." Surveillance does not simply show what is happening: it also "hails" the viewer to interpret the image in a particular way (McGrath 22–23). The allure of surveillance is "in watching people think that they are not being watched" and this produces "another space—a watched space, which prior to our watching did not exist" (McGrath 48). This watched space further produces "a feeling of power over the video's subjects" (McGrath 48). Similarly, in the context of narrative films, the surveillance frame often "hails" the viewer to anticipate violence (Turner 97). Nonconsent is critical to the creepshot and filmed sexual assault, making the image valuable and erotic, where nonconsent is the very enactment of gendered violence and domination (Burns 30; Oliver, "Rape"). Indeed, as Burns notes, "creepshots are not just about looking at others, but also concern forcibly taking something from them" (35). The creation of domination is wherein the "revenge" that the Tri-Lambs seek lies, which establishes and asserts the dominant white "masculinity" of Lewis and his friends in Mardorossian's structural, gendered relationship of violence. Thus, the surveillance image is not a neutral image: its very enframing *as* a moment of concentrated surveillant watching informs how we interpret the image. The surveillance images of the sorority sisters "hail" us to interpret surveillance as *sexualizing*, where the process of sexualization is understood to be structured by the violence of nonconsent.

To explore the nature of this gendered relation of domination more deeply, we can consider how intimacy functions within it. Drawing on Georg Simmel, Staci Newmahr[6] argues in her study of S&M that "intimacy is most fundamentally about *access*. It is constituted by and through access to another's secrets, another's private or new expressions of self, and another's resources" (171). Intimacy is not always a positive relationship: violence can also be an act of intimacy because it breaches boundaries (175–176). Newmahr also observes that obtaining intimacy with another is a kind of domination, a "competitive process" that "represents conquest" because the underlying desire is "to be the only one to gain it" (172). Intimacy, then, plays a role in how the nonconsensual image may be (e)valuated, because it is the outcome of a struggle that achieves a prized visual intimacy without the other's consent.

The creation of visual intimacy as the outcome of nonconsent is a critical point in understanding how the image fits into this situation. In her analysis of the strengths and weaknesses of Catharine MacKinnon's anti-pornography arguments, Frances Ferguson asserts that MacKinnon's strongest observation is related to her thinking on the use of pornography in a harassing way. In this context, "a representation may become an action by being watched" (690). Ferguson points out that representations can be used to accomplish an action (673). In a related vein, Phil Carney insists on recognizing the Austinian "performative" ability of photographs (282). Thus, "the harassing image is harassing not so much because of its content, what it says, but rather because it uses an image as a conspicuous expression of the difference between the parties who view it" (Ferguson 690). In terms of IBSA and *Revenge of the Nerds*, images may become a harassing or abusive action when they are used to enact domination of the viewer over the viewed, or the image-maker over the imaged.

Conclusion: Analog "Revenge Porn"

Although it may seem to be a problem born from our contemporary digital context, IBSA is not just an abstraction of digital images affecting digital subjectivities—it is also material and has material effects. The apparent " 'weightlessness' " with which some may characterize Deleuze's late-capitalist, digitally driven, dispersive control society still cannot be separated from the material bodies that populate, animate, and power it (Randell-Moon and Tippet 80). *Revenge of the Nerds* serves as a reminder of this materiality, as a film that predates the widespread use of the internet and depicts what might be considered an "analog" foreshadowing of so-called "revenge porn" in its contemporary form. The following scene from the film demonstrates the parallels between the nerds' use of Betty's image and contemporary "revenge porn."

After the panty raid, the Tri-Lambs participate in a money-raising competition between the sororities and fraternities that will also determine control of the Greek council. The Tri-Lambs' strategy is to sell "pies": aluminum pie plates filled with whipped cream, underneath which is the photograph of a topless Betty. This image has been gleaned from the nerds' surveillance-camera footage, printed and copied hundreds of times. When a shocked Stan sees this, he says, "That's *my* pie"—or, perhaps, "That's *my* Pi." The name of the Tri-Lambs' sales booth is "Eat a 'Pi' for Charity," where "Pi" is a play on the sorority's name, "pie" as food, and the slang term "hair pie." "Eat a 'Pi' for Charity" also refers to the "consumption" of Betty's image, the notion of sexually "consuming" women, and their cultural association with food (being called "sweetie pie," "sweet cheeks," "tart," or "cupcake," for example). Betty's image proves so popular that the Tri-Lambs raise the most money to win the competition, and eventually win control of Greek council.

Contextualized within the usually restricted access to Betty's desirable white body and its nakedness, the image is understood to be rare and difficult to procure. The public sale of this image simultaneously exploits Betty's high value—resulting in wide distribution and thus profit—while also decreasing it through exposure and circulation. Her decrease in social value serves to increase the Tri-Lambs' social value and (masculine) status where the valuable image's procurement demonstrates their superior intellectual and technical skills, as well as their ability to perform and claim a dominant, heterosexual masculinity (Kendall 269). Similarly, in the context of creepshot communities, Mantziari notes how "the skillful use" of technology is indexed to "the voyeur's ego" (401). Coupled with the "authenticity" of the surveillance frame and the domination it implies, the nonconsensually procured and distributed surveillance image of a naked Betty is understood as highly valuable, both economically and socially. In the online "political economy of reputation," such nonconsensual sexualized images are similarly invested with real value on "revenge-porn" sites, commanding both advertising revenue and fees for online "reputation management" (Langlois and Slane 120, 128, 131–132).

As suggested earlier, "revenge" in the title of this film is notable in the context of so-called "revenge porn," in that this film is very much concerned with white male entitlement[7] to white female bodies and the narrative's dramatization of what are essentially pre-internet "revenge-porn" tactics—nonconsensually procured and distributed sexualized images whose circulation plays into economies of gender, race, and financial profit. Examining the film's narrative, then, reveals that what we currently understand as image-based sexual abuse is not a phenomenon particular to our contemporary digital culture but rather has emerged from a long legacy of raced and gendered cinematic and surveillance practices that I argue require further excavation.

As Kendall notes, the word "revenge" also refers to an idea that was already in popular play at the time of the film's release: nerds may be nerdy, but they can grow up to be rich precisely because of those very qualities identified as "nerdy" (266). Such notions of social "revenge" in today's climate, however, have perhaps taken a markedly sinister turn. In her description of Elliot Rodger's explanation for his 2014 attack in Isla Vista, California, which killed several people (including himself), Amia Srinivasan writes:

> He [Rodger] writes of dyeing his hair blond (Rodger was half-white and half-Malaysian; blond people were "so much more

beautiful"); . . . being shoved by a pretty girl at summer camp ("That was the first experience of female cruelty I endured, and it traumatised me to no end"); becoming incensed by the sex lives of his peers ("How could an inferior, ugly black boy be able to get a white girl and not me? I am beautiful, and I am half-white myself. I am descended from British aristocracy. *He* is descended from slaves"); . . . and fantasising about a political order in which he ruled the world and sex was outlawed ("All women must be quarantined like the plague they are"). The necessary result of all this, Rodger said, was his "War on Women," in the course of which he would "punish all females" for the crime of depriving him of sex. He would target the Alpha Phi sorority, "the hottest sorority of UCSB," because it contained "the very girls who represent everything I hate in the female gender . . . hot, beautiful blonde girls . . . spoiled, heartless, wicked bitches." He would show everyone that he was "the superior one, the true alpha male." (Srinivasan)

Elliot Rodger has since taken on an elevated status within the so-called incel community. Indeed, Alek Minassian referred to Rodger as "the Supreme Gentleman" in a Facebook post purportedly written before the former allegedly drove a van into pedestrians in Toronto in April 2018 (Yang and Gillis); in March 2021, Minassian was found "guilty of 10 counts of first-degree murder and 16 counts of attempted murder" (Carter).

Clearly, the value of the idealized blonde white sorority woman and the struggle of masculinities engaged in *Revenge of the Nerds* continue to play out in North America. And rape culture more broadly is, unfortunately, alive and well. Brett Kavanaugh's remarks on the influence of 1980s popular cinema on him and his college-age peer group, then, suggest that the raced and gendered cinematic pleasures of looking are deeply entangled with privilege, entitlement, sexual violence, and rage—the echoes of which we still experience today.

Notes

1. While this hashtag was publicized in 2017 by American actor Alyssa Milano, its creation and the Me Too movement itself is attributed to American activist Tarana Burke and her organization Me Too, which was founded in 2006. See metoomvmt.org/about/#history.

2. This is a reference to a highly publicized trial in Steubenville, Ohio, in which two teenage boys raped a teenage girl and circulated images of it.

3. For example, see bell hooks's essay "The Oppositional Gaze: Black Female Spectators."

4. Creepshots are a form of nonconsensual sexualized images that often concentrate on particular body parts filmed or photographed surreptitiously, usually in public places.

5. It should be noted that "involuntary celibate" was actually coined by a bisexual woman, who built a website in the early 1990s called Alana's Involuntary Celibacy Project, which was meant to be "a home for all incels"—that is, a supportive place all kinds of people who were involuntarily celibate for a variety of reasons. After Alana stopped hosting the site a few years later, the term and its associated community have since narrowed into its contemporary iteration of misogyny (Baker).

6. Thank you to Morgan Oddie for suggesting Newmahr's discussion of intimacy to me.

7. The film also suggests the nerds' entitlement in a general sense. The text of the DVD back-cover description claims that *Revenge of the Nerds* has finally gotten the respect it deserves" and that the film ends with the nerds taking "their rightful place at the top of the social ladder!"

Works Cited

Baker, Peter. "The Woman Who Accidentally Started the Incel Movement." *Elle*, March 1, 2016. *Hearst Magazine Media Inc.* www.elle.com/culture/news/a34512/woman-who-started-incel-movement

Bart, Peter. "Pundits Say the Entertainment World Is Ripe for a Twee-peat: 'Revenge of the Nerds' Was an '80s Icon; Now Some Portend a Groundswell of Geekdom." *Variety*, August 5, 2014, p. S18. *Academic OneFile.* link.galegroup.com.proxy.queensu.ca/apps/doc/A381405139/AONE?u=queensulaw&sid=AONE&xid=b52a9d42

Bartlett, Melanie Elizabeth. "4 Coming-Of-Age Classics That Celebrate Rape Culture." *BlastMagazine.com*, September 3, 2013. blastmagazine.com/2013/09/03/4-coming-age-classics-celebrate-rape-culture

Baudry, Jean-Louis. "Ideological Effects of the Basic Cinematographic Apparatus." In *Film Theory and Criticism*, edited by Leo Braudy and Marshall Cohen. New York: Oxford University Press, 2004. 355–365.

Bell, David. "Surveillance is Sexy." *Surveillance & Society* 6, no. 3 (2009): 203–212. *Surveillance & Society.* ojs.library.queensu.ca/index.php/surveillance-and-"society/article/view/3281/3244

Burns, Anne. "Creepshots and Power: Covert Sexualised Photography, Online Communities and the Maintenance of Gender Inequality." In *The Evolution of the Image: Political Action and the Digital Self*, edited by Marco Bohr and Basia Sliwinksa. New York: Routledge, 2018. 27–40.

Calvert, Clay. *Voyeur Nation: Media, Privacy, and Peering in Modern Culture*. Boulder, CO: Westview Press, 2000.

Carney, Phil. "How Does the Photograph Punish?" In *Routledge International Handbook of Visual Criminology*, edited by Michelle Brown and Eamonn Carrabine. New York: Routledge, 2017. 280–292.

Carter, Adam. "Judge finds Toronto van attack guilty of murder." *CBC.ca*, March 3, 2021. www.cbc.ca/news/canada/toronto/van-attack-trial-decision-1.5933687

Cherniavsky, Eva. *Incorporations: Race, Nation, and the Body Politics of Capital*. Minneapolis: University of Minnesota Press, 2006.

Chun, Wendy Hui Kyong, and Sarah Friedland. "Habits of Leaking: Of Sluts and Network Cards." *differences: A Journal of Feminist Cultural Studies* 26, no. 2 (2015): 1–28. *E-Duke Journals Scholarly Collection*. doi:10.1215/10407391-3145937

Cocca, Carolyn E. *Jailbait: The Politics of Statutory Rape Laws in the United States*. Albany, NY: SUNY Press, 2004.

Crenshaw, Kimberle. "Demarginalizing the Intersection of Race and Sex: A Black Feminist Critique of Antidiscrimination Doctrine, Feminist Theory and Antiracist Politics." *University of Chicago Legal Forum*, no. 1, Article 8 (1989): 139–167. chicagounbound.uchicago.edu/uclf/vol1989/iss1/8

Driscoll, Catherine. *Teen Film: A Critical Introduction*. Oxford: Berg, 2011.

Ferguson, Frances. "Pornography: The Theory." *Critical Inquiry* 21, no. 3 (Spring 1995): 670–695. jstor.org/stable/1343941

Freeman, Hadley. "Times Move Pretty Fast! Rewatching 80s Favourites in the Age of #MeToo." *TheGuardian.com*, April 13, 2018. theguardian.com/film/2018/apr/13/80s-films-molly-ringwald-john-hughes-metoo

Ging, Debbie. "Alphas, Betas, and Incels: Theorizing the Masculinities of the Manosphere." *Men and Masculinities* (May 2017): 1–20. *SAGE Journals*. doi:10.1177/1097184X17706401

Hargreaves, Stuart. " 'I'm a Creep, I'm a Weirdo': Street Photography in the Service of the Male Gaze." In *Surveillance, Privacy and Public Space*, edited by Bryce Clayton Newell, Tjerk Timan, and Bert-Jaap Koops. New York: Routledge, 2018. 179–196.

Hasinoff, Amy Adele. *Sexting Panic: Rethinking Criminalization, Privacy and Consent*. Champaign: University of Illinois Press, 2015.

Karaian, Lara. "Lolita Speaks: 'Sexting,' Teenage Girls and the Law." *Crime, Media, Culture: An International Journal* 8, no. 1 (April 2012): 57–73. *Scholars Portal*. doi:10.1177/1741659011429868

Karaian, Lara. "Policing 'Sexting': Responsiblization, Respectability and Sexual Subjectivity in Child Protection/Crime Prevention Responses to Teenagers' Digital Sexual Expression." *Theoretical Criminology* 18, no. 3 (2014): 282–299. *SAGE Publications*. doi:10.1177/1362480613504331

Kavanaugh, Brett. "'My Friends and I Cringed' Over High School Yearbook, Says Kavanaugh." *YouTube*, uploaded by PBS News Hour, September 27, 2018. www.youtube.com/watch?v=ZA71Ycw3Ba0

Kendall, Lori. "Nerd Nation: Images of Nerds in US Popular Culture." *International Journal of Cultural Studies* 2, no. 2 (1999): 260–283. *Scholars Portal.* doi:10.1177/136787799900200206

Kiesel, Laura. "What My '80s Childhood Taught Me about Rape Culture." *BUST.com.* October 12, 2018. bust.com/feminism/195239-1980s-childhood-rape-culture.html

Koskela, Hille. "'You Shouldn't Wear That Body': The Problematic of Surveillance and Gender." In *Routledge Handbook of Surveillance Studies*, edited by Kirstie Ball, Kevin Haggerty, and David Lyon. New York: Routledge 2012. 49–56.

Kunyosying, Kom, and Carter Soles. "Postmodern Geekdom as Simulated Ethnicity." *Jump Cut: A Review of Contemporary Media* 54 (2012). www.ejumpcut.org/archive/jc54.2012/SolesKunyoGeedom

Langlois, Ganaele, and Andrea Slane. "Economies of Reputation: The Case of Revenge Porn." *Communication and Critical/Cultural Studies* 14, no. 2 (2017): 120–138. *Scholars Portal.* doi:10.1080/14791420.2016.1273534

Levin, Thomas Y. "Rhetoric of the Temporal Index: Surveillant Narration and the Cinema of 'Real Time.'" *CTRL[SPACE]: Rhetorics of Surveillance from Bentham to Big Brother*, edited by Thomas Y. Levin et al. Cambridge, MA: ZKM Centre for Art and Media and the MIT Press, 2002. 578–593.

McGlynn, Clare, Erika Rackley, and Ruth Houghton. "Beyond 'Revenge Porn': The Continuum of Image-Based Sexual Abuse." *Feminist Legal Studies* (March 2017). link.springer.com/article/10.1007/s10691-017-9343-2

McGrath, John. *Loving Big Brother: Performance, Privacy and Surveillance Space.* New York: Routledge, 2004.

Mantziari, Despoina. "Sadistic Scopophilia in Contemporary Rape Culture: *I Spit On Your Grave* (2010) and the Practice of Media Rape." *Feminist Media Studies* 18, no. 3 (2018): 397–410. doi:10.1080/14680777.2017.1367700

Mardorossian, Carine M. *Framing the Rape Victim: Gender and Agency Reconsidered.* Rutgers University Press, 2014.

Massanari, Adrienne. "#Gamergate and The Fappening: How Reddit's Algorithm, Governance, and Culture Support Toxic Technocultures." *New Media & Society* 19, no. 3 (2015): 329–346. *SAGE Journals.* doi:10.1177/1461444815608807

Metz, Christian. Translated by Celia Britton, Annwyl Williams, Ben Brewster, and Alfred Guzzetti. *The Imaginary Signifier: Psychoanalysis and the Cinema.* Bloomington: Indiana University Press, 1982.

Miller-Young, Mireille. *A Taste for Brown Sugar: Black Women in Pornography.* Durham, NC: Duke University Press, 2014.

Mulvey, Laura. "Visual Pleasure and Narrative Cinema." In *Film Theory and Criticism*, edited by Leo Braudy and Marshall Cohen. New York: Oxford University Press, 2004. 837–848.

Newmahr, Staci. *Playing on the Edge: Sadomasochism, Risk, and Intimacy*. Bloomington: Indiana University Press, 2011.

Oliver, Kelly. "The Male Gaze is More Relevant, and More Dangerous, than Ever." *New Review of Film and Television Studies* 15, no. 4 (2017): 451–455. *Scholars Portal*. dx-doi-org.proxy.queensu.ca/10.1080/17400309.2017.1377937

Oliver, Kelly. "Rape as Spectator Sport and Creepshot Entertainment: Social Media and the Valorization of Lack of Consent." *American Studies Journal*, ASJ Occasional Papers no. 10, 2015. *American Studies Journal*, op.asjournal.org/rape-as-spectator-sport-and-creepshot-entertainment

Osucha, Eden. "The Whiteness of Privacy: Race, Media, Law." *Camera Obscura* 24, no. 24 (2009): 67–107. *Academic Search Complete*. doi:10.1215/0270 5346-2008-015

Prince, Stephen. "Introduction: Movies and the 1980s." *American Cinema of the 1980s*, edited by Stephen Prince. New Brunswick, NJ: Rutgers University Press, 2007. 1–21.

Projansky, Sarah. *Watching Rape: Film and Television in Postfeminist Culture*. New York: New York University Press, 2001.

Quail, Christine. "Nerds, Geeks, and the Hip/Square Dialectic in Contemporary Television." *Television & New Media* 12, no. 5 (2011): 460–482. *Scholars Portal*. doi:10.1177/1527476410385476

Randell-Moon, Holly, and Ryan Tippet, eds. *Security, Race, Biopower: Essays on Technology and Corporeality*. New York: Palgrave Macmillan, 2016.

Roberts, Johnnie L. "Field Marshal." *Newsweek.com*, February 9, 1997. newsweek.com/field-marshal-174696

Rose, Steve. "Animal House and Rape Culture: What Brett Kavanaugh's Teen-Movie Viewing Taught Us." *TheGuardian.com*, October 1, 2018. theguardian.com/film/shortcuts/2018/oct/01/animal-house-rape-culture-brett-kavanaugh-teen-movie-viewing

Shary, Timothy. *Generation Multiplex: The Image of Youth in Contemporary American Cinema*. Austin: University of Texas Press, 2002.

Shohat, Ella, and Robert Stam. *Unthinking Eurocentrism: Multiculturalism and the Media*. New York: Routledge, 1994.

Speed, Lesley. "Loose Cannons: White Masculinity and the Vulgar Teen Comedy Film." *The Journal of Popular Culture* 43, no. 4 (August 2010): 820–841. *Scholars Portal*. doi: 10.1111/j.1540-5931.2010.00772.x

Srinivasan, Amia. "Does Anyone Have the Right to Sex?" *London Review of Books* 40, no. 6 (March 2018). www.lrb.co.uk/v40/n06/amia-srinivasan/does-anyone-have-the-right-to-sex

Thompson, Chrissy, and Mark A. Wood. "A Media Archaeology of the Creepshot." *Feminist Media Studies* (2018): 1–15. doi:10.1080/14680777.2018.1447429

Traube, Elizabeth G. *Dreaming Identities: Class, Gender, and Generation in 1980s Hollywood Movies*. Boulder, CO: Westview Press, 1992.

Tropiano, Stephen. *Rebels and Chicks: A History of the Hollywood Teen Movie.* New York: Back Stage Books, 2006.

Turner, John S. "Collapsing the Interior/Exterior Distinction: Surveillance, Spectacle, and Suspense in Popular Cinema." *Wide Angle* 20, no. 4 (October 1998): 93–123. *Project MUSE.* muse.jhu.edu/article/36227

Wise, J. Macgregor. *Surveillance and Film.* New York: Bloomsbury, 2016.

Yang, Jennifer, and Wendy Gillis. "Shadowy Online Subculture in Spotlight after Toronto Van Attack." *Toronto Star*, April 28, 2018. www.thestar.com/news/gta/2018/04/28/shadowy-online-subculture-in-spotlight-after-toronto-van-attack.html

CHAPTER 7

"Nothing happened to her that she didn't invite"

Wes Craven, Rape Culture, and the *Scream* Trilogy

Brittany Caroline Speller

We had the MPAA [Motion Picture Association of America] tell us on this one [*The Last House on the Left* (2009)] that the problem with the rape isn't so much that it's rape but that it's so real, which just tells you everything. That's one step short of saying it should be entertaining, or it shouldn't upset you.

—Wes Craven, "Wes Craven Talks *The Last House on the Left*"

Long considered one of horror's maverick directors, Wes Craven has been a staple of Hollywood since his breakout first film *The Last House on the Left* (1972) until his death in 2015. In between, Craven became known for consistently redefining the horror genre with major franchises like *A Nightmare on Elm Street* and the *Scream* trilogy. Part of what made Craven's work so innovative was his unfailing ability to redefine the limits of violence, terror, and cultural critique in his horror films. Whether it was his tale of homicidal desert mutants in *The Hills Have Eyes* (1977), or his sociological fable of a pair of burglars trapped inside their landlord's house in *The People Under the Stairs* (1991), Craven's films have often been read for their forethinking social commentary by both scholarly and popular critics.

Indeed, by the time of his death, Craven was heralded as a foundational proponent for feminist horror films, as evidenced with the title of elegiac pieces like Claire Lobenfield's "Looking Inside the Genre-Bending, Feminist Horror of the Late Wes Craven" for *Paper Magazine* and Andi Zeisler's "The King of Horror's Secret Feminism" in *The Cut* to name a few. Popular critics are not alone in seeing Craven as a forerunner of feminism in what has traditionally been labeled a misogynistic genre. In one of her multiple articles on the *Scream* films, Valerie Wee frames the saga as "rewriting the sexual and gender conventions of the genre" (2005, 57). Meanwhile, Kathleen Karlyn examines the trilogy's relationship with second- and third-wave feminism, arguing that *Scream* "enable[s] girls to reject codes of femininity familiar to them from the highly conventionalized genre of the teen slasher film in order to rewrite them in more empowering ways" (181). Sezin Koehler (2018) even goes so far as to suggest that *Scream 3*, with its "scathing indictment of how women are treated behind-the-scenes in Hollywood," is an important foreshadowing of the #MeToo movement. It is with these interpretations of Craven's oeuvre that I align my own reading of the director's legendary career.

Rather than considering how Craven's films may or may not be feminist in their politics or presentation, I instead contemplate the manner in which the director addresses rape in his works. More than perhaps any other horror director, Craven has incessantly portrayed rape on screen with a variety of depth and purposes. This solidifies him as a necessary figure to examine in a post-#MeToo movement environment. Craven's importance for study is further amplified by his extensive relationship with Dimension Films, a subsidiary studio of The Weinstein Company headed by Bob and Harvey Weinstein, the latter of which is at the epicenter of the Time's Up movement's efforts to remove sexual predators from film and other industries. Although the connection between Craven, Dimension, and the Weinsteins becomes significant for Craven's later career, the director's treatment of rape predates this association. In his earlier films, and their successive remakes, sexual assault serves as a basis for vengeful murder and to heighten audience terror, with critics habitually placing these films squarely within the rape-revenge subgenre. Craven's franchise work, however, approaches rape with increasing attention to its larger social contexts. His franchise films not only avoid the explicit representations of assault common in his previous work but also define rape as the origin of evil itself. For instance, the villainous Freddy from *A Nightmare on Elm Street* is the child of a rape, as is Roman, the orchestrator of all of protagonist Sidney's suffering in the *Scream* trilogy. By examining the latter of these series, I argue that the overall narrative structure of the trilogy shows Craven's growing interest in questioning and in confronting the consequences of rape culture as opposed to simply the act of assault itself.

Interestingly, Craven's filmmaking career sprang from depicting rape on screen. His first film *The Last House on the Left* (1972), both written and directed by him, was an exploitation style reconfiguring of Ingmar Bergman's famous rape-revenge film *The Virgin Spring* (Bergman 1960). *Last House* depicts the plight of two teenage girls who are kidnapped, raped, tortured, and eventually murdered by a group of criminal drifters, who later unknowingly seek lodgings for the night at the home of one of the slain girls, ultimately leading the girl's parents to take retribution. Critics who have explored the film have often done so through the lens of the rape-revenge genre. In her book *Revisionist Rape*, Claire Henry identifies *Last House* as a "canonical text" that helped to define the "generic elements of rape-revenge" (27). Alexandra Heller-Nicholas considers the film to be a watershed moment for rape-revenge films due to its spawning of endless imitators (82). The film was also one of the examples used by Carol Clover in her discussion of the genre. She asserts that prior to *Last House*, the tendency was for horror to treat rape as merely "a side theme" (Clover 137). With Craven's film, however, Clover notes that "rape moved to center stage and the rape-revenge story as a drama complete unto itself came into its own" (137).

Visually, there are two instances of sexual assault in *Last House*. Craven, however, does not dwell on those scenes. The first of two instances of sexual assault in *Last House* takes place entirely off camera, with only the sound of whimpering heard, while the other lasts less than two minutes of the runtime and lingers on close-up shots of the actors' faces, refraining from showing any nudity or graphic simulations. Screen time is largely spent on other acts of violence with plenty of gore to shock contemporary audiences. Censorship could be involved in Craven's minimized display of assault, but this seems unlikely given the extremity and graphic quality of similar scenes in films from the same period, such as *Straw Dogs* (Peckinpah 1971) or *Deliverance* (Boorman 1972). Within this frame of mind, then, *Last House* was clearly not intended to function as a wider commentary on rape, but rather employed assault as simply one of the many violent actions human beings enact on one another and as a suggested ploy to terrorize audiences.

Craven's next horror project was *The Hills Have Eyes* (1977), the story of a band of mutant mountaineers who terrorize an urban family on an RV vacation in the desert. Like its predecessor *Last House*, *The Hills Have Eyes* is often categorized as a rape-revenge film. Clover lists this Craven work as another example of the rape-revenge genre, outlining how socioeconomics plays into who is the rapist and who is the assaulted (126). Emily Brick, meanwhile, builds on Clover's sociopolitical reading to assert that movies like *The Hills Have Eyes* influenced later French rape-revenge films that feature heightened and complex intra-political violence (98). In her chapter about the nuclear family and ideological formations, Lorena Russell considers *The Hills Have Eyes* to be a rape-revenge film that dramatizes the "violent transgression of patriarchal spaces" (116).

Among the numerous creative means the mutants find to torture their victims, which includes burning the father Big Bob alive as a diversion, one of the mountain men sneaks into the camper and assaults the youngest daughter Brenda while her family is busy outside trying to save Big Bob. The effectiveness of this scene lies in its illustration of the chaos and terror the family experiences at seeing the immolation of its patriarch; audiences are not privy to Brenda's fear for long, nor to any assurances that an assault occurred. Considering the brevity and ambiguity of the scene, with the rape being more a presumption than an explicitly seen act, sexual assault in this instance functions in a similar manner to that in *Last House*, as just one of the increasingly horrific offenses enacted on the Carter family. This formula was also replicated in each film's successive reboot.

In the mid-2000s, both films were remade under other directors, with Craven involved in a behind-the-scenes capacity. Serving as producer, for example, Craven oversaw the reboots *The Hills Have Eyes* (Aja 2006), *The Hills Have Eyes II* (Weisz 2007), and *The Last House on the Left* (Iliadis 2009). He even co-wrote the script for *The Hills Have Eyes II* with his son Jonathan. Each of these remakes mimics their predecessors in employing sexual assault to demonstrate the severe viciousness of the antagonists and remain within the rape-revenge genre. Unlike their source material, however, these remakes feature extremely graphic sexual assaults with the camera remaining on the event rather than looking away as before. This feature keeps them strictly in line with the amplified violence of post-9/11 horror cinema but emphasizes the issue of rape and male control over women's bodies, which was often overlooked in other horror films of the period.

A critical point to consider in regard to Craven's rape-revenge films is that like most films in the genre they are predominantly, if not exclusively, white environments. Each feature traditional white families of middle-class status traumatized and terrorized by lower-income members of a white nonfamilial group. Daughters or women of the families who are victimized are always heterosexual. The fact that both the victims of assault and the perpetrators are white impacts the endings and the conceptualization of justice in these films. It is arguable that had the rape victims in these films been women of color, the use of violence and its supposed righteousness would be dramatically different, as would the approach to the perpetrators had they been people of color. This solely white framework is consistent throughout Craven's career, even into his higher-profile franchise films.

Craven's franchise work has taken a different approach to the subject of rape altogether. While his earlier films use sexual assault to prove the complete depravity of their villains, the director's franchise pieces consider rape with attention to its larger moral ramifications for individuals and society. Furthermore, this point is demonstrated in the way that Craven does make some efforts to show rape visually in his earlier films yet refuses to give any screen time to visualize sexual assault in his franchises. Although *Elm Street* and *Scream* are both about rape at their core, neither film sees even a single shot to depict such acts. Craven's *Elm Street* films never threaten Nancy with rape, nor do viewers witness the assault of any other female characters. As the first of Craven's two major franchises, then, the *Elm Street* series is a prime example of the director meditating on rape from a new angle.

Originally imagined in Craven's screenplay as a serial pedophile haunting the dreams of his now teenaged former victims, the dream-leaping villain Freddy Kruger became a child murderer in *A Nightmare on Elm Street* (1984) after serious concerns voiced from New Line Studios president Robert Shaye about mentioning molestation. In his initial idea for the script, Craven had the molested protagonist Nancy destroy Freddy through denying him any power over her dreams and thoughts, deciding to simply turn her back on Kruger and move forward with her life. This ultimately undermines Freddy's power as her former abuser and allows Nancy to have a happy ending. Following serious edits from Shaye, however, Craven had to rewrite the script deleting both Freddy's past as a child molester and the cheerful finale for Nancy, which belittles the optimistic rape survivor narrative initially intended by Craven (Farrands). Despite this former reframing of the *Elm Street* series, Craven managed to work rape back into the storyline when he returned for the third *Elm Street* installment, *Dream Warriors*.

A Nightmare on Elm Street 3: Dream Warriors (1987) is the second of three *Elm Street* films Craven was personally involved in. Often butting heads with Shaye during production of the first film, coupled with his vehement opposition to doing a sequel, Craven declined involvement with most of the subsequent installments in the franchise. He decided hesitantly to return for this third film, but only as a writer and executive producer, surrendering the role of director over to Chuck Russell. With Craven co-writing the screenplay alongside Bruce Wagner, sexual assault again became a major plot point, central to mythology of both Kruger and the series as a whole.

In this entry, Nancy returns to help a gang of tormented teenagers in a mental hospital defeat Freddy via learning his origins. Allied with another psychologist at the hospital, Nancy and the group find out that Kruger is the progeny of a nun who was assaulted by multiple criminally insane inmates before the hospital became a home for troubled teens. Through discovering and speaking out on the covered-up story of a young woman who was sexually assaulted, the Elm Street kids are able to find out more about how Freddy came into being, which helps them learn how to stop him. Furthermore, branded in the film "the bastard son of a hundred maniacs," Freddy's evil nature is explained through his patriarchal heritage as the son of rapists, much like Roman, the core villain of *Scream 3* and the *Scream* trilogy.

For his next franchise venture, Craven took on the role of director for a slasher film written by then up-and-coming screenwriter Kevin Williamson called "Scary Movie," the title of which Dimension Film chairman Bob Weinstein later changed to *Scream* (1996). With the film's immediate box office success, Weinstein ordered two further entries of Williamson, who had already begun drafting the sequel during the filming of *Scream*, along with an offer to Craven to direct the next pair, solidifying the film's fate as the opening act of a trilogy.

The trilogy as a whole features rape culture as one of the core themes without ever explicitly stating as much until the third film, and without showing the act visually, yet even within *Scream* this focus on sexual violence and its ramifications are evident. Set in a small, fictional town called Woodsboro, *Scream* depicts what happens when teenager Sidney Prescott and her friends are stalked and butchered by a masked killer as the one-year anniversary of her mother Maureen's rape and murder approaches. By the end, Sidney's boyfriend Billy Loomis and his friend Stu are revealed to be the killers, and also are responsible for her mother's grisly death the year before.

Although viewers never see Maureen's assault or her death, these events loom large in the imagination of everyone in Woodsboro, evidenced in reporter Gale Weathers commenting to Sidney, "Your mother's murder was last year's hottest court case, somebody was gonna write a book about it." It is worth briefly pointing out here that Maureen's positionality as a middle-class suburban, white woman in part guarantees the sensationalism and rabid reporting on the case that Gale acknowledges. Had Maureen been a woman of color, of a different sexuality, or a lower income status, arguably the crimes against her would not have gripped the national news media or created a kind of collective traumatic memory of the event for the town. Craven goes on to clarify why "this whole theme of Sidney's mother" is so vital to the overall structure of the film by pointing out that "[Maureen's] sort of kept as this wonderful, pure mother that was lost," making "the whole course of the movie [sic] Sidney's readjustment of her reality based on other people's information about [her] mother" ("Commentary"). One aspect of this reeducation involves revelations and rumors about Maureen's supposed promiscuity, which Sidney buffets against in relation to her own burgeoning sexuality.

Sex serves as a source of tension in Sidney's life even in the introduction of her character. In her first scene, Billy sneaks through Sidney's bedroom window hoping to convince her to "do some on top of the clothes stuff" despite his acknowledgment that Sidney has a no "underwear rule." This instance is the first of many where Billy pressures or attempts to guilt the virginal Sidney into sexual activity, something she has expressed increasing discomfort with in their relationship following the rape of her mother. Billy realizes what has caused this anxiety yet ignores her uneasiness as early as this initial conversation, complaining that two years ago the couple "started off hot-and-heavy, nice solid R rating, on our way to an NC-17," and how after the circumstances of Maureen's death, "things have changed, and lately, [they are] just sort of edited for television," meaning abstinent.

A little later, when he confronts her again about sex, Billy coldly diminishes the traumatic impact Maureen's assault has on Sidney, telling her "I think it's time you got over that." Sidney originally refuses this perspective, rebuffing him with, "I am sorry if my traumatized life is an inconvenience to you and your perfect existence," but in another scene with best friend Tatum, Sidney belittles her own instinctive discomfort and blames herself for not giving in to Billy's entitled advances. She tells Tatum, "Billy's right you know, I just can't relax when he touches me . . . he's been so patient with me . . . how many guys would put up with a girlfriend who's sexually anorexic," to which Tatum replies, "Billy and his penis don't deserve you." Picking up on the apprehension around sex in the film, Wee notes that Sidney's discovery that Billy murdered her mother only after she sleeps with him "introduces another concern," namely, "the boyfriend who turns against his girlfriend after sex" ("Resurrecting" 57). Wee's comment here inadvertently highlights the exclusively heterosexual perspective of the film on sexual violence, which does determine its narrative on patriarchy and violence. While she does not develop these last ideas in her article, Wee could easily be talking about a common practice in heterosexually driven patriarchal rape culture, that of slut-shaming, something *Scream* confronts head on.

It is through Maureen's alleged promiscuity that the film interrogates a form of victim blaming known as slut-shaming, which is a common practice of rape culture designed to dispel culpability from assailants. One such occurrence of slut-shaming comes when Sidney overhears two fellow classmates gossiping about her mother in the bathroom. The dialogue in this brief scene illustrates the damaging effects victim blaming has on Sidney. The camera cuts back and forth between the two gossipers and Sidney's increasingly distraught reaction. The first girl theorizes that Sidney could be the killer of first victims Casey Becker and Steven Orth out of jealousy, to which her friend replies skeptically that Sidney has a boyfriend. The first girl nastily replies, "maybe she's a slut just like her mother . . . it's a common fact, her mother was a tramp." When the scene faced being cut for time, Craven fought to keep it, explaining, "it tells so much about Sid and her growing confusion about who and what she really is, and where she's come from," referencing Maureen and her sexual history ("Commentary").

Another example of slut-shaming arrives at the final bloody show-down between Sidney and the killers, Billy and Stu. The whole reason Billy offers Sidney for why he murdered Maureen is "your slut mother was fucking my father," which he thinks led to his parents' divorce and his mother's abandonment of the family. Embodying a gendered double standard, instead of trying to kill his father, Billy solely displaces responsibility on to the women in the film, particularly Maureen and Sidney. Initially blaming Maureen, after he has killed her, he remains unsatisfied and transposes Maureen's alleged culpability onto Sidney. Holding a knife to her throat, Billy distorts his own guilt in the crime, claiming, "We did your mom a favor, Sid, that woman was a slut-bag whore who flashed her shit all over town like she was Sharon Stone." This dialogue will later reappear verbatim in *Scream 3* to further emphasize the trilogy's sustained critique of rape culture, but first, the second film bridges these two through its own consideration of victim blaming.

Taking place two years after the events of the first film, *Scream 2* finds the surviving Woodsboro teens away at Windsor College. Sidney has seemingly moved forward from her traumatic past and is happy with a new boyfriend, a fresh group of friends, and a leading part in the school play. Someone soon starts killing students at the college, mirroring the Woodsboro murders, and getting ever closer to Sidney and her friends. Eventually, the killers are revealed to be Sidney's new friend Mickey and Mrs. Loomis, Billy's mother. At the climax, Mrs. Loomis shoots Mickey in order to frame him and to have her revenge on Sidney alone. It is in this exchange between Mrs. Loomis and Sidney where the motive is revealed. Rape culture again comes to the fore through the way Billy's mother refuses to blame anyone but Sidney and Maureen for her and son's actions.

Despite the fact that her son murdered six people, raped Maureen, and tried to kill four others at Woodsboro, Mrs. Loomis denies that her son did anything wrong. She tells Sidney, "You killed my son, and now I kill you," totally ignoring the fact that Sidney killed Billy in self-defense. When Sidney fights back against this claim, saying, "You're as crazy as your son was," Mrs. Loomis loses control, hysterically asking, "Was that a negative, disparaging remark about my son?!," which begins a fanatical speech about why others are responsible for Billy's rampage: "I was a good mother. You know what makes me sick? I'm sick to death of people saying it's all the parents' fault, that it all starts with the family. You wanna blame someone? Why don't you blame your mother!? She's the one who stole my husband and broke up my family. And then you took my son." Throughout the dialogue with Sidney, she denies Sidney's claims that Billy raped her mother or that he was a psychopath.

Mrs. Loomis's response to criticism of Billy is highly characteristic of rape culture through its victim blaming and denial of sexual assault as a serious crime, notably coming from a woman and a mother. This practice can be found in the infamous case of Brock Turner, who was convicted of raping a fellow student at Stanford University, but only "[served] three months of a six-month sentence" with the narrative being that he was an otherwise upstanding young man who simply made a mistake (Rennison and Dodge 23). As Rennison and Dodge note, downplaying the viciousness of sexual assault makes it harder to get "offenders to acknowledge the magnitude of the violence they committed," which leads to higher recidivism rates and a whole host of negative social consequences for survivors of rape (23). By rewriting the memory of her son as a victim of the women he harmed, Mrs. Loomis contradicts survivor Sidney's trauma at having unknowingly had sex with the man who raped and murdered her mother, then tried to kill her, a trauma addressed elsewhere in the film, as well as the brutality of what Billy did to Maureen. This denial of the seriousness of sexual assault, and the culpability of the rapist, is taken up again in more depth in *Scream 3*, along with a larger repudiation of rape culture.

Scream 3 (2000) is the most conceptually ambitious of the three films, containing the self-reflexive metacommentary of having the story intermingle the Hollywood studio set and actors of *Stab 3: Return to Woodsboro* (*Stab* is the metacommentary film-within-a-film retelling of the Woodsboro murders, introduced in *Scream 2*) with the real actors of the *Scream* series. The narrative follows Sidney and the other Woodsboro survivors as they are drawn into a mystery revolving around old photographs of Maureen left behind at the murder scenes of *Stab 3* actors. Eventually, the group discovers that the real killer is *Stab 3* director Roman Bridger, revealed to be Sidney's long-lost half-brother, who is the product of Maureen's rape at the hands of studio executives when she was a young, aspiring actress.

This self-referential movie-within-a-movie arrangement allows Craven a number of avenues in which to examine aspects of rape culture, such as victim blaming and offender accountability, in both the film itself and the trilogy as a whole. By setting the story within the filming of a major Hollywood blockbuster, *Scream 3* examines the systemic elements within economic power structures, like production companies, that enable serial abusers to thrive at the detriment of the community at large, with Maureen as the historical epicenter. The man at the center of Maureen's sexual assault is *Stab 3* producer John Milton, who worked with Maureen during her missing Hollywood years. Milton is a figure who could arguably be a stand-in for Harvey Weinstein or other powerful men exposed in both the Time's Up and #MeToo movements, rendering Craven's portrayal of such a character intriguing in hindsight.

Many critics have recently picked up on the likenesses between Weinstein, Milton, and the toxic Hollywood power structures seen in the film. Adam White calls *Scream 3* an "early warning shot" for the narratives of abuse come to light with #MeToo. Writing for *Slate*, Matthew Phelan acknowledges that the Weinstein allegations alter the way audiences should understand *Scream 3*, seeing it as a film with a "parasitic symbiosis with reality" for those on the set who knew anything about Weinstein's behavior. This question of how much the cast or crew knew about Weinstein has in some sense been answered by a few cast members of the trilogy. Rose McGowan, who played Sidney's sidekick and Dewey's younger sister Tatum in the first film, has gone on to be an outspoken accuser of Weinstein and activist for #MeToo. She even recounts the full details of her assault at Weinstein's hands in her autobiographic book *Brave*. Meanwhile, in an interview with *Cosmopolitan* in 2017, Skeet Ulrich admits that not only did he know of Weinstein's reputation but that "most people knew" (Greco). When asked by interviewer Patti Greco why he remained silent, Ulrich details the sense of powerlessness that comes from facing "someone with that power" (Greco). He explains:

> There is nothing you can do. I mean, what am I gonna do? I can't step up, certainly then, on allegations. Honestly, and I think it's what most people faced: How do you cut your livelihood from a very powerful corporation . . . Now that it's starting to come out and people are finally stepping up and saying stuff, I'm glad. That's what it takes. Because one person stepping up and making allegations is gonna hurt that one person and not help anyone.

Accounts like those included here certainly highlight the similarities between *Scream 3*'s villainous producer John Milton and Miramax's Harvey Weinstein. Furthermore, it is perhaps not an accident that Milton's crimes take place in the 1970s, which is not only when Craven began making rape-revenge films but is also when Weinstein began his career in Hollywood. Recently, the *New York Times* reported on several allegations from women who detail abuse and sexual violence from Weinstein as far back as the 1970s, lending more credibility to the idea of Weinstein as an inspiration for Milton (Gabler, Twohey, and Kantor).

Whether Milton was a purposeful representation of Weinstein or not, either way the film speaks volumes on how abusive men use power to create damaging environments for women in both the past and present.

With this in mind, Milton embodies several aspects of rape culture, ranging from his devaluation of the victim's trauma to his silent complicity in Maureen's sexual assault. When Gale questions him about Maureen's time working for him, Milton tries to downplay the event by calling Maureen "a bit player" and "a nobody." His devaluation suggests a hierarchy in victimization, where because Maureen was not a famous actress when he knew her, what happened to her is not significant. He even asks Gale insolently, "What does it matter?" Yet, as another character points out, Milton has "made millions off the story of her murder" and does not admit to the police that he knew Maureen or recognized her pictures left at the crime scenes. Milton also refuses to admit that Maureen was assaulted, despite Gale's probing of "are you saying she was—," with him interrupting before she can say the word rape. He then attempts to validate his complicity by saying "it was in the '70s" and "everything was different" back then, before finally admitting "things got out of hand."

He next tries to completely deny any responsibility for both himself and the other men involved by displacing culpability onto Maureen: "I was well known for my parties, [she] knew what they were. It was for girls like her to meet men, men who could get them parts, if they made the right impression. Nothing happened to her that she didn't invite, in one way or another, no matter what she said afterwards." As Gale and the others stand openly aghast and disgusted at Milton's outburst, he continues, "Maybe they did take advantage of her! Maybe the sad truth is, this is not the city for innocence. No charges were brought. And the bottom line is, [Maureen] wouldn't play by the rules. You wanna get ahead in Hollywood, you gotta play the game, or go home." In this view, Milton benefits from the fear many victims may understandably have about reporting their assaults to the police, especially when powerful men and corporations are involved as in this case. Susan Caringella describes this anxiety, pointing out that "the unique barriers those victimized by rape face dissuade them from reporting and prosecuting offenders," something made even more complicated when socioeconomic or racial factors are considered (10). Therefore, one of the many reasons why Milton's perspective is disturbing is because of its reliance on formal legal charges as a scale to assess blame, a confidence at odds with the aforementioned hesitancy in rape reporting.

The second major figure to represent the toxic effect of rape culture in the film is the killer Roman Bridger. His revelatory exchange with Sidney at the film's conclusion explains not only why he started killing in this movie, but also offers background on how he persuaded Billy Loomis to rape and murder Maureen, the goal being to destroy both Sidney and her mother. With the failure of his initial plan to have Sidney die at Billy's hand, and the subsequent media attention she receives after the events of *Scream 2*, Roman plots to murder Sidney himself. Moreover, his speech above shows his absolute denial of responsibility for his actions, choosing instead to blame Maureen and Sidney for everything, all while slut-shaming Maureen to justify his actions.

Roman mimics the earlier slut-shaming seen in Billy's and Mrs. Loomis's tirades against Maureen. His warped, rape culture logic is evident in his argument that "what [Milton] did to her made her a slut," and his taunt to Sidney, "Seems Maureen, mom, she really got around." Refuting the validity of Roman's insult, Sidney defiantly yells at him, "God, why don't you stop your whining and get on with it, I've heard this shit before!" meaning the language of victim blaming that has repeatedly been used by the trilogy's killers toward her mother.

Roman then explains that he intends to frame Sidney for all the killings as revenge for a host of imagined wrongs done to him. The main sins Roman accuses the two of committing are denying him the family environment he feels entitled to, maintaining that Sidney by her mere existence is guilty, and blaming Maureen for putting him up for adoption. Just like Billy and Mrs. Loomis, Roman rants his alleged justification beginning with Maureen, declaring:

> I searched for a mother too, an actress named Rina Reynolds. I tried to find her my whole life . . . Knocked on her door thinking she'd welcome me with open arms, but she had a new life and a new name, Maureen Prescott! You were the only child she claimed Sidney. She shut me out in the cold forever, her own son . . . She slammed the door in my face, Sid, said I was Rina's child and Rina was dead. And it struck me, what a good idea!

Despite knowing about Maureen's rape and his connection to it, Roman clearly has no sympathy for the trauma meeting him must have caused her, no sense of empathy for what happened to Maureen, and moves immediately into seeking revenge for the denial of his entitlement to both her and her family. Resembling Billy's double-standard perspective, Roman does not exact vengeance on Milton or any of the men who he acknowledges raped Maureen; he only later kills Milton in order to frame Sidney, orchestrating the producer's murder to look like Sidney killed him in retribution for Maureen.

This move to lay blame on Sidney for all his wrongdoings is perhaps not surprising considering the particular vitriol he saves for her, as well as his own refusal to take responsibility for his actions. Not only does Roman fault her for having the family life he wanted, but also for what he perceives to be her stardom as the survivor of several massacres. He jealously rants about how Sidney is going to "pay for the life you stole from me," specifying that all of this violence was "for the mother, and for the family, and for the stardom, and for, goddammit, everything you had that should've been mine!" The two then start a back-and-forth shouting match where Sidney refuses to allow Roman's victim blaming, rebutting him with, "You know why you kill people, Roman, do you? Because you choose to, there is no one else to blame! Why don't you take some fucking responsibility?!" to which Roman merely covers his ears with his hands, shouting, "I don't want to hear it!" Through the dialogue during this final showdown between she and Roman, Sidney rejects once and for all the narrative of rape culture as she refuses to accept Roman's shifting of responsibility for his actions onto her and her mother.

Craven's work on the *Scream* trilogy is a perfect example of the director's use of film to interrogate rape culture. His storied career as a horror film director, writer, and producer has left an indelible legacy on the genre. Although his early films, such as *The Last House on the Left*, fall squarely within the rape-revenge genre, the director's franchise ventures question rape culture in a multitude of ways. Through franchises like *A Nightmare on Elm Street* and *Scream*, Craven makes rape the foundation of all evil, demonstrating the profound impact such crimes have on society at large. Interestingly, Craven's work has recently been reevaluated in light of the #MeToo movement and the conviction of Harvey Weinstein, who acted as a producer for the *Scream* trilogy. *Scream 3* in particular contains blatant parallels between the abusive environments created by men in positions of power, like Weinstein, and the film's villain, producer John Milton. This single entry of the trilogy, however, is only one part of a larger narrative on the intersections of power, complicity, and sexual violence. As I have argued here, *Scream* is at its core a story less about the terror of a serial murderer in a small town than an example on how sexual violence can cyclically impact victims and their families, all while perpetrators are protected by the intricacies of rape culture. The fact that all of the main characters in the trilogy are white does have an impact on the violence and its aftermath as covered by the films. Maureen's privileged race and class allow her to occupy such a strong position of almost mythical remembrance and attention. The trilogy itself can be reasonably reinterpreted at the end as Sidney and her friends ultimately try to seek justice for Maureen, marking her as the crux of these rape culture critiques. By having mostly white males like Roman and Billy as the initiators of sexual violence, their protection under traditional rape culture narratives is almost certainly guaranteed, just as Maureen's positionality determines how much public value is given to her victimhood. With these considerations in mind, Craven, having been a director who regularly included rape in his films, must be paid new attention in order to understand how sexual assault functions in his oeuvre, especially in light of movements like #MeToo and their focus on dismantling various aspects of rape culture.

Works Cited

Aja, Alexandre, director. *The Hills Have Eyes*. Craven-Maddalena Films, 2006.

Brick, Emily. "Baise-moi and the French Rape-Revenge Film." In *European Nightmares: Horror Cinema in Europe Since 1945*, edited by Patrick Allmer, Emily Brick, and David Huxley. New York: Wallflower Press, 2012. 93–102.

Clover, Carol. *Men, Women, and Chainsaws: Gender in the Modern Horror Film*. Updated edition. Princeton, NJ: Princeton University Press, 2015.

Craven, Wes, director. *A Nightmare on Elm Street*. New Line Cinema, 1984.

Craven, Wes, director. *The Hills Have Eyes*. Vanguard, 1977.

Craven, Wes, director. *The Last House on the Left*. Sean S. Cunningham Films, 1972.

Craven, Wes, director. *Scream*. Dimension Films, 1996.

Craven, Wes, director. *Scream 2*. Dimension Films, 1998.

Craven, Wes, director. *Scream 3*. Dimension Films, 2000.

Craven, Wes, and Capone. "Wes Craven Talks *The Last House on the Left* remake, 25/8, and *Scream 4* with Capone!!!" *Ain't It Cool News*.Com. http://legacy.aintitcool.com/node/40358

Craven, Wes, and Michael Banka. "Interview on Elm Street: An Interview with Wes Craven." *Cinéaste* 17, no. 3 (1990): 22–25. www.jstor.org/stable/41686985

Farrands, Daniel, and Andrew Kasch, directors. *Never Sleep Again: The Elm Street Legacy*. 1428 Films, May 4, 2010.

Gabler, Ellen, Megan Twohey, and Jodi Kantor. "New Accusers Expand Harvey Weinstein Sexual Assault Claims Back to '70s." *The New York Times*, October 30, 2017. www.nytimes.com/2017/10/30/us/harvey-weinstein-sexual-assault-allegations.html

Greco, Patti. "Skeet Ulrich Went from '90s Heartthrob to Struggling TV Actor. Now He's Back." *Cosmopolitan Magazine*, October 17, 2017. www.cosmopolitan.com/entertainment/tv/a13030127/skeet-ulrich-riverdale-profile

Heller-Nicholas, Alexandra. *Rape-Revenge Films: A Critical Study*. Jefferson, NC: McFarland and Co., 2011.

Henry, Claire. *Revisionist Rape-Revenge: Redefining a Film Genre*. New York: Palgrave MacMillan, 2014.

Ilias, Dennis, director. *The Last House on the Left*. Rogue Pictures, 2009.

Karlyn, Kathleen. "Scream, Popular Culture, and Feminism's Third Wave: 'I'm Not My Mother.'" *Motherhood Misconceived: Representing the Maternal in U.S. Films*, edited by Heather Addison, Mary Kate Goodwin-Kelly, and Elaine Roth. Albany, NY: SUNY Press, 2009. 177–196.

Koehler, Sezin. "'Scream 3' Foreshadowed Hollywood's #MeToo Movement." *Bitch Media*, March 20, 2018. www.bitchmedia.org/article/scream-three-and-me-too

Lobenfield, Claire. "Looking Inside the Genre-Bending, Feminist Horror of the Late Wes Craven." *Paper Magazine*. August 31, 2015. www.papermag.com/looking-inside-the-genre-bending-feminist-horror-of-the-late-wes-crave-1427637285.html

Phelan, Matthew. "How the Harvey Weinstein Scandal Changes the Way We Watch Scream 3." *Slate*, October 31, 2019. slate.com/culture/2019/10/scream-3-harvey-weinstein-producer-character.html

Rennison, Callie Marie and Mary Dodge. *Introduction to Criminal Justice: System, Diversity, and Change*, 3rd edition. Thousand Oaks, CA: Sage, 2019.

Robb, Brian J. *Screams and Nightmares: The Films of Wes Craven*. New York: Harry N. Abrams, 1999.

Russell, Lorena. "Ideological Formations of the Nuclear Family in *The Hills Have Eyes*." In *The Philosophy of Horror*, edited by Thomas Fahy. Lexington: University Press of Kentucky, 2010. 102–120.

Wee, Valarie. "Resurrecting and Updating the Teen Slasher: The Case of *Scream*." *Journal of Popular Film and Television* 34, no. 2 (2006): 50–61.

Wee, Valarie. "The *Scream* Trilogy, 'Hyperpostmodernism,' and the Late-Nineties Teen Slasher Film." *Journal of Film and Video* 57, no. 3 (2005): 44–61.

Weisz, Martin, director. *The Hills Have Eyes 2*. Craven-Maddalena Films, 2007.

White, Adam. "Scream 3 was a Manic Misfire—in the Wake of Weinstein, it Now Feels Like an Early Warning Shot." *The Independent*, February 3,

2020. www.independent.co.uk/arts-entertainment/films/features/scream-3-harvey-weinstein-wes-craven-rose-mcgowan-a9298696.html

Zeisler, Andi. "The King of Horror's Secret Feminism." *The Cut*, September 3, 2015. www.thecut.com/2015/09/king-of-horrors-secret-feminism.html

CHAPTER 8

Survivors in Rape-Revenge Films

Melancholic Vigilantes

Amanda Spallacci

The rape-revenge film was established as a popular film genre during the 1970s, participating in a culture that saw activist groups protest sexual violence and radical feminists create rape crisis centers, a culture demarked by an influx in the production of material content such as published books, zines, newsletters, and film that underlined rape as a primary topic.[1] For its part, the Women Against Pornography (WAP) movement, founded by radical feminists in New York City in the mid-1970s, followed Kate Millet's feminist literary criticism in *Sexual Politics* (1970), arguing that representation in pornography imitates reality and vice versa (Allen 2016, 51). In an effort to protest pornography through Civil Rights, Andrea Dworkin partnered with lawyer Catharine MacKinnon and tried to establish the Anti-Pornography Civil Rights Ordinance. Their rationale was that pornography violates women's civil rights because it leads to violence against them inflicted by men who watch it. Despite these public efforts to outlaw pornography, it was never formally prohibited, and the production of pornographic media has increased significantly in quantity and across various digital platforms. Relatedly, graphic depictions of rape in film may have previously horrified audiences, purporting an ethical stance against rape, but due to the influx of violent pornography, perhaps the rape-revenge film emerged in an effort to pair violent images with negative consequences to reestablish the ethical imperative against rape.

This ethical stance against rape in popular culture is necessary because the criminal justice system is not equipped to obtain justice for rape survivors. In most cases of rape, the only form of evidence is the survivor's testimony, and this evidence is restricted by conventions of legal testimony and myths about rape. The effects of the rape trauma on survivors' memory may prevent survivors from forming a linear and comprehensive account, making them look as if they are not telling the truth when they explain that they were raped. While these effects of trauma may prevent survivors from adhering to the conventions of legal testimony, the pervasiveness of what feminists and scholars refer to as "rape culture" also undermine their statements. Molly Ann Magestro defines rape culture as a "pervasive set of socially accepted ideas that increase tolerance for a normalization of rape and sexual violence" that include "fixed and rigid gender roles for women in particular, and the long list of rape myths that proliferate in society and popular culture" (13). The effects of rape trauma as well as prominent rape myths create a bias against survivors in the criminal justice system—an institution that is supposed to support and protect survivors—and creates favorable conditions for perpetrators, abusers, defense lawyers, and the public to discredit testimonies about rape. Perhaps in response to this injustice against survivors, the rape-revenge film provides an alternative jurisdiction in which the protagonist must achieve her own justice because survivors rarely obtain justice through the legal system.

Depictions of sexual violence in rape-revenge films tend to establish an ethical stance against rape through the genre's narrative structure: the woman is violently raped and must avenge this injustice through violence. As I have argued previously, rape scenes are problematic because the position of the camera mostly situates the viewer as a voyeur, and much like the photograph, the scene serves as evidence of the traumatic event, setting an impossible precedent of witnessing that does not exist in reality, since a survivor's testimony is often the only form of evidence of a rape (Spallacci 6). Furthermore, cinematic choices employed throughout the rape scene, such as presenting the protagonist's face in close-up, can evoke sympathy, an affect that Carl Plantinga has argued is "self-interested" because viewers take pleasure in being on the right side of morality (4); moreover, depicting the rape scene in long shot coupled by close-up shots of the protagonist's body parts can evoke feelings of horror and disgust, which dehumanize the protagonist and ultimately homogenize women as rape victims, resulting in a failure to produce any critical thought about how a woman's position in society makes certain women more vulnerable to rape than others (Spallacci 5). As a result, scholars tend to evaluate the rape scene—and more specifically, the affects produced by these cinematic images, such as disgust or empathy—rather than the effects of trauma on the survivor. The impulse to critique the event as opposed to the effects of trauma on the survivor is in line with Ruth Leys's claim that the most central contradiction within trauma studies is the conception of mimetic and anti-mimetic theories of trauma (8).

Ruth Leys has claimed that, previously, trauma was defined by dissociation, in which the subject was absent from the self, and under hypnosis the subject "unconsciously imitated, or identified with the aggressor or traumatic scene" (8). During hypnosis the subject embodied "an experience of hypnotic imitation of identification" (8), which Leys categorizes as mimesis. This hypnotic trance "appeared to shatter the victim's cognitive perceptual capacities [and] made the traumatic scene unavailable for a certain kind of recollection" (9), and, as a result, hypnosis seemed to demonstrate the effects of trauma on the subject. For Susannah Radstone, the mimetic model suggests that memories are linked to "the unconscious, unbiddable processes of the inner world" (14). While this model seemed to represent and explain the "victim's suggestibility and abjection," early theorists of trauma began to see the theory as a "threat to an ideal of individual autonomy" (9) that "tended to call into question the veracity of the victim's testimony as to the veridical or literal truth of the traumatic origin" (9). These doubts led to a new theory, what Leys refers to as the "anti-mimetic theory," which sought to "re-establish a strict dichotomy between the autonomous subject and the external trauma" (9). In this model, "memories are understood to be the unmediated, though unassimilable records of traumatic events" (Radstone 14). The rejection of the mimetic model explains why a significant, but overlooked, component of the rape-revenge film—the sequence immediately following the rape, in which the protagonist tries to cleanse herself of the negative affects transferred to her from the perpetrator, followed by a sequence in which the protagonist appears as a double of the perpetrator—has been excluded in scholarship pertaining to rape-revenge films. Often, these mimetic representations of trauma appear through cinematography, mise-en-scène, and dialogue, rather than the narrative. This chapter thus focuses on the scenes of mimetic representations of trauma in Patty Jenkins's *Monster* (2003), David Fincher's *Girl with the Dragon Tattoo* (2011), and Quentin Tarantino's *Kill Bill vol. 1* (2003); the scenes in question focus on the effects of trauma rather than on the traumatic event itself and depict each individual rape as part of a larger chain of historical violence against women.

From Historical Narrative to Genre: The Critical Reception of Rape-Revenge Films

Current scholarship pertaining to rape-revenge films tends to focus on reading practices: specifically, whether the film should be read as a genre, based on its narrative structure, or through a postfeminist lens. Claire Henry argues that rape-revenge films should be categorized as their own genre, one classified by its own salient characteristics and regarded as a "cultural key that can help reveal and interrogate the meanings of rape and the political, ethical, and affective responses to it" (3). Alternatively, Jacinda Read reads rape-revenge films as responding to a "historically, rather than generically, specific cycle" (23), with these historical roots having been established during second-wave feminism. For Henry, rape-revenge films have expressed a specific narrative structure, and this breaking away from historicism explains the rise in rape-revenge films produced since the publication of Read's text (2). Similarly, Alexandra Heller-Nicholas suggests that this recent spike in the release of rape-revenge films and the ubiquity of rape-revenge across genre and history should have put "an end to any suggestion that rape-revenge is a historically or generally specific cycle" (155). Henry responds to Heller-Nicholas's claim that rape-revenge films are too ubiquitous to subscribe to a specific genre or narrative structure by arguing that rape-revenge is a hybrid genre with its own loose narrative structure (3). Conversely, rather than reading rape-revenge through a genre or narrative perspective, Sarah Projansky argues that "postfeminism intersects, in at least some way, with the vast majority of films that include rape or the threat of rape" (13) and interrogates the role that the ubiquitous representations of rape in cinema plays in popular culture. For Projansky, the intersection of representations of rape and discourses of postfeminism "is a dominant means through which contemporary popular culture discursively defines feminism" (13). Genre, narrative, and postfeminist approaches to rape-revenge films have generated fruitful readings of these films; yet, Henry argues that the tension between "contextual and psychoanalytic readings" (8) of rape-revenge films has produced a gap in the critical literature on the rape-revenge genre (14).

Among other scholars, Tanya Horeck reads rape-revenge films through a psychoanalytic framework. Horeck, who borrows from J. LaPlance and J-B. Pontalis's definition of fantasy as "scripts of organized scenes which are capable of dramatizations—usually in visual form" (308), considers the role that fantasy plays in rape-revenge films. These readings of fantasy are reductive: for example, reading rape fantasies as "patriarchal fantasies" of men who want to rape helpless women (3). Horeck also questions whether "this [reading is] the only way to think of fantasy" (3) in rape-revenge films. Freud suggested that collective fantasies such as the original primal fantasy are shared by everyone: in this fantasy, the child observes their parents engaging in sexual intercourse, initially perceiving the father to be wounding the mother; later, the look of pleasure on the mother's face confuses the child, producing an ambivalent scene. Expanding on the concept of collective fantasy, Horeck argues that scholars who study rape-revenge films should consider "what sort of wishes or desires are being played out in and through [rape-revenge] texts" (7). For Horeck, representations of rape expose "a double meaning of representation insofar as it is often made to serve as a sign for other issues" such as a means to express "ideological and political questions concerning the function of the body politic" (7). This chapter is concerned with the representation of trauma in rape-revenge films, specifically with respect to the role of doubles and repetition following the rape scene, not only as a depiction of individual violence but also as a comment on the history of collective violence against women.

Scape Goats, Doubles, and Mimesis: Trauma in the Rape-Revenge Film

In his scholarship, David Humbert takes up Freud's work on mirrors, doubles, repetition, and déjà-vu alongside René Girard's method for literary analysis that "bypasses almost all of the standard aesthetic categories" such as genre, narrative structure, and poetics to instead focus on "the ways in which texts conceal or reveal violence and or mimetic desire" (Bubbio and Fleming 4). Humbert argues that violence in cinema, specifically in Stanley Kubrick's films, represents both individual and historical memory.

Rather than apply Freud's reading that doubles represent "a return of primary narcissism . . . by means of the repetition compulsion" (qtd. in Humbert 17), Humbert relocates the repetition and doubling of violence from the unconscious and argues that they have a real foundation in human history. For Humbert, culture's inability to acknowledge certain forms of systemic violence "constitutes a very real [cultural] repression" (117), and representations of violence in film have a double meaning because they link characters to historical victims of violence who are "scapegoats for the unbounded, retributive violence that regularly crops up in human affairs and that are routinely repressed and forgotten" (126). According to Paolo Diego Bubbio and Chris Fleming, films are cultural artifacts capable of directly or indirectly approving of different kinds of violence through representation by making "these kinds of violence either invisible or natural" (2); in other words, they can make certain acts of violence against specific victims legible and others invisible.

Rape-revenge films and the rape scene, in particular, tend to normalize violence against particular groups of women who are disenfranchised in contemporary culture; however, the doubling that appears within the space of transition between the rape scene and the subsequent acts of revenge that ensue for the remainder of the film are representations of mimetic trauma that demonstrate not only the individual trauma of the rape survivor but also reveals the history of systemic violence against women. Specifically, the depiction of the protagonist mimicking the perpetrator in the scene that follows the rape scene has not yet been thoroughly considered, perhaps due to the discomfort with the mimetic model of trauma; however, I argue that this scene is the closest visual representation of trauma in the context of films in which rape is the subject.

While trauma theorists argue that trauma is not representable (Caruth 1996; Felman and Laub 1992), I suggest that the rape scene is a presentation of the traumatic event, and the scene that follows the rape scene is the closest possible representation of trauma in a rape-revenge film. The scene that follows the rape scene can be analyzed using the mimetic model of trauma: Bubbio and Fleming propose that "directors and screenwriters might end up expressing meaningful contents *even beyond their own intension*" (7), and that "one of the motivating orientations of mimetic theory" is that it can discern "traces of violence in texts, as well as the perpetrator's attempts to disguise or naturalize these [traces]" (2). By analyzing the representation of the survivor's trauma in the scene that directly follows the rape in rape-revenge films, through the mimetic model of trauma, Teresa Brennan's (2003) concept of the transmission of affect, and Jane Caputi's (2003) adaptation of Brennan's theory in the context of rape, I argue that these scenes reveal that the desire for revenge is not through the individual's will for retribution, but rather is part of a historical chain of structural violence against women, in the form of rape, that society would rather forget.

Capitalism as Mimetic Desire: A Case of Rape

René Girard deconstructs the mimetic mechanism and argues that tracking the components of this mechanism can reveal the roots of violence. The mimetic mechanism begins with mimetic desire, and if another person possesses the object of desire, mimetic desire becomes mimetic rivalry. As the rivalry consumes the subject, the desire for the object becomes irrelevant, denoting a mimetic rivalry that "transforms into a sickness that can spread through the community like a plague" (136). The direct consequence is mimetic crisis that can be resolved only through the scapegoat resolution, in which the outbreak of violence is directed toward a community or person who absorbs the violence. These scapegoats are mimetic figures in that they symbolize a double: they are the subject in which hate and violence are directed, as well as sacrificial figures who absorb the violence, restoring the order of the community. Rape, as scholars have demonstrated, is intrinsically linked to capitalism; therefore, and borrowing from Girard, I argue that the power that capital affords is the object of mimetic desire. For instance, in relation to more women entering the workforce, Diana Russell points out that men, "are no different from any other ruling class in resisting threat to their monopoly of power" (258). Masculinity may thus be classified as socially powerful, but Jane Caputi claims that "masculinity is terrifyingly delicate, fundamentally insecure, and consistently susceptible to challenge" (2). According to Girard, competing for the desired object will be achieved through "violence if need be" (n.p.), which helps to explain why sexual violence toward women has increased as more women enter the workforce, cultivating power and acquiring capital—two objects to which men believe they are entitled (Russell 258; Dowd Hall 342).

The mimetic desire to obtain capital through violence appears to be connected to notions of masculinity and identity, and rape becomes a tool to subordinate women.

Investigating the theory that violence is connected to masculine identity, James Gilligan interviews men in prisons and psychiatric hospitals who have committed violent atrocities, and reports that the inmates describe feeling a loss of identity that they hoped to resurrect through acts of violence (1153). Masculinity is connected to capitalism because patriarchy has assigned the realm of capitalism to men, and because masculinity is tied to identity, once women enter the workforce, men experience a threat to their capital, which is not only linked to their masculinity but to their identity as well. To resolve this crisis, Girard would propose that men become consumed by the mimetic desire to reclaim their capital by means of violence, and Gilligan would argue that, in an attempt to bring their dead self "back to life," they would turn to violence (1153); however, violence against women is not distributed equally.

Both Girard and Gilligan draw attention to the desire for an object—in the case of rape, the object is capital, identity, or a mix of both—and the connection between this desire and violence; yet, neither Girard nor Gilligan appears to address the fact that, during mimetic rivalry, violence is not directed at all rivals equally. In the context of rape, it is important to note that assumptions about certain groups of women make them increasingly vulnerable to rape. In other words, as women enter the workforce in increasing numbers, the most vulnerable women—racialized, poor, queer, disabled women—become scapegoats toward whom men direct their violence. Referencing Girard's concept of the scapegoat resolution, John O'Carroll explains that scapegoat figures "emerge as the resolution to conflict and this conflict results from the interactions of mimetic desire" (21). The three protagonists in the rape-revenge films work in industries that place them outside of the margins of society and are gender nonconforming and occupy a nondominant sexual orientation, making them increasingly vulnerable to violence. The rates of sexual violence against women increase as more women emancipate themselves from men and generate their own capital, and while the protagonists are not the women who acquire this type of capital in the public sphere, Russell argues that violence is not necessarily "directed towards the particular women who gain this access" (258). Girard seemingly addresses the disparity of violence by asserting that the mimetic theory "allows the definition of difference in what is similar without renouncing the latter" (19); however, during the discussion of doubles, Girard explains that "the word double is the very symbol of desymbolization, and it means undifferentiation: the absence of all differences" (50–51). Girard's attempt to address a subject's positionality and their subsequent vulnerability to violent acts is confusing and convoluted. Conversely, scholarship by Angela Davis provides a nuanced perspective of difference within the case of rape and explains the relationship between rape and capitalism.

Angela Davis, for example, as a Black scholar and activist, critiques white feminists, like Susan Brownmiller, who wrote about rape during the 1970s' anti-rape movement for maintaining that "rape is a natural product of male anatomy and psychology" (39). According to Davis, these white feminists ignore the link between the "institution of lynching" Black men and women (42) and the "systematic rape of Black women," both of which are tools used by the oppressor to ensure the "exploitation of Black labour and political domination of Black people" and to guarantee "prosperity of whites" within the capitalistic system (40). Rape, like lynching, was used as a tool to inflict fear and violence on Black communities; yet, narratives to justify this racism would also need to be constructed. Society used the myths of the dangerous Black rapist and the promiscuous Black woman to rationalize the lynching of Black men and the rape of Black women, and these acts of violence would become the "essential ingredient[s] of the strategy of terror which guaranteed the over-exploitation of Black labour" and the "political domination of Black people" (42). Establishing an inextricable link between capitalism and white supremacy, Davis signals the need to examine the contemporary legacies of slavery, segregation, and white supremacy in order to end the rape of Black women.

While all three protagonists in the rape-revenge films are white, they are increasingly vulnerable to violence because of multiple forces of oppression such as their socioeconomic class, and in Aileen and Lisbeth's case, their sexual identity. The following section establishes capital as the mimetic object of desire and the relationship between capitalism and rape in all three films. Then, it demonstrates that the dialogue as well as the cinematic and stylistic techniques in the three films depict the rapist transferring his negative affects onto the survivor; despite the survivors' attempts to cleanse themselves of these negative affects, the revenge sequences reveal the ways in which the survivors exhibit the mimetic model of trauma.

The Historical Chain of Violence against Women: Trauma, Memory, Affect

Each of the rape scenes in the rape-revenge films establish a parallel between sexual violence and capital. In the most direct sense, in *Monster*, the protagonist, Aileen Wuornos, is a sex worker who enters a man's car to have sex for money, and this encounter ends in a brutal rape. This narrative presents a clear connection between rape and money. Similarly, Lisbeth Salander, the protagonist of *Girl with the Dragon Tattoo*, is a ward of the state, and, as a result, she cannot access her finances without permission from her state-appointed guardian, Nils Bjurman. In this case, Nils has complete power to prevent Lisbeth from acquiring any capital and also exploits this power to force Lisbeth to have oral sex in exchange for her finances, again demonstrating an association between capital and violence. The Bride in *Kill Bill vol. 1* was previously part of the Deadly Viper Assassination Squad; once she tries to quit the Squad, her boss shoots her in the head at her wedding and she remains in a coma for four years. While in a comatose state, the Bride is repeatedly raped by Buck, an orderly who works at the hospital, who also sells the Bride's body to truck drivers who want to rape the unconscious woman. The rape of the Bride is literally and figuratively a way in which Buck can reassert his masculinity because her body is an object that he uses to obtain capital, but also a receptacle for him and the men to reestablish their masculinity through violence. All three examples demonstrate that these protagonists become the scapegoats in which the rapists can obtain, through rape, their mimetic desire for capital.

The placement of the actors, dialogue, and the cinematography depict the rapist in a position of power compared to the protagonist during the rape scene, demonstrating their social position in relation to these women who are vulnerable based on multiple, intersecting forms of oppression. Following the rape scene, however, these same stylistic choices are employed throughout the revenge scene, presenting the mimetic switch from the rapist's mimetic desire for capital to the survivor exhibiting mimetic effects of trauma. This switch not only presents these individual cases of violence but also speaks to the larger systems of power that permit this violence. *Monster's* Aileen, a queer, homeless sex worker who, in an effort to obtain money for her upcoming date with Selby, enters a man's car to have sex for money. Once he drives into the forest, he parks, punches Aileen in the face, and rapes her with a crowbar. Throughout the rape, Aileen and the rapist are depicted in medium close-up; both face the camera as Aileen is forced to lie on her stomach across the car seats, as the rapist is positioned behind and above Aileen. Right before the rapist punches Aileen, he turns to her and says, "You know, women, I love 'em and I hate 'em." As he rapes Aileen, the rapist repeatedly asks: "Do you want to die?" The rapist's question can be read as a desire for power that he obtains through deciding whether or not to kill Aileen, and his dichotomous love and hatred for women is ironic given that some heterosexual men require the use of women to assert their masculinity through sexual power, yet women can also pose a threat to their masculinity.

After Aileen is raped, the rapist pours gasoline all over her, planning to light her on fire and kill her. Managing to escape, Aileen shoots the rapist repeatedly; in this revenge scene, the rapist is depicted in medium close-up on the ground with bullet wounds in his chest, as Aileen stands above him. Aileen, appreciating that she barely escaped death, turns and spots an ax in the trunk of the rapist's car, and the close-up of her face depicts her horror as she realizes that this event is part of a pattern of violence enacted on women. By shooting the rapist numerous times, she avenges her own rape, and once Aileen finds the axe she runs back over to the rapist, who is lying on the ground, and repeatedly kicks him, shouting, "Fuck you! You fucking piece of shit!" While the narrative structure, typical of most rape-revenge films, denotes the reversal of power, the mode of revenge in *Monster*—specifically, the bullets penetrating the rapist's body—is symbolic of the transfer of mimetic violence.

In *GWTDT*, Lisbeth works as an investigative hacker, identifies as bisexual, and presents as gender queer. Nils Bjurman, her state-appointed guardian, consistently exploits the power he holds over Lisbeth and in one scene orders her to perform oral sex in his office in exchange for access to her money; in another scene, she enters his home and he tases her, ties her up, and anally rapes her. In the scene, Lisbeth is tied to Nils's bed and positioned lying on her stomach, while Nils kneels over her back, preparing to rape her. Part of this scene is recorded behind

the bed from the perspective of the camera placed in Lisbeth's backpack
that is propped on a chair behind the bed. The position of the camera
captures Lisbeth's entire body in long shot from behind. Preceding the
rape scene, Nils tells Lisbeth, "You're so cute when you're surly," which
echoes a popular rape myth that women often "play hard to get" in an
effort to create a game of chase because they want men to dominate them.
Following this declaration, the guardian states, "I forgot to ask: do you
like anal sex?" seemingly mocking the imperative that men must ask for
consent, as he has Lisbeth tied up and is not interested in her response.

Later, Lisbeth returns to Nils's home, tortures him, negotiates her
finances, and forces him to lift her declaration of incompetence. An
aerial shot captures Nils's naked body as he is tied on the ground, which
mimics the long shots of Lisbeth's naked body while she was tied to the
bed and raped. Lisbeth hovers above the rapist and threatens, "If I find
a girl in here, whether she came of her own free will or not, I will kill
you." Not only is Lisbeth avenging her own rape, but as she penetrates
Nils's skin with ink, tattooing the words "I am a rapist Pig" across his
torso, Lisbeth ensures that Nils will never be around another woman.

Last, once the Bride wakes up from the coma in *Kill Bill*, she
immediately hears two men walk into her room, so she pretends to be
asleep and listens to their conversation. The Bride lies flat on her back as
Buck, an orderly—who has raped and sold the Bride's body for sex while
she was in a coma—as well as a truck driver—who is a new client that
pays Buck for sex with the Bride—are depicted in medium shot standing
at the foot of the hospital bed. Buck dictates the rules of raping the
Bride to the truck driver, who pays Buck for access to the Bride's body;
the rules include "no punching" or "leaving marks of any kind" because
the nurse will uncover the abuse and the "jig will be up." The fact that
Buck has to state the rules demonstrates an understanding between the
men of a mutual desire to abuse women. Before Buck leaves the room,
he informs the truck driver that the Bride's "cooch can get drier than
a bucket of sand," and gestures toward a container of Vaseline, stating
that, if he "lubes up, [he] will be good to go." The Bride is in a coma
and does not experience arousal; yet, the men still want to rape her,
indicating a complete negation of women's pleasure. Once Buck leaves the
room, the truck driver leans in to kiss the Bride, and a close-up depicts
the Bride biting and stretching his lip, almost completely removing it
from his face. The Bride hides, and Buck returns to the room to check
on the reason for the commotion, and when the Bride slashes his ankle,

he falls to the ground. The Bride's legs are weak from her coma, so she sits up, still above the orderly, who lies flat on the ground. She spots Buck's keychain that reads "Pussy Wagon" and looks down at Buck in disgust, yelling, "Pussy Wagon, you fucker!" and slams his head between the door repeatedly. Similar to Aileen, who steals the rapist's car after she kills him, and begins to enact revenge on others, the Bride steals the "Pussy Wagon" and begins enacting her revenge. This key chain, displaying a term from the song "Greased Lightnin'" from the 1978 film *Grease*, symbolizes that Buck's sexist views against all women is part of a larger popular discourse that reduces women to objects for masculine pleasure.[2] The survivors' desire to enact violence on others—beyond the rapists—surfaces because, as men rape women to reestablish their masculinity, they transfer their negative affects onto women.

Scholars who study affect, such as Teresa Brennan, claim that women—or "feminine beings"—carry "the negative affects for the other" (15) because people are not self-contained in terms of their energy (29); rather, the energy that oscillates between and among human subjects is what Brennan calls the transmission of affect (34). Jane Caputi adopts Brennan's framework to explain the transmission of affect in the context of sexual violence. For Caputi, the transmission of affect—or "dumping"—refers to "those needing to relieve themselves of negative and toxic affects—can transmit those to another who then carries the affect" (2), and this process is marked by power, since women who are "poor, and those who are stigmatized by racism, sexuality, and so on" tend to be the target (2). Aileen, Lisbeth, and the Bride are marginalized based on intersecting forms of oppression: Aileen's class and sexuality, Lisbeth's gender and sexuality, and the Bride's gender and ability make them increasingly vulnerable to sexual violence. These intersecting forms of oppression create an imbalance of power between the rapists and the protagonists, and establish all three women as scapegoat figures, who carry the rapists' negative affects and experience the effects of mimetic trauma.

The doubling of the rape scene and revenge scene visually demonstrates Humbert's claim that "violence spreads like a kind of contagion and the means is imitation . . . because of the automatic prestige [violence] confers, the charismatic authority it commands and the protection it seems to afford" (119–120). As the rapists transfer their negative affects onto the protagonists, the women attempt to rid themselves of contamination through a cleansing ritual. Caputi explains that the "ritual bath" is a common metaphor that appears in testimonies of survivors of sexual violence and that this cleansing ritual "provides an exorcism of some of the toxic affects that are contained and transmitted via the sense of smell, carried in and by bodily fluids, skin, tone of voice, touch" (4). Once Aileen and the Bride kill the rapists, they are covered in blood, and both find jugs full of water to dump all over their bodies in order to rid themselves of the blood. Humbert argues that "blood is a signifier not only of violence, but fatal pollution as well," and that because blood stains, attempts to clean up the blood are in vain, just as society tries to repress the history of violence, but it remains (123). Similarly, Lisbeth performs two cleansing rituals: first, in a scene in which she visits Nils's office to obtain her money, he forces her to perform oral sex in exchange for her own money, and afterward, she enters the bathroom and forces herself to purge. Second, following the rape at Nils's home, Lisbeth returns home, and is depicted in long shot as she undresses and enters the shower. As Lisbeth takes a shower, bruises on her arms, back, and wrists are shot in close-up, and the camera pans down her shaking legs. Like blood, the images of ruptures and injuries are significant in visual representations of trauma, and Jill Bennett argues that because skin is permeable, and it is "precisely through the breached boundaries of memory that skin continues to be felt as a wound . . . it is here in sense memory that the past seeps back into the present, becoming sensation rather than representation" (36). The woman cannot get rid of the negative affects because they are social and systemic: these systems of oppression are ineluctable. The cleansing scenes, in which the protagonists attempt to purify themselves of blood and other bodily fluids, accompanied by images of trauma on the skin, represent the physical effects of trauma on the body following the rape, and mark the transition in which the protagonists decide to begin their violent revenge: Aileen decides to kill every man who wants to pay her for sex, Lisbeth constructs a plan to re-enter Nils's home to enact her revenge, and the Bride retaliates against every member of the Viper Assassination Squad. These scenes not only denote a reversal of power, but the parallelism between the rape and revenge scenes, established by cinematic and stylistic choices, also demonstrate the mimetic model of trauma.

The scene in which Nils forces Lisbeth to give him oral sex is depicted by an aerial shot; during this scene, Nils tilts his head back and his face appears in close-up. After this scene, Lisbeth arrives home, and an aerial shot shows her sitting cross-legged on the floor of her apartment listening to heavy metal music; Lisbeth tilts her head back, and a close-up of her face follows. The graphic match of Nils and Lisbeth represents the transfer of negative affect, and the moment in which Lisbeth decides to construct a plan for revenge on Nils. The scenes in which Aileen and the Bride are represented as a double of the perpetrator are more explicit than in *GWTDT* and are constructed through the use of costume and props. Once Aileen completes the cleansing ritual, she searches the perpetrator's car for new clothes; this scene is followed by a cut to Aileen driving in the rapist's car, wearing his uniform, gloves, and hat as she drinks from his flask. Similarly, following a flashback of Buck at the foot of the Bride's bed right before he rapes her, the Bride repeatedly slams his head in the door, steals his car keys, and escapes the hospital in Buck's Pussy Wagon wearing his uniform.[3] With respect to experiences of trauma, Brennan asserts that trauma is directly linked to the transmission of affect because "some of its victims testify with extraordinary activity concerning the experience of something infiltrating their psyches as well as their bodies" (121). Violence is fluid (119), as Humbert argues, and since "identities are unstable," (41) as Girard (2000) claims, the protagonists become visual embodiments of their perpetrators, essentially their doubles, representing the effects of trauma through mimesis, and this mimesis demonstrates that rape is a part of larger systems of oppression that work to subordinate women.

Conclusion

With the exception of the mimetic representation of trauma in *Monster*, *GWTDT*, and *Kill Bill vol. 1*, all three films provide limited readings of rape. As previously stated, the three protagonists are either gender nonconforming or identify as lesbian or bisexual, and all three films present rape as a means of correcting the protagonists' gender or sexual orientation to adhere to dominant and normative expectations of gender and sexuality. This "correction" is evident following the revenge sequences; Aileen ends up in jail, Lisbeth forms a romantic relationship with Mikael, and the Bride ends up with her long-lost daughter. While these films demonstrate how these three disenfranchised women are not only more vulnerable to acts of sexual violence but also are unable to obtain any formal version of justice, the narratives make their rape and the material discourses that script this violence legible. Conversely, far fewer rape-revenge films that feature a Black protagonist circulate in the public sphere, suggesting that

Black women's narratives of sexual assault are not rendered legible in society. Kimberle Crenshaw (1991) argues that, today, Black women are least likely to be believed when reporting sexual assault to law enforcement, see the perpetrator arrested, charged, tried in court, and convicted. To engage with representations of rape, then, scholars must consider the oppressive systems of power, beyond patriarchy, that are responsible for shaping the material discourses of rape in the United States.

As personal testimony and political activism about rape have begun to saturate popular culture across a variety of media, and these discourses expose issues such as the suspicion and disbelief with which rape testimony is often met in juridical settings and the public sphere, relatedly, scholarship regarding depictions of rape in contemporary Hollywood cinema ought to switch from a focus on the presentation of a graphic rape scene to a representation of rape trauma. Jill Bennett proposes a framework to understand visual representations of trauma and suggests that one "should read fragments of memories written on the body" using a dialectic relationship" between common memory which consists of experiences that can be transcribed into narrative frameworks, and sense memory, which is the physical imprint or bodily effects of trauma felt in the present (31). Reading representations of rape trauma through this dialectic of common memory and sense memory is crucial "so [that] affective experience of viewing can be understood in relation to a larger set of political and moral issues" (31). While the construction of the graphic rape scene can generate affects such as disgust or sympathy, a representation of traumatic memory using the mimetic model of trauma presents rape trauma not as an individual occurrence but as part of a larger chain of violence against women. This chapter has demonstrated that melancholia, as a form of sense memory, provides a framework for understanding representations of rape trauma beyond an individual event but as part of a larger system of intersecting forms of oppression.

Anne Anlin Cheng, citing Freud, explains that melancholia's ambivalence occurs because the relationship between the ego and object shatters when the "ego wishes to incorporate this object into itself . . . by devouring it" (8). This mimetic consumption produces a state of melancholia in which the subject enters, and according to Freud the subject, unable to complete the process of mourning, becomes psychically stuck in a pathological and perpetual state of mourning; yet, Cheng claims that this continuous consumption of the other can also be nurturing (8). In the case of rape-revenge films, the survivor enters a state of melancholia; the protagonist consumes the aggression of the rapist, and through this identification of violence the survivor enacts violence not only out of self-preservation and to avenge their own rape but also to avenge the rape of past victims and to ensure that women are protected against future predation.

Notes

1. Rape-revenge films are also commonly referred to as rape and revenge films and rape/revenge films.

2. In "Greased Lightnin,'" Travolta sings "she's a real pussy wagon," which feminizes the car in a masculine car culture. Furthermore, according to Travolta, this feminized car ensures that "chicks'll cream" and that he can "got off [his] rocks." Interestingly, the song also aligns the feminized car with capital, as the group of men harmonize the lyrics: "I'll get the money, I'll kill to get the money."

3. By stealing the Pussy Wagon and using it as a means of mobility to enact her revenge, the Bride repurposes the car from an object men use seduce women, as the song "Greased Lightnin'" explains, to a vehicle of female empowerment. Ironically, in an interview with Maureen Dowd (2018) at the *New York Times*, Uma Thurman reveals details of her allegations of sexual abuse against Harvey Weinstein, disclosing that on the set of *Kill Bill* she refused to perform a driving sequence in which she felt uncomfortable, and director Quentin Tarantino forced her to perform her own stunt; she crashed and suffered serious injury. She recalls confronting Tarantino after the accident, and claims that they "had an enormous fight, and [Thurman] accused him of trying to kill [her]" (n.p.).

Works Cited

Allen, Leah Claire. "The Pleasures of Dangerous Criticism: Interpreting Andrea Dworkin as a Literary Critic." *Signs* 42, no. 1 (2016): 49–70.

Bennett, Jill. "The Aesthetics of Sense Memory: Theorising Trauma Through the Visual Arts." In *Memory Cultures: Memory, Subjectivity, and Recognition*, edited by Susannah Radstone and Katharine Hodgkin. New York: Routledge, 2005. 27–39.

Brennan, Teresa. *The Transmission of Affect*. Ithaca, NY: Cornell University Press, 2003.

Bubbio, Paolo Diego, and Chris Fleming. "Introduction." *Mimetic Theory and Film*. New York: Bloomsbury Academic, 2019. 1–14. http://dx.doi.org/10.5040/9781501334863.0004

Caputi, Jane. "'Take Back What Doesn't Belong to Me': Sexual Violence, Resistance and the 'Transmission of Affect.'" *Women's Studies International Forum* 26, no. 1 (2003): 1–14.

Caruth, Cathy. *Unclaimed Experience: Trauma, Narrative, and History*. Baltimore: Johns Hopkins University Press, 1996.

Cheng, Anne Anlin. *The Melancholy of Race*. New York: Oxford University Press, 2001.

Crenshaw, Kimberle. "Mapping the Margins: Intersectionality, Identity Politics, and Violence against Women of Color." *Stanford Law Review* 43, no. 6 (1991): 1241–1299. jstor.org/stable/1229039

Davis, Angela Y. "Rape, Racism and the Capitalist Settling." *The Black Scholar* 12, no. 6 (1981): 39–45.

Dowd, Maureen. "This is Why Uma Thurman is Angry." *New York* Times, February 3, 2018. www.nytimes.com/2018/02/03/opinion/sunday/this-is-why-uma-thurman-is-angry.html

Dowd Hall, Jacquelyn. "The Mind That Burns in Each Body." In *Powers of Desire*, edited by Christine Stansell, Ann Barr Snitow, and Sharon Thompson. New York: Monthly Review Press, 1983. 328–349.

Felman, Shoshana, and Dori Laub. *Testimony: Crisis of Witnessing in Literature, Psychoanalysis and History*. New York: Routledge, 1992.

Freud, Sigmund. 1917."Mourning and Melancholia." *The Standard Edition of the Complete Psychological Works of Sigmund Freud, Volume XIV (1914–1916): On the History of Psycho-Analytic Movement, Papers on Metapsychology and Other Works*, translated by James Strachey, edited by Anna Freud, Alix Strachey, and Alan Tyson. New York: Vintage, 2001.

Freud, Sigmund. "The Uncanny." *Studies in Parapsychology*. Rdited by Philip Rieff. New York: Macmillan, 1963, 19–60.

Gilligan, James. "Shame, Guilt, and Violence." *Social Research* 70, no. 4 (2003): 1149–1180. www.jstor.org/stable/40971965

Girard, René. *Evolution and Conversion: Dialogues on the Origins of Culture with Pierpaolo Antonello and João Cezar De Castro Rocha*. New York: Bloomsbury, 2000.

Girard, René. *The Scapegoat*. Translated by Yvonne Freccero. Baltimore: Johns Hopkins University Press, 1982.

Girard, René. *Violence and the Sacred*. Translated by Patrick Gregory. Baltimore: Johns Hopkins University Press, 1977.

Girard, René. "What Is Occurring Today Is a Mimetic Rivalry on a Planetary Scale." Translated by Jim Williams, *Le Monde*, November 6, 2001. www.uibk.ac.at/theol/cover/girard/le_monde_interview.html

Girl With the Dragon Tattoo. Directed by David Fincher, Columbia Pictures, 2011.

Grease. Directed by Randal Kleiser, Paramount Pictures, 1978.

Heller-Nicholas, Alexandra. *Rape Revenge Films: A Critical Study*. Jefferson, NC: MacFarland and Company, 2011.

Henry, Claire. *Revisionist Rape: Redefining a Film Genre*. London: Palgrave Macmillan, 2014.

Horeck, Tanya. *Public Rape: Representation Violation in Fiction and Film*. New York: Routledge, 2004.

Humbert, David. "Eyes Wide Shut: Mimesis and Historical Memory in Stanley Kubrick's The Shining." In *Mimesis, Movies, and Media: Violence, Desire, and the Sacred*, vol. 3, edited by Scott Cowdell, Chris Fleming, and Joel Hodge. New York: Bloomsbury Academic, 2015. 117–127.

Kill Bill vol. 1. Directed by Quintin Tarantino, A Band Apart, 2004.

Leys, Ruth. *Trauma: A Genealogy*. Chicago: Chicago University Press, 2000.

Magestro, Molly Ann. *Assault on the Small Screen*. New York: Rowman and Littlefield, 2015.

Monster. Directed by Patty Jenkins, Zodiac Productions, 2003.

O'Carroll, John. "The Scapegoat Mechanism and the Media: Beyond the Folk Devil Paradigm." In *Mimesis, Movies, and Media: Violence, Desire, and the Sacred*, vol. 3, edited by Scott Cowdell, Chris Fleming, and Joel Hodge. New York: Bloomsbury Academic, 2015. 17–32.

Palaver, Wolfgang. "Mimetic Theory and Gender." *René Girard's Mimetic Theory: Studies in Violence, Mimesis and Culture*, translated by Gabriel Borrud. Ann Arbor: Michigan University Press, 2011. 297–307.

Plantinga, Carl. *Moving Viewers: American Film and the Spectator's Experience*. Berkeley: California University Press, 2009.

Projansky, Sarah. *Watching Rape: Film and Television in Postfeminist Culture*. New York: New York University Press, 2001.

Radstone, Susannah. "Trauma Theory: Contexts, Politics, Ethics." *Paragraph* 42, no. 2 (2007): 9–29. www.euppublishing.com/doi/10.3366/prg.2007.0015

Read, Jacinda. *The New Avengers: Feminism, Femininity, and the Rape-Revenge Cycle*. Manchester, UK: Manchester University Press, 2000.

Russell, Diana E. H. "From Witches to Bitches: Sexual Terrorism Begets Thelma and Louise." In *Making Violence Sexy: Feminist Views on Pornography*, edited by Diana E.H. Russell, New York: Teachers College Press, 1993, pp. 254–269.

Spallacci, Amanda. "Representing Rape Trauma in Film: Moving Beyond the Event." *Memory Affect, and Cinema*, special issue of *Arts*, vol. 8, no. 8, 2019, pp. 1–11, *MDPI*. https://doi.org/10.3390/arts8010008

Young, Alison. *The Scene of Violence: Cinema, Crime, Affect*. New York: Routledge, 2009.

CHAPTER 9

Painting Pain on Her Skin

Vigilante Justice and the Feminist Revenge Heroine in *The Girl with the Dragon Tattoo*

Nicole Burkholder-Mosco

"God should have made girls lethal
when he made monsters of men"

—Elisabeth Hewer from *Wishing for Birds*

The 2017 #MeToo movement—as well as the 2018 #TimesUp movement—can be attributed to a number of cultural shifts and altered societal norms in the decade or so proceeding their rise.[1] One such shift can be traced to the early 2000's large-scale import of Scandinavian Noir to an American viewer- and readership. Through these dark and gritty works, sexual assault—and misogyny in general—is shown unflinchingly and with sometimes shocking conclusions. In 2008, Stieg Larsson's *The Girl with the Dragon Tattoo* was published in English and took the English-speaking literary world by storm. The novel was originally published in Sweden in 2005 with the title *Män som hatar kvinnor*, which translates to "Men Who Hate Women." A Swedish film with the new *Girl* title followed in 2009, and an American remake in 2011.[2] For much of America, this was their introduction to Scandinavian Noir and to the character of Lisbeth Salander. The plot of this story revolves around men who treat women badly—very badly. In fact, multiple plot strains center on physical and sexual violence to women and show not only the varied and often horrific ways women can be harassed, coerced, or assaulted but also the ways surviving victims cope with such assaults. Lisbeth Salander becomes the example that stands for the whole as we see her story unfold. Her mistreatment by a more powerful man has no judicial recourse, so she takes justice into her own hands.

The original source material of the book, the Swedish film, and the American film—all written or directed by men—show women who have no hope of official retribution *for* or even prevention *of* abuse. With no optimistic expectations from a system that often fails them and a society that dismisses them, we see in fiction examples of vigilante justice served by women in unconventional, albeit violent, ways. The story of *The Girl with the Dragon Tattoo*—especially its sleek American film that infiltrated the mainstream with high box-office sales and critical regard (including an Oscar nomination for actress Rooney Mara)—serves as a backdrop to the American society that nurtured the #MeToo and #TimesUp movements; this dark tale with its unforgettable female protagonist also demonstrates how early twenty-first-century fiction responded to the age-old disparity between violent men and the women whom they violate.

Textual Spaces in Fairy Tales and Dragon Tattoos

From a historical narrative perspective, this plot—of women who are fearful of men and who seek to find solutions for their predicaments—is as old as the first mythologies and oral stories humankind has shared. In fact, fairy tales, often told by women in the centuries before the written versions by men, centered on women, the home, and marriage: specifically, the fears of leaving the relative safety of one's home for the dangerous one of an older man or the persecution of young girls in their homes from the very people whom they should be able to trust. While too often disregarded as children's narratives of little importance, fairy tales have been ever present over millennia precisely because they address issues of "significant social function" (Tatar 1999, xi) and the anxieties that have always existed in both children's and women's lives. Some tales, such as the Bluebeard cycle, show the horrific fate of women who might find themselves married to a monstrous man. Others, such as the Catskin cycle,[3] show the terror that exists at home due to an overly amorous father attempting to court and/or marry his daughter. In other related categories of tales, we see even more graphically violent family relationships. For example, in "The Maiden without Hands," we see an incestuous father who seeks to marry his daughter but, in these stories, the enraged father cuts off his daughter's hands, breasts, or tongue as retaliation for her refusal. In an Italian version recorded by Giambattista Basile in 1634 entitled "Penta of the Chopped-Off Hands," we see a girl, Penta, who discovers her brother seeks to molest and violate her instead of providing her protection; he notes that in particular her beautiful hands are what most attracts him to her. In this version, Penta has her own hands severed from her body and, to address her brother's dubious fetish, delivers them to him with a note encouraging him to "enjoy what delighted him most" (qtd. in Tatar 1992, 122).

If these stories seem dark and twisted, they are—just like the genre of Scandinavian Noir,[4] which is generally identified as fiction set in bleak landscapes that confronts realistic brutality, often emphasizing rape, misogyny, and other types of violence to women (though the cruelty need not be confined to women). The events that transpire tend to occur in commonplace environments traditionally thought to be safe. There is a mystery to be solved that may—or may not—save others from pain and suffering. Like fairy tales, Scandinavian Noir is often grim and primordial, and these stories don't always have happy endings. We see here a resurrection of our original stories, tales told for thousands of years to serve as both warning and instruction. For girls, it was imperative in the past, as it is in the present, to understand the dangers that exist in the everyday world. Fairy tales and Scandinavian Noir often show women as victims but also as industrious, wily, and tough as they navigate patriarchal worlds filled with violent men who are twisted with magic, or magical thinking; both genres also include plots of entrapment and possession. If a girl is to survive, she must find her way out. Scandinavian Noir resurrected the fairy tale revenge heroine and gave voice to her silenced sisters.

The notion of women fearing men and finding they can turn to no one other than themselves in the face of threat and outright violence has never gone out of style since these early days of storytelling. However, these women who fight back complicate things; they are no longer passive victims who do as they're told and suffer—then die quietly. By embracing a defensive stance and, often, mimicking violence to combat that which is being done to them, the woman is often viewed as monstrous herself.

As Carol Clover says in her seminal 1992 examination of the "final girl" in twentieth-century horror films, the girl who steps up and fights back often becomes victim, hero, and monster: the final surviving girl "becomes a kind of monstrous hero—hero insofar that she has risen against and defeated the forces of monstrosity, monster insofar as she has herself become excessive" (4). Rape-revenge films have long gravitated toward scenes of gratuitous violence used as male-gaze entertainment. According to Gayatri Nair and Dipto Tamang, "such depictions are rarely critical in nature, adopting instead what . . . Laura Mulvey calls the male gaze, where the narrative is driven primarily by the male protagonist and a perceived male audience, while women serve a purely 'exhibitionist role' onto which men project their fantasies" (614).

However, *The Girl with the Dragon Tattoo*, with its utilization of fairy tale tropes, was one of the first to change the conversation.[5] While some viewers of the films, particularly the American one, will still argue the rape and retaliation scenes are unnecessarily graphic, others (including Rooney Mara and Noomi Rapace, who plays Lisbeth in the Swedish film[6]) have noted that Lisbeth embodies a more humane and fully rounded victim-turned-hero and, that by showing sexual assault in its unflinching ugliness, a conversation necessarily ensues since that's what sexual assaults so often are: ugly moments of extreme violence inflicted upon the victim in a dehumanizing manner. If filmic sexual assaults have traditionally been normalized as voyeuristic entertainment, these films challenge those norms just as they simultaneously challenge the viewer to not look away. If the stark rape of Lisbeth doesn't turn a viewer's pleasure to discomfort, then the revenge rape and retaliation scene perpetuated on her attacker should do the trick—there is nothing pleasurable in either scene; in the book and both films, rape and assault are shown as horrific, visceral, and disturbing.

In Larsson's book, we see a number of examples of men treating women badly. This makes the title change, from the Swedish *Men Who Hate Women*, significant. When the English translation changed the title to *The Girl with the Dragon Tattoo*, the emphasis was also changed from the *men* who inflict pain to a *woman*—a "girl" in this case—who fights back. In fact, Larsson's intent when writing the *Millennium* trilogy, the first three books of what was originally planned as a series of ten novels before his death in 2004, was to show a series where independent entries focused on different types of dangerous and monstrous men: men who hurt women in their private lives, human trafficking, and society's implicit role in condoning the violence and degradation to which women might find themselves subjected.[7] The three novels taken together provide a comprehensive overview of violence against women that "tie together intimate partner abuse with organized crime and the institutionalization of social stigma" (Mollegaard 349). These books, in fact, might be an attempt to correct a wrong Larsson felt keenly. According to lore surrounding Larsson's life, he witnessed a gang rape at the age of fifteen but did nothing to prevent the assault. According to a friend, Larsson later begged forgiveness from the assaulted girl: she refused his request (Acocella).

In his first novel, Larsson begins each section with Swedish national statistics for violence against women. And before any significant plot strains involving Lisbeth Salander, the "girl" of the title, we are shown multiple examples of violence against women that often goes unanswered: a security company's newest and most lucrative service for affluent, professional women who seek protection from former male partners or stalkers (35); the male protagonist, Mikael Blomkvist, whose sister is an attorney specializing in family law as well as a women's rights advocate, publicly representing battered women on television (75); and even Lisbeth's personal history that includes sexual assault and unfair targeting due to her perceived promiscuous sexuality[8] (160). Lisbeth, who is under a court-ordered psychiatric guardianship that includes oversight of her assets, has a deep mistrust of authority and is most likely afflicted with Asperger syndrome. After a childhood filled with trauma, foster families, and unpleasant stays in psychiatric clinics, the courts are resistant to remove her guardianship; this is bearable for Lisbeth when her trustee is Advokat Holgar Palmgren, who becomes a sort of kindly father figure to her—one of a series of men who, unlike their many counterparts, shows consistent compassion and respect for women throughout the novel. However, when Palmgren suffers a debilitating stroke, Lisbeth is assigned a new guardian: Advokat Nils Bjurman.

The book outlines first a sexual harassment and grooming session followed by two distinct assaults on Lisbeth by Bjurman. At first, Bjurman asks Lisbeth inappropriate and sexually motivated questions (*How often do you have sex? What's your favorite position? Do you enjoy oral sex? Have you ever had anal sex?*), making clear all the while that he holds significant power over her, including the power to have her institutionalized if she does not play his game (Larsson 200–201). This quickly escalates to sexual assault when, at another meeting, Bjurman begins by massaging her neck, proceeds to groping her breasts, and, finally, culminates with forcing her hand—and then her mouth—onto his genitals. He tells her, "If you're nice to me, I'll be nice to you" (Larsson 222). Lisbeth, meanwhile, fully understands her vulnerable position and realizes that she has little recourse at this point—she notes that she never does anything without "first weighing the consequences" (Larsson 221), a lesson taught to her many times as a poor young woman caught in an indifferent social system that has labeled her as "trouble."

The next meeting with Bjurman goes even more terribly wrong. Lisbeth believes herself prepared this time; using her computer and security skills, she rigs a small camera inside her bag to record what she assumes will be another assault of the variety she endured at the previous meeting—another groping and forced oral sex. However, Bjurman, perhaps heady with the power he feels he has over women like Lisbeth, moves the goal posts. This time, he violently attacks her, slapping her and throwing her to the bed. He rips off her clothing and handcuffs her to the frame, then hideously rapes and sodomizes her for hours. He keeps her chained to the bed and once even suffocates her with a pillow until she almost passes out. Unwilling to go to the authorities who have always seen her as a troublemaker and who have consequently put her into this position as a ward of the state in the first place, she takes matters into her own hands. First, she spends a week recovering. If the passage in the text about the many assaults Bjurman perpetrates on Lisbeth is brief, her recovery makes the attack unflinchingly clear: she stays in bed a week with injuries that include pain in her abdomen and bleeding from her rectum. During her recovery, she studies American research on sadists, which tells her that they will choose dependent individuals as their victims. This bothers Lisbeth immensely, who is above all things a survivor. She concludes that others see her as the type of woman who can be abused, a woman with no power. This knowledge perhaps motivates her next actions more than does simple revenge for her attack. However, she first marks this moment by getting another tattoo—a painful one on her ankle. A reader might, at this point, start to reevaluate Lisbeth's many tattoos and body piercings; if we see her memorializing her pain with body modification, what might we conclude about her early life and the multitude of other traumatic events she has endured? Kirsten Mollegaard finds that the tattoos, "emblematically inked onto Salander's body as warnings, signal meaning and identity in a borderline space" (351). Just as Lisbeth has existed in a liminal space for most of her life, being between spaces and places but belonging to none, her skin also demarcates the liminal positioning of her body; while she has often lost control of her body—to the state, to violent men—she controls the liminal surface of her skin that separates her inside from outside and uses its surface to mark her identity and her history in a permanent manner.

Lisbeth does get revenge on her attacker. Instead of going to the authorities, she enacts vigilante justice that will both punish her tormentor and get her the independence both he and the state have denied her. The next time she meets with him at his apartment, she is prepared: she tasers him, uses his own sex toys against him, makes him watch the DVD she has made of her rape, then tattoos his chest all the way down to his groin. This is a crucial point of Lisbeth's ideology: she knows a man like Bjurman will assault other women and this isn't acceptable to her. She wants to make sure he is marked and branded to any woman he encounters. Bjurman's tattoo will also serve as a reminder to him: his body now reads, "I AM A SADISTIC PIG, A PERVERT, AND A RAPIST" (Larsson 262). Lisbeth, by this act, possesses his liminal space and uses it to serve as a reminder to him of his trespass. Interestingly, this scene in the book is interposed with another story, that of Cecilia Vanger—one of the members of the prominent family Mikael Blomkvist is investigating—who is recalling both her husband, who physically abused her, and her father and brother, who psychologically and emotionally abused her. She recalls that when she finally got the courage to leave her husband after his abuse sent her to the emergency room one afternoon, her father, rather than offering any support, berated her, telling her she was a "whore" who could not keep a man. She looked to her brother who was also present and hoped for some compassion; instead he laughed and humored their father. Cecilia, holding a gun, tells the reader that she closed her eyes and felt that "her only option at that moment seemed to be to raise the gun and fire both barrels. She wanted to kill them both" (Larsson 257).

Certainly, this story, situated the way it is, tells us several things. First, this kind of treatment can happen to any woman—it's not class contained. Cecilia Vanger belongs to one of the wealthiest families in Sweden; she is formally educated and respected. Yet her husband, father, and brother feel that she is an object, subhuman, to be treated with cruelty, brutality, or simple indifference. Second, this episode reminds us that any woman can be pushed to retaliation and violence. In that moment, Cecilia seriously considered the murder of her father and brother. The violence that we see explode with Lisbeth is not unique to her; all women can be capable of such violence in response to men's treatment of them. And finally, this chapter highlights the pervasive nature of violence to women, something that Larsson goes to great lengths in his narrative to make clear. In all spaces of life—at home with her husband, in the woods with her father and brother, or in a scheduled meeting with her court-appointed guardian—women can find themselves in vulnerable positions that allow men to assert physical or societal pressure onto them. Notably, Cecilia's story is just a side anecdote to the central plot; what Mikael eventually uncovers through his investigation is that two *other* men in the Vanger family (another father and brother) were serial rapists and killers over the course of at least forty years. Lisbeth, when she enacts revenge on her attacker using her computer savvy, her bravery, and downright nerve, displays a type of fantasy fulfillment for any woman who has been victimized by a man but has not found reasonable recourse; such a reader might feel validation in Lisbeth's brand of justice. Larsson is showing his readers how pervasive and successful men can be at hurting and coercing women and how often women have few tools at hand to fight back.

The Girl with the Dragon Tattoo on the Big Screen

The message about women who are treated badly by men, so carefully articulated in the book, came roaring to life when David Fincher released his 2011 version of the film. Known for films like *Se7en*, Fincher set out to create a dark yet stylish, atmospheric film. The book had already been adapted in Sweden in 2009 by director Niels Arden Oplev. Fincher, like Oplev, follows the novel closely in his adaptation, but you can tell from the opening credits that this is a big-budget Hollywood film seen through Fincher's expressive eye. The opening montage, which uses Led Zeppelin's "Immigrant Song" covered by Trent Reznor, Atticus Ross, and Karen O, is a sleek, nightmarish collision of images that feels simultaneously erotic and unnerving. Images of love and passion are interspersed with the obscene and violent. As a black, viscous fluid oozes over the screen, the viewer is stimulated with imagery: flowers, sex, violent phallic symbols, dragons, wasps, computer parts, and even a man on fire. A Larsson fan will note that these images tell a story that extends beyond the borders of the first novel in the *Millennium* trilogy; instead, this opening sequence contains allusions to Lisbeth's life story that will be expounded upon in the subsequent sequels. The opening montage takes us beyond her skin made famous in the title and into the depths of her nightmares.

Fincher's Lisbeth (Mara) is a more androgynous character than is Oplev's Lisbeth (Rapace). Fincher's "girl" is also more socially awkward than her Swedish predecessor. Both films treat their subject material in a more general way than does the novel, which feels intensely personal; Larsson creates Lisbeth as a dysfunctional hero, individual in her looks and abilities, who can right the wrongs of her world. The filmic texts both utilize seemingly unique female characters but want them to clearly stand for the whole; these filmic women, despite looking different and having rare skill sets, are both easy to connect to, quick to inspire empathy. Fincher especially takes his time establishing Lisbeth as the trickster character, a surprising yet formidable victim/hero; unlike the more common "fighting fuck toy," so dubbed by Caroline Heldman who identified this trope as a powerful woman in a visual space whose power is sublimated by her oversexualization, Lisbeth is able to outthink *and* outfight the men without a tight skirt or a low-cut shirt.[9] In a scene from Fincher's film, we see Lisbeth rushing through a subway station and, through Mara's effective body language, it is obvious she wishes to remain as unobtrusive as possible, clearly avoiding interaction with others. A man targets her, however, grabbing her computer bag and taking off for the escalator. It's apparent he doesn't think this diminutive, inconsequential girl provides a threat; as he gets on the escalator, he visibly slows his pace and relaxes. That's a mistake. Lisbeth comes hurtling at him from behind; she fights like a banshee and gets her bag back. Not only is the larger, fit man no match for Lisbeth in the fight but she also outruns him, nimbly jumping onto the steeply declining panel between escalators and sliding to safety with her possessions. The scene is a powerful one. The attack on Lisbeth comes out of nowhere, reminding all of us how vulnerable we might look to others and, frankly, how vulnerable we might actually be. Women will view this scene with a cringing nod; it's the attack we all suspect when we hear the rapid footsteps behind us. But just as shocking is Lisbeth's retaliation. She is all energy and determination; she has no fear. Fincher makes her look like a slight, defenseless child, then shows us her explosive agency.

This scene does not exist in the book, though there is a brief mention of a different type of assault, a sexual one, when a man gropes

Lisbeth three weeks before her eighteenth birthday and it's noted that
when she kicked the man, the police chose to charge her with assault
and battery despite witnesses supporting her testimony (Larsson 159).
This tableau is part of her background that puts her at the mercy of the
state and shows direct correlation to her mistrust of authority. Interestingly, this scene is also reworked in yet another way in the Swedish film.
Here, the attack on Lisbeth is sudden but terribly violent. A gang of
drunk, belligerent men converge on Lisbeth after she brushes against one
of them. They hit her, throw her against a wall, dump a bottle of beer
on her, and surround her with mounting threats of sexual exploitation.
They yell, urging each other on to greater acts of brutishness against
Lisbeth. It's a terrifying moment in the film. Lisbeth, of course, saves
herself. She grabs a broken bottle of beer and, screaming incoherently,
slashes at them. The men suddenly see her as something other than a
victim—crazy, perhaps, but not a victim—and they back off. She walks
away, covered in beer and bloodied by the attack, but also with the res-
ignation that suggests this is to be expected, that such acts of violence
against women are unavoidable.

The rape scene[10] and subsequent revenge scene from the novel
become the central episodes of the film (both the American and Swedish
versions). These are also the scenes that brought so much consternation
to the media after the American film's release. Most reviews of the film
mention the scenes, and a heated debate grew about the "gratuitous"
nature of the attack on Lisbeth and whether it was necessary. A quick
Google search of the film's title shows a predominance of outraged viewer
response to seeing a woman raped in what was otherwise marketed as
a mainstream film. It is as striking then as it is now that all manners
of violence, sometimes unrealistic in the extreme, can be depicted in
Hollywood film, but a realistic representation of sexual assault is where
some viewers draw the line. Notably, the rape scene in Fincher's film
is handled much like Larsson's in the book: details are sparse, forcing
the viewer to imagine the worst. Yet it is a very uncomfortable scene.
Lisbeth's attacker, Bjurman, is not lean and fit as described in the book;
rather, he is large and fleshy. In the earlier assault scene when Lisbeth is
forced to perform oral sex, the camera utilizes an upshot from Lisbeth's
perspective to show the man towering over her, his grotesque, rounded
stomach lunging toward her face. When he pushes her head to his crotch,
his hand looks monstrously large as it thrusts the back of her small head
forward. In the second assault scene, the focus is less on Lisbeth's nudity

and more so on her anguish. The camera focuses on Mara's face as she allows Lisbeth to comprehend what is happening to her: the surprise, the rage, the panic, and the pain. To call the scene gratuitous—when it is possibly one of the more realistically based plot twists in the entire story—shows the great unease American audiences had in 2011 with the reality of rape. In fact, the film also shows stills of women's bodies after their horrific murders and, strikingly, there are virtually no reviews that remark on those images at all.

The discomfort audiences were made to feel during the rape scene serves as a turning point in Hollywood cinema. That so many viewers were even having a debate about the scene's inclusion served to move the conversation forward, providing a breeding ground to finally bring to light the many instances of sexual harassment and assault that are the norm in Hollywood on the other side of the camera. To see a young woman fighting back against such depravity served as yet another example of reality mimicking art. It is significant, though, that Fincher's film, which is so honest in its portrayal of Lisbeth's assault, did flinch elsewhere in his retelling. At the end of the novel there is a clever, empowering gender reversal when Mikael is captured by the serial killer he seeks, the man who kills women, and Lisbeth comes to his rescue. In the scene, Mikael is forced to the basement cell of the killer, Martin. Martin strings him up like the women he normally victimizes, and Larsson takes great care in making Mikael feel the fear his female predecessors would have felt in his place. Mikael asks Martin why he's gone to all this trouble and taken all this risk to rape and kill so many women. He answers, "Because it's so easy . . . Women disappear all the time. Nobody misses them" (Larsson 448). The scene becomes increasingly erotically charged: Martin strokes Mikael's cheek tenderly, he lights two cigarettes and places one between Mikael's lips, and he strips Mikael as he hangs defenseless with a noose tightening around his neck. After Martin strips Mikael's pants from his body and cuts the t-shirt from his chest, he confesses that he's never had "a boy" (455) in his murder room. Then, before he pulls the strap that will tighten the noose around Mikael's neck, he says, "I've always wondered how a man tastes" (456) and leans forward, kissing Mikael on the lips. It is into this scene—where Mikael is fully embodying the role of the bound, molested, female victim—that Lisbeth, the avenging heroine, erupts.

It's a brilliant scene that shows the potential of assault on men and positions Lisbeth in the role of hero after already being cast as victim and monster. As she bounds into the room, she becomes the alpha female staking claim to her sexual territory: "Hey, you fucking creep, in this shithole I've got a monopoly on that one" (456). She attacks Martin, releases Mikael, then proclaims "I'm going to take him" (458) and heads out in mad pursuit of Martin, who has fled the room. She ultimately chases him on her motorcycle and he—seeing the end to his schemes—intentionally drives into oncoming traffic, killing himself on impact. The role reversal is complete, and we've come to accept and even anticipate Lisbeth as our hero and Mikael as our helpless victim, saved at the last moment from his fate.

This is a scene waiting for a visual display on the big screen. And it is at this point that Fincher wavers. Lisbeth still saves Mikael in the film; however, his feminization is minimized, and she becomes more of Mikael's attack dog then her own agent. Here Martin doesn't sexualize Mikael in the same manner as in the book. Mikael is placed into the same position as Martin's female victims but only out of expedience since Martin wants Mikael eliminated. It's necessity for Martin, not pleasure. Mikael is never stripped naked. His shirt is opened, but only, it appears, so Martin can choose the best place to cut. When Martin reaches toward Mikael's jeans button, he hesitates, stops, then walks away as he reflects on the molestation by his own father. Martin does connect Mikael to his female victims when he tells Mikael he's fallen prey to a classic female error of being afraid to offend: he asks Mikael why he came into the house earlier in the evening when it was obvious Mikael felt something was wrong. He continues, "Fear of offending can be stronger than the fear of pain." Like women who are conditioned to please rather than offend, Mikael too is feminized by his own reactions that put him in harm's way. Yet, there is significantly less male homoeroticism in this filmic scene than its source material. The same film has no reservations about showing the homoeroticism, even homosexuality, between two women—Lisbeth and her lover, Mimmi—earlier in the film. It's also noteworthy that after the other visual representations of sex, violence, and pain inflicted upon women in this film, the male protagonist is saved from that same fate of sexual exploitation unlike his character in the book.

There is a convincing statement being made about the limits of male sexualization in this 2011 film that might reflect the reality of men in Hollywood and the power they are unwilling to relinquish. Ultimately, this scene in the film gives Mikael yet more power when, after Lisbeth attacks Martin and saves Mikael, she—instead of *telling* him that she's going after the murderer—asks his permission: "May I kill him?" It's a great line, no doubt, and shows her ability to compartmentalize things into black and white without any pesky ethical concerns, but it also lessens her agency when she seeks permission from the man whom she, instead, declares ownership of in the same scene in Larsson's novel.[11]

Fincher's film ends with the mystery Lisbeth and Mikael are investigating being solved. They find the missing girl and discover why she ran all those years ago. This uncovers yet another tale of hideous family abuse at the hands of men. Like "The Maiden without Hands" fairy tale cycle, Harriet Vanger fled the family estate at age sixteen because after years of sexual and physical abuse at the hands of her father, she murdered him in retaliation—only to have her brother Martin, who also abused her, blackmail her into further submission. She led a horrific life and ran away to survive. When this sad and sordid tale comes to light, Lisbeth's only response in the film is to say, "Harriet fucking Vanger." Without reading the book, it might be unclear why Lisbeth responds in such a way to a girl who suffered so much. The book, though, elaborates in a conversation between her and Mikael:

"Bitch," she said

"Who?"

"Harriet Fucking Vanger. If she had done something in 1966, Martin Vanger couldn't have kept killing and raping for thirty-seven years." (499)

Lisbeth looks out for other women as much as she does for herself. Her revenge on Bjurman and the tattoo she painted all over his chest illustrates her desire to create bodies as textual spaces and her ability to ensure such a text for others to see and to use as warning. In Fincher's film, the hook Mikael uses to snare Lisbeth when he approaches her for help is to tell her that he wants her to help him "catch a killer of women." This works: she's eager to do what she can. There's a suggestion here—in the filmic and textual narratives—of the importance of community. As happened with the birth of the #MeToo and then the #TimesUp movements, we see that one woman alone isn't usually enough to make a difference when it comes to rising up against powerful men. However, a community of women can make all the difference. When women stand with each other, real change can occur. In the 2011 film, Lisbeth Salander served as an empowering symbol and helped Americans glimpse the David and Goliath moment that was around the corner for women in Hollywood and beyond.

Feminist Revenge Heroines before and after
#MeToo and #TimesUp

Before #MeToo and #TimesUp, films that showed women in situations that defied the traditional male gaze or complicated it with uncomfortable narrative turns were often found to be critical failures or completely dismissed. For example, in 2009, two years before the American *The Girl with the Dragon Tattoo* film, the box-office bomb *Jennifer's Body* was released. The film's director, Karyn Kusama, often tells stories about grief and trauma and, as Christine Smallwood explains in a *New York Times Magazine* profile on Kusama, films like *Jennifer's Body* "explor[e] how women internalize their drama by externalizing it physically." *Jennifer's Body* features a beautiful young woman (Megan Fox) and her equally attractive-though-nerdy friend (Amanda Seyfried) as they navigate the aftermath of a vicious attack. The online digital media and entertainment platform *Refinery29* published an updated review of the film in 2018—well into the middle of the above-mentioned movements. In this 2018 review, the author, Anne Cohen, discusses how viewing such a film with the benefit of a decade of movement, allows a new evaluation of the work: "In a post-MeToo context, the idea of a woman's body being used for men's gain . . . and her coping with this violation by using her sexuality to entrap and feed on those who once objectified her, feels like something to be celebrated, not mocked. Had this film been made a decade later, it's possible Fox could have been heralded as the feminist revenge hero of our time."

The movie, a campy film about demonic possession, was often tagged upon its release simply as bad horror with timid sex scenes. However, those seem to be particularly male perspectives of the plot. As Cohen notes—and both Kusama and producer Jason Reitman confirm—the film aims to be something else: a film exploring communities of women, their friendships, and female empowerment. In fact, the film was intended to be marketed to a young female audience but was instead marketed to young men by the film's distributor (Nichols; Smallwood). The succeeding years, though, have transformed opinions of the movie so that it is now considered a feminist film in the horror genre. Megan Fox, in a 2019, ten-year anniversary interview, reiterates that the film wasn't meant to be just about a hot girl and teen sex. She explains that the film was "about sexualizing somebody who doesn't want to be sexualized, about all of these other things, about powerlessness as young girls and women and nobody was ready to hear that" (qtd. in Nichols).[12]

Like *The Girl with the Dragon Tattoo*, scenes like the rape scene—often called gratuitous upon the film's release—can now be reevaluated with the passage of time and alongside the #MeToo revolution. Moreover, the films that were released in the decade or so before this movement (and #TimesUp) served to initiate a new conversation and, as in the case of the storyline found in Larsson's novel and the films, pushed the genre of rape-revenge films to a discussion that refused to be satisfied with only vigilante justice. Too often, in films and real life, the onus is on women to simply react to inequity and violence instead of there being an expectation that the warped institution that houses such injustice should change. #MeToo is a response to the exploitation of women that insists on righteousness. The fictional revenge fantasy of women taking justice into their own hands serves as a warning that rape and abuse can no longer be normalized. What #MeToo does is insist on legal recourse and institutionalized justice.[13] Unsurprisingly, this goal of legal restitution is one that is sometimes questioned. Perhaps influenced by fantasy fulfillment in fiction and film, there is now a strain of criticism that suggests #MeToo is (or could devolve into) vigilante justice. One such example was raised around the 2016 firing of Professor Steve Galloway from the University of British Columbia amidst allegations of sexual harassment and the subsequent support for him by writers, including Margaret Atwood.[14] There is a legitimate concern that #MeToo might encourage a less violent form of retribution that exists in the form of job loss and reputation destruction. #MeToo, though, is not intended for further injustice nor the mob-mentality of modern-day witch hunts. Pulitzer prize–winning investigative reporter Ronan Farrow, who became an integral part of #MeToo when publishing accounts of Hollywood mogul Harvey Weinstein's predatory behavior, reminds us that "there are Harvey Weinsteins everywhere, because these kinds of abuses of power are endemic" (Farrow). What #MeToo activists want is accountability and systemic change: a world where women can be heard, where allegations are taken seriously, and where these abuses are not so prevalent in the first place. The movement also makes critical the need for women (and men) to stand together in the face of such abuse. Upon finishing the final pages of Larsson's novel, a textual space that tries to right these types of wrongs, the reader can't help but focus not on the atrocious acts of the men who hurt and kill women, but rather on the young woman who refuses to be a compliant victim and feels unmitigated fury for any passive acceptance of that violence. Her rage at other women who save themselves and not the community is palpable, reminding us that acceptance of the age-old story of abuse and murder of women is no longer an option: silence and seclusion is not the way to win this war.

Our cultural narratives have all continued to evolve, rewriting and revising stories of women and girls, finding new ways for them to fight against violence and oppression. In 1979, Angela Carter published a collection of her revisionist fairy tales in *The Bloody Chamber*: here Carter returned to the oral roots of fairy tales, telling her stories the way they were meant to be told back when women wove their yarns for other women: the way they were before men appropriated them, making victims and cautionary tales out of the girls caught in their narratives. In Carter's collection, she resurrects the women who had to save themselves through their wits and their bravery. In her title story, we see a re-telling of "Bluebeard." As the girl is about to be killed by her much older, sadistic, and murderous husband, her hero bursts through the gates—her mother:

> You never saw such a wild thing as my mother, her hat seized by the winds and blown out to sea so that her hair was her white mane, her black lisle legs exposed to the thigh, her skirts tucked round her waist, one hand on the reins of the rearing horse while the other clasped my father's service revolver . . . Now, without a moment's hesitation, she raised my father's gun, took aim, and put a single, irreproachable bullet through my husband's head. (39–40)

Like some earlier Bluebeard tales that position the wife's sister as savior, this story sends no man to save our young narrator; it's another woman, her mother, who is the avenging vanquisher come to save her child and slay the monster. Scandinavian Noir understands the darkness and the light of our communal fairy tales, and also reminds us of the importance of communities of women who save one another. The genre additionally reminds us that we can change the narrative and make our stories our own. We see in Lisbeth Salander a modern heroine, a sister to those fairy tale girls who came before; Lisbeth rejected the fictional status quo at a pivotal moment and her refusal reverberated through the world—and especially through Hollywood—as women, often powerful women and some men as well, who had been assaulted, harassed, or coerced now felt empowered to say, "No more." By standing together, as Lisbeth would understand, a defense could finally be mounted against those who would otherwise continue to harm. In real life and in fiction, we now see a different way forward: a way that encourages community rather than isolation as we advance into a more equitable and judicial future.

Notes

1. I refer specifically here to the #MeToo hashtag movement that went viral in 2017 and not the original 2006 Me Too movement popularized via Myspace by Tarana Burke.

2. In May 2020, Amazon announced a project for a stand-alone series featuring Lisbeth Salander. No actress or director is attached to the project as of this writing; however, Andy Harries and Rob Bullock are serving as executive producers on the series.

3. Catskin tales are related to Cinderella tales; according to the Aarne-Thompson index, Cinderella tales are categorized as AT501A and Catskin tales as AT501B; "The Maiden without Hands" belongs to ATU706.

4. Nordic Noir is an often interchangeable term for Scandinavian Noir, differing only in its slightly larger inclusion of Nordic settings; Arctic Noir, also similar, refers to settings in the more northern regions of the Arctic Circle.

5. Maria Tatar also mentions Lisbeth Salander in connection to fairy tales; in her revised 2017 edition of *The Classic Fairy Tales*, she puts Lisbeth into the category of "warrior women who hunt, shoot, and seek revenge in today's cinematic re-fashioning of fairy tale figures" (122). For a longer discussion on what Tatar calls the new female trickster, see her "Sleeping Beauties vs. Gonzo Girls" (*New Yorker,* 8 March 2013).

6. See interviews with both actresses, including Steven Rea's "Scenes of Explicit Sexual Violence Essential to *Girl with Dragon Tattoo*" and Catherine A. Traywick's "The Rape of *The Girl with the Dragon Tattoo*" in *Ms.* magazine.

7. Kirsten Mollegaard discusses this and translation changes—as well as the impact of body modification, including tattooing—in her article "Signs Taken for Warnings: Body Modification and Visual Pleasure in *The Girl with the Dragon Tattoo*."

8. Lisbeth identifies most closely with pansexuality. It is likely that her nonbinary, androgynous appearance combined with her mental health issues (possibly Asperger's, probably PTSD) and sexual identity all coalesce to "other"

her in ways that make her a target for traditional mainstream institutions as well as deviant sexual predators.

9. The term "fighting fuck toy" became popular after Heldman's inclusion of it in the 2011 documentary film *Miss Representation*, released the same year as Fincher's *The Girl with the Dragon Tattoo*. The director of the film, Jennifer Siebel Newsom, launched the #NotBuyingIt campaign in March 2017 as a vehicle to call attention to misrepresentation in media.

10. For clarity's sake, I refer to the "rape" scene as the crucial extended rape scene Lisbeth endures that includes rape, sodomy, and physical abuse. Technically, Bjurman rapes Lisbeth twice, the first time being when he penetrates her mouth with his penis.

11. It should be noted that Fincher's film does more to position Mikael in the role of the female than does the Swedish film, which eliminates all homoerotic content. Also related to this franchise and its ongoing influence, the 2018 film *The Girl in the Spider's Web*, based on a spinoff of the original *Millennium Trilogy*, breaks new ground by using a transgendered actress to play a cisgender role: trans model and actress Andreja Pejić plays Sofia, Lisbeth's cisgender lesbian lover and partner in the film.

12. Megan Fox has also revealed her personal experiences with objectification and sexualization in Hollywood, starting when she was fifteen years old. In a 2019 interview, she said "I was sort of out and in front of the #MeToo movement before the #MeToo movement happened, I was speaking out and saying, 'Hey, these things are happening to me and they're not ok.'" See "All the Horrifying Ways Megan Fox has been Sexualised since she was a Child are Resurfacing," by Moya Lothian-McLean.

13. The guilty verdict of Harvey Weinstein on February 24, 2020, created a new dialogue that, on the one hand, provided validation for victims who might have once not believed legal justice could be served against one of the most powerful men in Hollywood. On the other hand, jurors in the case have clearly separated their decision to convict from #MeToo activism (see *CBS This Morning* interview with Gayle King, February 28, 2020).

14. See "Am I a Bad Feminist?" by Margaret Atwood (*The Globe and Mail*, January 13, 2018).

Works Cited

Acocella, Joan. "Man of Mystery: Why do People Love Stieg Larsson's Novels?" *New Yorker*, January 2, 2011, pp. 70–74. web.b.ebscohost.com.proxylhup. klnpa.org/ehost/detaildetail?vid=4&sid=0e47be7b-51bc-4758-ad81-786d7c da6386%40pdc-v-sessmgr03&bdat =JnNpdGU9Z Whvc3QtbGl2ZS ZzY29wZT1zaXRl#AN=57080429&db=asn

Atwood, Margaret. "Am I a Bad Feminist?" *Globe and Mail*, January 13, 2018. www.theglobeandmail.com/opinion/am-i-a-bad-feminist/article37591823

Carter, Angela. *The Bloody Chamber*. New York: Penguin Books, 1979.

Clover, Carol. *Men, Women, and Chainsaws: Gender in the Modern Horror Film*. Princeton, NJ: Princeton University Press, 1992.

Cohen, Anne. "*Jennifer's Body* and the Feminist Revenge Hero Who Came Too Early." *Refinery29*, August 3, 2018. www.refinery29.com/en-us/2018/08/206237/jennifers-body-review-defense-female-revenge-movie

The Girl with the Dragon Tattoo. Directed by David Fincher, Sony Pictures, 2011.

The Girl with the Dragon Tattoo. Directed by Niels Arden Oplev, Nordisk Film, 2009.

Hewer, Elisabeth. *Wishing for Birds*. UK: Platypus Press, 2015.

Jennifer's Body. Directed by Karyn Kusama, 20th Century Fox, 2009.

Kelly, Mary Louise. "Ronan Farrow Lauds #MeToo After Verdict: 'There Are Harvey Weinsteins Everywhere.'" *NPR*. February 28, 2020. www.npr.org/2020/02/28/810449415/ronan-farrow-lauds-metoo-after-verdict-there-are-harvey-weinsteins-everywhere

Larsson, Stieg. *The Girl with the Dragon Tattoo*. Translated by Reg Keeland. New York: Vintage-Random House, 2009.

Lothian-McLean, Moya. "All the Horrifying Ways Megan Fox has been Sexualised since she was a Child are Resurfacing." *Indy100 from Independent*, June 22, 2020. www.indy100.com/article/megan-fox-michael-bay-transformers-two-and-half-men-metoo-9579026

Malbin, Drew. Interview with Gayle King. *CBS This Morning*, February 28, 2020. www.cbsnews.com/news/harvey-weinstein-juror-verdict-not-message-about-metoo-movement

Miss Representation. Directed by Jennifer Siebel Newsom, Girls' Club Entertainment, 2011.

Mollegaard, Kirsten. "Signs Taken for Warnings: Body Modification and Visual Pleasure in *The Girl with the Dragon Tattoo*." *Journal of Popular Culture* 49, no. 2 (2016): 347–365. doi:10.1111/jpcu.12406

Nair, Gayatri, and Dipti Tamang. "Representations of Rape in Popular Culture: *Gone Girl* and *Badlapur*. *International Feminist Journal of Politics* 18, no. 4 (2016): 614–618. doi:10.1080/14616742.2016.1226401

Nichols, Mackenzie. "*Jennifer's Body* Turns 10: Megan Fox, Diablo Cody, and Karyn Kusama Reflect on Making the Cult Classic." *Variety*, September 11, 2019. variety.com/2019/film/news/jennifers-body-10th-anniversary-megan-fox-diablo-cody-1203323111

Rea, Stephen. "Scenes of Explicit Sexual Violence Essential to *Girl with Dragon Tattoo*." *Philadelphia Inquirer*, March 22, 2010. www.inquirer.com/philly/blogs/onmovies/=Scenes_of_explicit_sexual_violence_essential_to_Girl_with_Dragon_Tattoo.html

Smallwood, Christine. "The Filmmaker Karyn Kusama Explores the Many Dimensions of Women's Rage." *New York Times Magazine*, December 20, 2018. www.nytimes.com/2018/12/20/magazine/destroyer-movie-karyn-kusama.html

Tatar, Maria. Introduction. In *The Classic Fairy Tales*, edited by Maria Tatar. New York: Norton, 1999. ix–xviii.

Tatar, Maria. "Introduction: Sleeping Beauty." In *The Classic Fairy Tales*, 2nd edition, edited by Maria Tatar. New York: Norton, 2017. 117–123.

Tatar, Maria. *Off with Their Heads!: Fairy Tales and the Culture of Childhood*. Princeton, NJ: Princeton University Press, 1992.

Tatar, Maria. "Sleeping Beauty vs. Gonzo Girls." *The New Yorker*, March 8, 2013. www.newyorker.com/books/page-turner/sleeping-beauties-vs-gonzo-girls

Traywick, Catherine A. "The Rape of *The Girl with the Dragon Tattoo*." *Ms.*, April 14, 2010. msmagazine.com/2010/04/14/the-rape-of-the-girl-with-the-dragon-tattoo

CHAPTER 10

Taking Consent into Account

American Teen Films amidst #MeToo

Michele Meek

In an April 6, 2018, essay in *The New Yorker*, actress Molly Ringwald reflects on the 1980s John Hughes films that made her famous. Specifically, she revisits their depiction of sexual consent and finds that the films do not hold up well under #MeToo scrutiny. In *The Breakfast Club* (1985), for instance, she recalls how Bender and Claire (Ringwald) become a couple after Bender "sexually harasses Claire throughout the film," including a scene in which he crawls under her desk to peek up her skirt. Similarly, in *Sixteen Candles* (1984), the "geek" (Anthony Michael Hall) repeatedly sexually harasses Samantha (Ringwald) until she relents to giving him her underwear as evidence of a sexual "conquest" that never occurred, and the film's heartthrob Jake offers up his intoxicated girlfriend and car to the geek with the advice to "have fun." This trend of blatantly condoning sexual harassment and assault in such a way started to falter before #MeToo went viral. In the early twenty-first century, teen films routinely take sexual consent into greater account—often quite explicitly depicting affirmative consent. And yet, even since the #MeToo movement started, coming-of-age films at times incorporate sexual coercion in ways that run interference to the insistence that "no means no" and "yes means yes." In this chapter, I provide an overview of consent theory and chart a history of sexual consent in American teen films. I then turn to several more recent teen films, such as *Blockers* (Cannon 2018), *The Kissing Booth* (Marcello 2018), *Good Boys* (Stupnitsky 2019), and *Booksmart* (Wilde 2019) to examine specific moments that highlight troubling complexities of consent.

Sexual Consent in the #MeToo Era

There appears to be widespread support—in theory, if not always in practice—that consent is of utmost importance in sexual interactions. Every U.S. state has laws against nonconsensual sex, including specific guidelines for age-of-consent and marital rape, and the United States has federal laws against sexual assault and harassment. Alan Wertheimer notes in the chapter "Consent to Sexual Relations," in the 2009 book *The Ethics of Consent*, "It is commonly thought that we should regard it as morally and legally permissible to engage in sexual relations if and only if the parties consent" (Miller and Wertheimer, 195), and David Archard in the 1998 book *Sexual Consent* notes, the distinction between consent and nonconsent marks "the difference between the permissibility and impermissibility of some practice or activity" (1). In the twenty-first century, the "no means no" mantra has been adapted to emphasize "yes means yes." Affirmative consent is now routinely incorporated into definitions of consent, for example, in Planned Parenthood's consent acronym FRIES—"freely given, reversible, informed, enthusiastic, and specific" ("What Is Sexual Consent?"). The prioritization of both a fully aware and conscious consent has become the norm. This shift emphasizes that the lack of a "no" (or silence) does not imply a "yes." Consent must be clearly expressed without coercion.

The #MeToo movement has raised the stakes of getting consent right. Several perpetrators who have been publicly called out for repeated sexual harassment and assault have lost their jobs, prestige, and credibility. A few have seen civil and criminal charges brought against them—and several have faced prison time. In addition, the sheer number of individuals coming forward to publicly share their stories of sexual assault and harassment in the #MeToo movement has forced a public reckoning—suddenly, it became obvious that nonconsent is not something that affects only a small percentage of women, but rather is a widespread problem impacting many women's experiences in families, careers, and relationships.

However, a closer look reveals anything but a clear reading on how the public sphere values consent—even since #MeToo went viral. While criminal charges resulted from the outings of Harvey Weinstein, Bill Cosby, and Jeffrey Epstein, numerous other men, such as Donald J. Trump and Brett Kavanaugh, have proceeded to gain powerful positions despite multiple credible allegations of assault and harassment. There has also been much debate on how to draw a line between seduction and nonconsent. For example, upon allegations by an unnamed photographer against actor Aziz Ismail Ansari, a public debate ensued about whether their private sexual encounter was consensual or coerced. In addition, a letter signed by over a hundred celebrities in the French newspaper *Le Monde* ("Nous défendons une liberté d'importuner, indispensable à la liberté sexuelle") argued against the momentum of #MeToo, stating that "insistent or clumsy flirting is not a crime, nor is gallantry a chauvinist aggression" (Breeden and Peltier). As Milena Popova in the 2019 book *Sexual Consent* states, "If we have learned one thing from the #MeToo campaign, apart from just how pervasive sexual violence is, it is that we as a society do not have a clear, uncontested idea of what sexual consent looks like, and that we do not all universally and equally value it" (6). When we move beyond the more blatant cases of nonconsent, we often find ourselves in disconcertingly blurry territory. The #MeToo movement has exposed a need for us to understand where the line between consent and nonconsent should reside. As Tarana Burke, who started the #MeToo movement, states in a *Washington Post* interview, "Culture shift doesn't happen in the accusation; it doesn't happen in the disclosure. Culture shift happens in the public grappling with these questions. Because nobody has firm, definitive, perfect answers" (Ottesen). For this reason, scholars of and advocates of sexual consent often conclude that true consent is a worthy—but challenging—goal.

In the sex-critical approach to consent, scholars look to examine, call out, and rewrite "sexual scripts" that often represent "one particular, dominant idea of how sex works" (Popova 81). Rather than defining sexuality as a purely biological or psychological drive, the sex-critical approach emphasizes how sex is a culturally produced desire and practice. Ideas about sex, in other words, are developed and maintained through sexual scripts or repeated scenarios, which, Popova says, "are another way in which power operates in our society to shape how we think and act in relation to sex" (79). And with a dearth of comprehensive sexual education in the United States, Popova suggests, "culture serves as our main sex educator" (100). Films, TV, and other media become a formidable means to perpetuate, examine, and rewrite these sexual scripts. Certainly, one of the most repeated sexual scripts has been the seduction story, which, as Popova notes, "generally implies persuading someone to have sex with you when that person has expressed unwillingness to do so" (56–57). The prevalence of this predominantly heterosexual narrative—boy meets girl, boy pursues girl, boy gets girl—means that the line between courting and sexual harassment (in the pursuit) and seduction and rape, or consent and nonconsent (in the conquest) have often remained indistinct.

Sex in Teen Films before #MeToo

Teen and youth-centric films often address how young people begin to negotiate consent, and, as such, they become important texts for investigating how dominant sexual scripts are reiterated or resisted. Scholar Timothy Shary identifies "love/sex films" as one of the five subgenres within American youth films that typically "cater to romance or sexual titillation, but rarely both at once" (2003, 40). Shary states, "Youth sex films tend to focus on the arduous attainment of sex or the negative consequences of it; love films consistently portray youth trying to establish relationships that are nonetheless thwarted by outside forces or differences, such as parents, age and class" (48). Shary notes that *Blue Denim* (Dunne 1959) is part of the "early evolution" of the teen sex film, and we might even trace its roots to as early as Dorothy Arzner's pre–Production Code film *The Wild Party* (1929) depicting college girls who are more interested in partying than studying. The film industry's self-regulation through the Production Code, or Hays Code, caused films from the 1930s through the 1950s mostly to avoid the combination of teens and sex. Only in the later years of the Code did studios begin attempting risqué subject matter as part of cautionary dramas like *Blue Denim*, about two teenagers who have intercourse, which results in a pregnancy and the quest for an illegal abortion, or *Susan Slade* (Daves 1960) about a girl whose premarital teen pregnancy leads to a series of tragic events including the baby's father's death, her attempted suicide, and her father's death. Although both of these films end on a somewhat upbeat note for melodrama—in both cases, it appears that the girls will be married to end their single parenthood—they highlight dire life consequences for teen sex. Even the more comedic film *Where the Boys Are* (Levin 1960), which contains the first manifesto by a teen about premarital sexual behavior, depicts sexual consent as dangerous terrain for girls. The boys relentlessly pursue sex, while the girls desperately pursue marriage—and when one of the girls, Melanie, does decide to "play house before marriage," she winds up being raped by another boy on a subsequent evening. So, the film's message is clear: girls who fail to uphold their role as gatekeepers invite disaster.

In the 1970s, as sex ceases to be as taboo and the film industry starts to push boundaries with the option of R- and X-rated films, the "teen sex comedy" begins to depict more blatant teen sexual exploits. But these initial depictions of sex often portray a mixing of sexual consent with coercion. In teen films of the late 1970s and 1980s, a "no" is often read as "try harder," and male subterfuge to obtain sex is routinely depicted as humorous or romantic. Numerous scholars and journalists have since lambasted the scene in *Porky's* (Clark 1981) where the boys spy on the girls in the shower. Commonly critiqued scenes that occur in *Revenge of the Nerds* (Kanew 1984), in which one of the "nerds" has sex with a girl while wearing a mask to guise as her boyfriend, and *Sixteen Candles*, in which the heartthrob Jake offers his car and his intoxicated girlfriend to another teenager, are deeply troubling. Other films mirror such scenarios, and they do not seem limited to white male aggressors. For example, in *Fame* (Parker 1980), several Black and white male high school students repeatedly peer into the girls' locker room through a crack in the wall and ogle topless girls. And the film *Class Act* (Miller 1992) depicts two Black teens, Duncan (the "nerd") and Blade (a "bad" boy failing high school), who switch identities, each pursuing a different girl, while posing as the other boy. Blade even has sex with Ellen while she is under the misconception that he is the brilliant, straight-A Duncan. Such scenes are presented without irony or critique, depicting consent as either entirely unimportant or attainable through some form of coercion. In all of these cases, we are led to believe, the girls are not raped or assaulted because they do not see themselves as raped or assaulted.

But what about the more ambiguous breaches of consent in teen films of this era? Anne Barnhill in the chapter "Just Pushy Enough" in *Dating Philosophy for Everyone*, attempts to draw a line between egregious assaults and what she calls "strategic and morally permissible" pursuits. Although she acknowledges such scenes "are influenced by regrettable gender norms and retrograde romantic notions" in which "we find it romantic and fitting for the man to violate the woman's boundaries, despite her protests" (91), she ultimately argues, "How does John Cusack always get the girl? It's not by scrupulously respecting her boundaries. It's by violating her boundaries" (99). Barnhill defends "these particular boundary violations [as] unproblematic" (91) because the male characters "are acting like boundaries don't exist, in the hope that the boundaries will cease to exist" (92). However, I would argue Barnhill's position, published in 2010, does not align with current thinking on consent. Consent is not moot because boys want long-term relationships, and there is nothing "morally permissible" about pursuing girls against their will, despite the fact that it certainly might be "strategic." As a result, many of our favorite teen comedies of the 1980s, now, with a more critical look, seem fraught with inappropriate and unethical boundary transgressions. Of course, exceptions exist in this era, as well. The film *Dirty Dancing* (Ardolino 1987), for example, unabashedly portrays a high school girl's burgeoning sexual desire and agency and the romance develops through mutual attraction.

Problematic depictions of consent in teen films appear to transcend racial boundaries—although there are simply less Black teen comedies to examine. In the book *Teen Movies: American Youth on Screen*, Shary (2005) notes that in the 1980s, "African-American youth were shown in films fighting for their lives, under the hegemony of a racist legal and political system, under difficult family and class conditions, and under the influence of the media" (82). These issues did not make for light comedic fare, and films featuring Black teens in this era tend toward the dramatic, such as Spike Lee's *School Daze* (1988) and John Singleton's *Boyz n the Hood* (Singleton 1991). Even the film *Cooley High* (Schultz 1975), which starts like a traditional teen comedy with a group of Chicago Black male teens looking to party and hook up with girls, ultimately ends with one of the boy's tragic death. In the moments that do emerge, it seems consent remains fraught for Black teens too. In *Cooley High*, protagonist Preach bets his friends a dollar that he will "get" the uppity Brenda. Preach pursues her throughout the movie despite her numerous protests—at one point, she even asks him, "Don't you understand the meaning of the word 'no'?" Later, when he finds the key to piquing her interest (her love of poetry), they do wind up having sex. The scene that unfolds appears as one of mutual desire, but it ends abruptly after Preach lets it slip about the bet, and Brenda storms off. Another troubling scene takes place in the Black teen film *Just Another Girl on the*

I.R.T. (Harris 1992) when Ariyan and Ty are about to have sex, and she asks him for a condom. He says he doesn't have one but will "pull out," and when she says no, he gets angry saying, "At the party you were acting like such a tough girl. What was that just an act or what?" She insists on not being a tease, and they have sex—which leads to her unintended pregnancy. Of course, a few other depictions of Black teens countered this pervasive narrative. For example, in *House Party* (Hudlin 1990), Kid and Sydney discover he only has one old, torn condom, so they mutually decide to wait to have sex.

In the 1990s, films began to depict teen sex with more caution, or even doom; widespread attention on such issues as teen pregnancy and AIDS shifted the types of depictions possible. Sure, teen romance comedies persisted with films like *Clueless* (Heckerling 1995), *She's All That* (Iscove 1999), and *10 Things I Hate About You* (Junger 1999), but sex is absent from them. In fact, the teen sex comedy appeared to be on a hiatus until its comeback with *American Pie* (Wietz and Wietz) in 1999. Instead, when sex did make an appearance in most '90s films, it often had dire consequences—unintended pregnancy in *Just Another Girl on the I.R.T.* and HIV in *Kids* (Clark 1995). One exception is the genre of the openly lesbian/gay teen comedy, which finally made its appearance in American teen films in the '90s, with teen romances such as *The Incredibly True Adventures of Two Girls in Love* (Maggenti 1995), *But I'm a Cheerleader* (Babbit 1999), and the drama/comedy *Edge of Seventeen* (Moreton 1998). However, *Edge of Seventeen* still depicts a minefield of consent for teens. The protagonist Eric experiences numerous disappointing sexual interactions—a brief encounter with someone he meets at a bar, uncomfortable intercourse with his college-aged co-worker Rod, and an awkward heterosexual experience with his friend Maggie, which ends their friendship. *The Incredibly True Adventures of Two Girls in Love*, on the other hand, presents a teen romance that culminates in a mutual first sexual experience between two girls—Randy and Evie—who come from different racial and socioeconomic backgrounds. *The Incredibly True Adventures of Two Girls in Love* is a rare film on many levels: its depiction of openly queer characters, a Black protagonist who falls in love with a white girl without race being an issue, and its emphasis on clear mutual consent.

Several independent films of the 1990s also tackle some complexities of consent. In Colette Burson's *Coming Soon* (1999), for instance, the protagonist Stream embarks on a quest to have an orgasm. Here, the obstacles for this desiring girl are boys who appear to have only their own sexual satisfaction in mind. In one scene, Stream and her boyfriend kiss on his couch, and he pushes her head down to give him fellatio—and after resisting twice, she relents. In the documentary episode "Indie Sex: Teens," director of *But I'm a Cheerleader* Jamie Babbit describes this scene, stating, "I think all girls can relate to that scene . . . because they've all been through it. I mean it's like, hello? Can you put *your* head down?" Babbit suggests it was no accident that *Coming Soon* found neither widespread distribution nor received acceptance into major film festivals, stating that "the culture wasn't quite ready to deal with" a movie about girls who just "want to come, they want to come, they don't want to just be fucked, they want to come." *Coming Soon,* for whatever reason, remained on the fringe.

The Impact of #MeToo on Teen Films

It would be impossible to pinpoint an exact moment that the #MeToo movement began impacting media depictions of consent. Films, even independent films, typically take many years from the initial writing of the script to the actual release. For example, the film *Booksmart* began as a screenplay written by Emily Halpern and Sarah Haskin in 2009. Several iterations later, the film was eventually made and premiered at the SXSW Film Festival in 2019. In any case, during the early twenty-first century, even before #MeToo went viral, sexual consent started to be taken into account in teen films. For example, the film *The Edge of Seventeen* (Craig 2016) depicts a teen boy's respect for a girl's "no," despite confusing circumstances. Protagonist Nadine accidentally sends a text to her crush Nick detailing all the sexual acts that she would like to do with him. To her surprise, he agrees to meet her. When he picks her up, he takes her to a deserted parking lot. They kiss, but when he tries to take off her underwear, she resists, first saying quietly, "I don't know if . . ." but then yelling "No get off!" He immediately stops, and they then sit uncomfortably in the car. When she kisses him again, he slides his hand up her thigh, and again she stops him. Nick then says, "Fuck, I don't understand you, what do you want? What do you want?" and she says, "To talk, to get to know you, not just do it in the first five seconds." He responds, "You wrote me a novel about how you were dying to blow me in Petland, you psycho, I'm not here to get to know you." The scene ends soon after, and she angrily gets out of the car. Despite the fact that Nick feels Nadine is giving him mixed signals, he respects her "no." And Nadine here articulates her "no" clearly several times, despite being pressured to follow through on what she "promised." This scene, thus, rewrites a sexual script that had come to be a fixture in teen films of the late twentieth century—one that obliged a girl to "consent" after consistent pressure or the accusation of being a tease.

In the era before #MeToo went viral, even blockbuster teen sex comedies like *American Pie* and *Superbad* (Mottola 2007) take consent into account and disrupt the traditional narrative of seduction—despite their reductive portrayals of sex-crazed male behavior. Although both of these films contain the standard sex comedy premise of male teenagers desperate to lose their virginity, they also demonstrate how male sexual aggression backfires. In *American Pie*, the protagonist Jim sets up a webcam to spy on an exchange student Nadia, as she undresses in his room. When Jim returns to the room while Nadia is masturbating, it is Jim who ultimately becomes the object of ridicule, when he accidentally broadcasts their interaction to his classmates who witness him prematurely ejaculate twice from touching Nadia's leg and breast. Of course, in the aftermath, the boys suffer no reprimanding for their actions, and Nadia, who has now been seen naked by her classmates without her permission, is sent back to her home country. In a recent reflection on the twenty-year anniversary of the film, actress Shannon Elizabeth (Nadia) notes, "If this had come out after the #MeToo movement, there would definitely be a problem. I think that it would have gone down differently" (Kupfer). It is clear that Nadia is sexually objectified in this scene for both her classmates and the film's audience. Nonetheless, the film turns the tables on male subterfuge working to obtain sex, at least in this moment.

Superbad takes this disruption a step further. At the beginning of the film, Seth tries to convince his friend Evan that they should get the girls they like drunk to have sex with them. Seth says, "You know when you hear girls saying 'Aw, I was so shitfaced last night. I shouldn't have fucked that guy'—We could be that mistake!" But part of the humor of this scene is that Seth's point-of-view is untenable and unethical. Unlike in earlier films where the male protagonists succeed in such a quest for sex, neither Seth nor Evan lose their virginity in the film. As it turns out, Jules (the girl Seth wants) doesn't drink, and Becca (the girl Evan likes) gets so intoxicated at the party that she winds up vomiting all over the bed as they make out. Furthermore, it is clear that Evan does not want to have sex with Becca while they are both intoxicated. When they are kissing, he stops her saying, "Becca, I don't think you want to do this. You're really drunk." Although she insists that she is fine and even shames him by calling him a "little bitch," Evan stops them before she throws up. So, although *Superbad* initially presents the familiar setup of boys' pursuing sex from girls, the film ultimately disrupts this plot arc, in particular through the character of Evan, who embarks on the journey reluctantly and does not wish to see it through in its culmination. In the end, the boys "get the girls," but they don't get the sex.

Over a decade after writing *Superbad*, Seth Rogen and Evan Goldberg teamed up again to produce the post-#MeToo film *Good Boys*, which critics called "Superbad, Jr." (Travers) and "Superbad with no pubic hairs" (Simonpillai). Once again, the premise of the film seems to be one based on boys' overriding the consent of girls. As the writers describe in an interview, "I think the first thing we talked about was a couple of twelve-year-old boys spying on some sixteen-year-old girls with a drone" (Swinson). The setup is clear: boys want something girls would not consent to, and so the boys solve their problem by simply . . . doing it anyway. In this way, the notion of nonconsent remains fundamental to the narrative structure of the story. Yet, it is quite obvious too how consent is taken into account in this film quite explicitly in other ways. In the film, the boys decide to practice kissing on what they think is a "really pretty CPR doll," but is actually a sex doll. When Max starts to lean in for a kiss, his friend Lucas yells, "Stop! What are you doing?" "Kissing her," Max replies. His friends explain, "You can't kiss someone without their permission. Remember from assembly?" and "Pretend it's Brixlee. Try to be a gentleman." Max replies, "OK," then asks the doll, "Brixlee, can I kiss you?" Lucas pretends to be the doll/ Brixlee as he asks to know what Max likes about her, and ultimately says in his imitation female voice, "I consent" so Max can move in for his kiss. This practicing of consent transfers over to the boys' personal interactions in the film, as well. When the "kissing party" takes place, each of the boys and girls can consent to participate, or they can choose to play VR games in another room of the house. Then when Max does have the opportunity to kiss Brixlee, he asks her, "Can I kiss you?" to which she responds, "Yes" before he does. These scenes demonstrate how the filmmakers sought to ensure consent was explicit in the film. In one interview, director and co-writer Gene Stupnitsky calls consent "very real and something that should be addressed," adding, "There's a long history of movies being on the other side of that, and I think going forward it's imperative for filmmakers, as the world evolves, to evolve with it" (Chuba). Interestingly, in the April 4, 2017, *Good Boys* version of the screenplay written by Lee Eisenberg and Stupnitsky, consent *does not* make an appearance—none of these scenes I mention above appear in the original script and the word "consent" is entirely absent (Eisenberg and Stupnitsky). In other words, consent was written into *Good Boys* somewhere between this 2017 iteration of the script and the film's release in 2019—very likely due to the post-#MeToo critical conversations about consent.

Several recent teen sex comedies, such as *The To Do List* (Carey 2013), *Blockers,* and *Booksmart,* have shifted girls into the position as the driver of sexual exploits—changing them from their more traditional gatekeeper role to the aggressor. The entire premise of *The To Do List,* for instance, is that A-student Brandy Klark decides to cram her sexual exploits into the summer before college by creating a sexual "to do list" and then pursuing boys to check off the items on her list. After declaring to her friends that she plans to tackle the "hand job" next, the scene cuts to Brandy and Cameron in a movie theater. Without asking, she takes his popcorn and unzips his pants. He asks, "What are you doing?," to which she responds, "What do you think I'm doing?" She then abruptly stops when she presumably sees his penis (we see only a shot of her looking down). He asks, "why'd you stop?" and she doesn't answer, but gets up, goes to the lobby, and calls her mom. Instead, she reaches her sister, who gives her advice on how to handle an uncircumcised penis. She returns to her seat after getting a handful of butter from the popcorn stand. Cameron asks her, "Is everything OK? Did I do something wrong? Are you sure?" She then unzips his pants again, and starts touching him again, at which point he asks, "Do you want me to touch you?" As he climaxes, he yells out, "I love you!" and he leans his head on her shoulder while she examines the semen in her hand. In the film, Cameron clearly has more than a sexual interest in Brandy—he appears to want a relationship with her—but to her, he is simply a convenient prop to check an item off of her list. As such, it would be difficult to imagine a contemporary teen film depicting this comedic scene with the genders swapped. The abruptness of Brandy's actions also directly contrasts with the way Cameron obtains consent from her in an earlier scene. While they kiss on the couch, she tells him "I'm so wet. Touch me," and then getting impatient she demands, "Finger me already," at which point he admits to being confused by her skorts—"are these shorts or a skirt?" and "over or under?" When she says "under," he again confirms her consent, asking "are you sure?," and she impatiently says, "Yes!" Only then does he proceed. Despite how carefully Cameron is depicted as checking for Brandy's consent to touch her, she neither asks nor tells him before she touches him. *The To Do List*, in other words, prioritizes affirmative consent by female characters, but not always the male characters. In failing to do so, it perpetuates the sexual script that men and boys are always consenting and that their consent does not need to be taken into account.

Blockers too pairs an ambivalent male teen with an aggressive female teen for a comedic effect. One of the characters, Kayla, has vowed to lose her virginity the evening of prom. When her date Connor offers her alcohol, she says, "Before I do drink this though, I just want to let you know that I am fully planning on having sex tonight—with you." He says, "Wherever the wind blows us," to which she responds, "Well, the wind's going to blow us there." Again, he expresses hesitance, saying, "Wherever the night takes us," and she says, "It's going to take your penis into my vagina." He then says, "OK, if the universe wills it," to which she responds, "And the universe *will* will it," to which he finally concludes, "Thanks for letting me know, I guess." Although these scenes depict an exaggerated form of female sexual empowerment for comedic effect, they explicitly fail to take male consent into account. Connor's consent seems to be a moot point—at least to Kayla. She seems to believe it's only her affirmative consent that needs to be addressed, which is why she states in advance of drinking that she consents to future sexual intercourse even if she gets drunk later (which, of course, is not how consent works). Although these scenes of female sexual aggression might at first glance be seen as "feminist" or empowering, they do not prioritize affirmative consent. Later in the film, the joke culminates with a scene in their hotel room as the two mutually decide not to have intercourse. However, Kayla says that she is "still down for pleasure" as she points where he should go. He smiles, kisses her, and then the shot cuts away as he begins to move his head down, presumably to perform cunnilingus on her. As we understand it later, no other sexual act besides this one occurs between them that night. Although this cannot be read explicitly as a scene of nonconsent, Kayla's forceful demeanor and their subsequent one-sided sexual interaction makes light of a troubling dynamic that has existed for decades, albeit with the genders reversed. One might recall how Mrs. Robinson's behavior in *The Graduate* was originally thought of as revolutionary and even feminist for placing a female character into the older predatory position. Yet, scenes of female sexual empowerment that simply swap gender roles by depicting girls' pursuing sexual conquest without mutual consent should be just as disturbing as when boys do it. According to the CDC, one in three women are sexually assaulted in their lives, but nearly one in four men are as well ("Preventing Sexual Violence"). Although we cannot count on mainstream films to depict ideal behavior, I would argue that it is an unfortunate (and even unimaginative) form of comedy to simply reverse the gender roles in this way.

Booksmart also makes the two female protagonists the drivers of the plot—Amy and Molly set out to pack all of the partying they missed out in high school into one night—but these girls do not pursue their conquests with the same level of aggressiveness. In the beginning of the film, Amy, as Molly puts it, has been, "out for two years" but "never kissed a girl." At the end of the film, Amy winds up crying in the bathroom at a party after she spots the girl who she has a crush on kissing a boy. One of her classmates, Hope, catches her crying and calls her "meek" and "Molly's little sidekick bitch," to which Amy retorts calling her a "basic hot girl who's going to peak in high school." Then unexpectedly, Amy leans in and kisses Hope—a move that surprises Hope and makes her smile. The two of them continue kissing on the bathroom floor, and as Amy takes off Hope's shirt, Amy pauses. Hope asks, "Are you all right?" and Amy responds, "Yeah, sorry I just got a little dizzy there for a second." Hope tells her, "We can stop if you want," and Amy replies, "We are *not* stopping." After more undressing and making out, Amy stutters asking Hope, "How . . . how . . . how is that for you?," and Hope responds, "It's OK." Amy, recognizing her own inexperience and wanting to please Hope, asks, "Is there another way you prefer?" and Hope hesitates, then admits, "Um, I don't think that's the hole you think it is." The scene then dissolves into a classic awkward teen sex comedy moment—with Amy stammering her apology, and Hope assuring her it's all right, until Amy drinks something from the wrong cup on the tub causing her to throw up all over Hope. Although Amy initially makes her move on Hope before obtaining affirmative consent, consent figures prominently in this scene for both characters—Amy in her earnestness of wanting to touch Hope the way she wants to be touched and Hope in her recognition that Amy might not be ready or sober enough to proceed. Consent also figures into the comedy of the scene, in that Amy mistakenly puts her finger into the "other" hole and then says she was not accustomed to coming from that angle and her "geometry was off."

Although this scene certainly emphasizes consent, the film is still filled with nonconsensual moments of the nonsexual variety. For instance, Amy and Molly are taken to a private boat party against their will by a male classmate, where they are given ecstasy by a female classmate also without their consent. In this way, the idea of nonconsent remains a central device for the plot—the girls try to get to a particular party, and the obstacles come in the form of characters who refuse to comply with the girls' desires. Nonconsent becomes a way to create an obstacle in the familiar plot structure—a character who wants something meets obstacles in trying to obtain their goal. Of course, as scholars we should be careful, as Catherine Driscoll suggests, not to fall into the trap of "judg[ing] films in the genre as good or bad in terms of a responsibility to represent adolescence in always that would be good for adolescents" (4). Plus, as Catherine Ashcraft in the essay "Adolescent Ambiguities in *American Pie*: Popular Culture as a Resource for Sex Education" states, "we must remember that teens are capable of engaging in critique of popular texts even when they enjoy these texts" (49). Still, it might be important to recognize that youth are learning about all types of consent—not just sexual—through films, which makes the violation of being given mind-altering drugs without your consent a narrative turn worth discussion.

The enormously popular Netflix original *The Kissing Booth* (2018), also a more recent teen film, harkens back to what we might have thought (or hoped) were the dark ages of sexual consent. Adapted from the young adult novel originally published online at WattPad by Beth Reekles, the film became, according to Netflix, "one of the most-watched movies in the country, and maybe in the world" (Adalian). The plot features teenaged Elle who has a secret crush on her best friend Lee Flynn's older brother Noah. What Elle doesn't know is that Noah has been threatening all the boys at school to stay away from her—whether he wants to "protect" her or because he wants to keep her for himself is unclear. One day, Elle comes to school with her old uniform skirt, which is short enough to reveal her underwear. Upon arrival, she starts getting ogled by boys and girls alike, and one of the boys, Tuppen, grabs her butt. First her friend Lee comes to her defense, but as he is about to be punched by Tuppen, Noah steps in and punches Tuppen first. All three of them (Tuppen,

Noah, and Elle) wind up in detention, and there Tuppen begins flirting with Elle, sending her a note saying, "What do I have to do to get your number?" Elle smiles back at him and writes back, while Noah shakes his head in disapproval at her. In other words, the film depicts Elle as interested in and attracted to a boy who has just sexually assaulted her and another who exhibits officious behavior toward her.

At a party later in the film, one of Elle's classmates, Warren, tells her that she needs a "hot tub," and although she says no twice, he grabs her hand and starts dragging her as she says "I'm not feeling well." Noah comes out of nowhere to step in and shouts, "She said 'No!' Warren!" Noah is ready for another fight (his trademark), and Elle pleads with him to just take her home. But as soon as Warren makes a snide remark to Noah, Noah takes the bait and punches him hard. When Elle runs away, Noah runs after her, yelling, "Elle, wait. Just get in the car Elle. Just get in the car, Elle." He then says it a *third* time while slamming his hand down on the car roof so hard that she jumps and stops in her tracks, looking afraid. He then says, "please," and we see her expression waver and soften. In the next scene, she's in his passenger seat. She soon realizes and articulates, "Wait this isn't the way home," and he tells her that he wants to show her something. He drives her to an isolated lookout to view the city from behind the Hollywood sign. Although she calls him out on his "player" moves, she still thinks to herself, "he's good." She then expresses a set of rules—no more fighting, no more telling her what to do, and "if we do this, nobody can know, at least until I can figure out a way to tell Lee." He agrees to her terms, and then they kiss. When he starts to unbutton her shirt, he pauses and says, "Um, you know we don't have to." She responds by unbuttoning *his* shirt. *The Kissing Booth* takes consent into account in this one minor moment—Noah will not proceed to have sex with Elle unless she consents, which she does. However, Noah's behavior before and after this moment suggests that he is actually a controlling and abusive partner, who cares little about her consent.

As indieWIRE reviewer Kate Erbland describes, the film is a "sexist and regressive look at relationships that highlights the worst impulses of the genre." Noah deceives and controls Elle—and her attempts to assert herself often seem futile and meaningless. The moment that he takes consent into account is but a blip in a stream of situations in which Noah acts on his own impulses with little to no regard for Elle's wishes or feelings. The innocent girl/bad boy theme mirrors other recent successes such as *Twilight* (Hardwicke 2008) and *Fifty Shades of Grey* (Taylor-Johnson 2015)—all of which suggest that the male love interest is not a stalker/abuser/violator because we see him protecting the girl from other men or boys who want to violate the girl. Worse than simply putting girls in the gatekeeper role, this trend suggests girls need and want protection from an older and stronger male figure who tells them where to go, what to wear, and how to behave. Noah constantly transgresses Elle's boundaries—and she falls for him either despite or because of his behavior. To think that this film came after the #MeToo movement started means that we might want to pause before declaring the eradication of the blurring of seduction and violence in teen films.

Undoubtedly many of the same patterns get reiterated in movies, perhaps without a lot of thought for the consequences other than what both works for the story and is marketable—and clearly *The Kissing Booth* succeeded at its goal for viewership. One in three viewers have rewatched the film on Netflix, and *The Kissing Booth 2* was released in 2020 and *The Kissing Booth 3* released in 2021 (Kaufman). The film's success might, in fact, be directly linked to its being an "intentional" "throwback" to "John Hughes classics" and the "kind of teen movie the film business rarely makes anymore" (Kaufman), complete with a cast starring Molly Ringwald, as Lee and Noah's mom. The film feels as if it were from some other era specifically because it seems oblivious to the formidable trend in teen romantic films to take consent, girls' sexual agency, and healthy relationships into account. In other words, nonconsent disguised as seduction has not quite been relegated to the past in teen films, but at least we have reached a moment when it seems like it should have been. Evan Goldberg, co-producer of *Superbad* and *Good Boys*, has said that he and co-producer Seth Rogen would make a teen comedy every ten years, joking "that's what we're allowed" (Chuba). Certainly, we can expect further changes in the genre on many levels, especially on how they incorporate and depict sexuality. Undoubtedly, the wide release and subsequent success of *Love, Simon* (Greg Berlanti 2018) marked a critical shift toward Hollywood's acceptance of the queer teen film. The transformation of the teen comedy over the past few decades suggests that the genre has been substantially impacted by the public's evolving perception of sexuality and consent, even while certain tropes persist. At this moment, the teen films of the future exist in various stages of development—and how they will take consent into account remains to be seen.

Works Cited

Archard, David. *Sexual Consent*. Boulder, CO: Westview Press, 1998.

Ashcraft, Catherine. "Adolescent Ambiguities in *American Pie*: Popular Culture as a Resource for Sex Education." *Youth & Society* 35, no. 1 (2003): 37–70.

Barnhill, Anne. "Just Pushy Enough." In *Dating Philosophy for Everyone*, edited by Kristie Miller and Marlene Clark. Hoboken, NJ: Wiley-Blackwell, 2010. 90–100.

Breeden, Aurelien, and Elian Peltier. "Response to French Letter Denouncing #MeToo Shows a Sharp Divide." *New York Times*, January 12, 2018.

Chuba, Kristen. "Seth Rogen, Evan Goldberg on How *Good Boys* Echoes *Superbad*." *The Hollywood Reporter*, August 15, 2019. www.hollywoodreporter.com/news/seth-rogen-evan-goldberg-how-good-boys-echoes-superbad-1232213

Driscoll, Catherine. *Teen Film: A Critical Introduction*. London: Bloomsbury, 2011.

Eisenberg, Lee, and Gene Stupnitsky. *Good Boys*. April 4, 2017. Draft script.

Erbland, Kate. "'*The Kissing Booth*': Netflix's Teen Comedy Sensation Is Sexist and Outdated—Review." indieWIRE, May 31, 2018. www.indiewire.com/2018/05/the-kissing-booth-netflix-teen-romantic-comedy-sexist-1201969234

Kaufman, Amy. "Must Reads: How *The Kissing Booth* became a pop culture sensation (even if critics hated it)." *Los Angeles Times*, June 28, 2018. www.latimes.com/entertainment/movies/la-ca-mn-kissing-booth-netflix-joey-king-20180628-story.html

Kupfer, Lindsey. "Shannon Elizabeth reflects on life-changing 'American Pie' role 20 years later." Page Six, July 9, 2019. https://pagesix.com/2019/07/09/shannon-elizabeth-reflects-on-life-changing-american-pie-role-20-years-later

Miller, Franklin, and Alan Wertheimer. *The Ethics of Consent: Theory and Practice*. New York: Oxford University Press, 2009.

"Nous défendons une liberté d'importuner, indispensable à la liberté sexuelle." *Le Monde*, January 9, 2018.

Ottesen, K.K. "#MeToo founder Tarana Burke reflects on the movement—and the reckoning." *The Washington Post*, November 6, 2018.

Popova, Milena. *Sexual Consent*. Cambridge, MA: MIT Press, 2019.

"Preventing Sexual Violence." CDC Violence Prevention. www.cdc.gov/violenceprevention/sexualviolence/fastfact.html

Ringwald, Molly. "What about *The Breakfast Club*?" *The New Yorker*, April 6, 2018. www.newyorker.com/culture/personal-history/what-about-the-breakfast-club-molly-ringwald-metoo-john-hughes-pretty-in-pink

Shary, Tim. "Course File for 'Film Genres and the Image of Youth.'" *Journal of Film and Video*, 55, no. 1 (Spring 2003): 39–57.

Shary, Timothy. *Teen Movies: American Youth on Screen*. New York: Wallflower 2005.

Simonpillai, Radheyan. "Review: *Good Boys* is *Superbad* with No Pubic Hairs." *Now Toronto*, August 14, 2019. https://nowtoronto.com/movies/reviews/good-boys-jacob-trembla

Swinson, Brock. "The Real Writing Is in The Outlining": Lee Eisenberg and Gene Stupnitsky Talk *Good Boys*." *Creative Screenwriting*, August 14, 2019. https://creativescreenwriting.com/the-real-writing-is-in-the-outlining-lee-eisenberg-and-gene-stupnitsky-talk-good-boys

Travers, Peter. "*Good Boys* Review: R-Rated Innocence." *Rolling Stone*, August 13, 2019. www.rollingstone.com/movies/movie-reviews/good-boys-review-r-rated-innocence-870783

"What Is Sexual Consent?" Planned Parenthood. www.plannedparenthood.org/learn/sex-and-relationships/sexual-consent

CHAPTER 11

Flipping the Script on Consent

Re-centering Young Women's Sexual Agency in Teen Comedies

Shana MacDonald

Feminist Re-Presentations in the MeToo Era: Setting the Scene

On October 19, 2017, *Elle* magazine published the "Women in Hollywood 2017: Power List," noting bleak statistics around Hollywood's lack of support and opportunities for women as directors, studio heads, and sole protagonists within major films (Rushfield). The article appeared just three weeks after the *New York Times* outlined Hollywood mogul Harvey Weinstein's decades-long history of sexual predation (Kantor and Twohey), and four days after #MeToo went viral. As a counterpoint, the article highlighted a list of key women in the movie industry, including presidents and CEOs of major studios like Disney and 20th Century Fox,[1] offering a forward-reaching vision of a post-Weinstein Hollywood (Rushfield). This cohort of women have tried to make incremental changes in the twenty-first century by ensuring greater visibility for women's representation in film, television, and popular culture more broadly. To an extent it is working; many new films and prestige television shows over the last five years offer strident critiques of sexism and reflect the rise of newly "emergent feminisms" in popular discourse (Keller and

Ryan 1–2). The Time's Up campaign, part of a "dramatic and unprece-dented cultural acknowledgment and conversation about sexual assault and harassment in Hollywood and beyond" (Cobb and Horeck 489), exemplifies this growing relationship between explicit feminist politics and the entertainment industry. And yet, as the startling lack of Oscar nominations for women filmmakers and artists in 2020 revealed, little has actually changed in terms of institutional recognition for women in Hollywood and women directors in particular.

What are we to make of these forward-reaching feminist goals and the lack of institutional support for them? While there are many ways into this conversation, one is to consider the feminist messaging within contemporary films that aptly reflect the discourse of the times. Here we may find some reason for hope. Since around 2014, women-directed, -written, and -produced films and television have notably shifted away from the postfeminist narratives of the early 2000s, which advanced neoliberal, individualist notions of women's empowerment (Brundson 2000; McRobbie 2004; Gill 2005; Negra 2008). Postfeminism is defined as a reductive belief system that delegitimizes feminist activism. Instead, it encourages women's self-surveillance, competitive individualism, and the myth of "empowerment" through a consumerist ethos (Gill 2007 149). Postfeminism evokes feminism's "cultural power" in order to "empty it of its radical critique" (Gill 74). This framework is being challenged by popular film and television at present. For instance, Jessica Jones in the Netflix series of the same name (Rosenberg 2015–2019) is not a postfeminist heroine but rather a feminist killjoy (Ahmed 2017). I have argued elsewhere that in fighting sexism and racism Jones is in fact a postfeminist failure insofar as she refuses individual empowerment and idealized femininity (see MacDonald 2019). Her character is one of many examples of representational change in Hollywood that deserve further consideration. Expanding upon this argument, I consider here feminist counter-narratives found in recent teenage romantic comedies written and directed by women. The films positively reflect popular and public feminist conversations in the media by refiguring the retrograde sexual politics largely associated with this rom-com genre for the last four decades.

While much has been written on the chick flick and its problem-atic ties to neoliberal, postfeminist ideals (Gerhard 2005, Cobb 2011), we must also examine such ideals in films directed at younger women. This is particularly important because "girls . . . as a social group . . . typically embody fears and desires of cultural transition" (Willis 242). In response, I explore how current iterations of feminism in the #MeToo era are being articulated in positive representations of consent within teen rom-coms. I compare three films: the Netflix original *To All the Boys I've Loved Before* (Johnson 2018), the Judd Apatow-esque raunch comedy *Blockers* (Cannon 2018), and Olivia Wilde's directorial debut *Booksmart* (2019). These films center on both straight and queer, as well as white and biracial, women protagonists in formative sexual and romantic encounters. The narrative arcs of these films reflect a broader cultural transition through their focus on young women's sexual agency and consent.

To All the Boys I've Loved Before was arguably the most popular teen romance of 2018 (Fang). With thousands of posts using the #tatbilb for fan memes on Instagram, Tumblr, and Twitter, the movie developed a large audience across millennial and generation Z audiences. Distributed by Netflix, the film boasts a core group of women creatives at the center of production. Directed by Susan Johnson, the film is based on the equally popular 2014 young adult novel of the same name by Jenny Han and was rewritten for the screen by Sofia Alvarez. Cited by Netflix as "one of its most viewed original films ever with strong repeat viewing" (Fang), the film represents the current resurgence in rom-coms being led by streaming services (Sandberg). The second installment in the film franchise, *To All The Boys: PS I Still Love You*, was released on February 12, 2020, and the final installation in the trilogy, *To All The Boys: Always and Forever*, was released on February 12, 2021.

In the first film, Lara Jean Covey (Lana Condor), a somewhat reluctant protagonist, is trying to find her place in the social spaces of her high school after her older sister leaves for college. Her younger sister sees her struggling and mails five love letters Lara Jean wrote to former crushes but never intended to send. These letters include one to her sister's ex-boyfriend and one to school jock Peter Kavinsky (Noah Centineo) who just broke up with popular mean-girl (and Lara Jean's former best friend), Genevieve (Emilija Benerac). Lara Jean and Peter agree to "fake-date" each other to solve their separate romantic problems and fall in love along the way.

Blockers, released in the same year as *To All the Boys*, is the directorial debut of Kay Cannon, who wrote for *30 Rock* between 2008 and 2010, and wrote and produced the *Pitch Perfect* franchise between 2012 and 2017 and Netflix's *Girlboss* in 2017. *Blockers* was produced by Seth Rogen and Evan Goldberg, the team behind *Superbad* (2007) and

Pineapple Express (2008), and distributed by Universal Pictures. *Blockers* premiered at South by Southwest in March of 2018 and its theatrical release came a month after. Cannon, who situates the film as part of a larger feminist project, is notably one of only six women to have ever directed a "big budget R-rated comedy movie in film history" (Holmes). It has an 83 percent rating on Rotten Tomatoes and made $94 million (USD) globally, which is impressive given it had a production budget of just $21 million (USD).

The film follows teenage best friends, Kayla (Geraldine Viswanathan), Julie (Kathryn Newton), and Sam (Gideon Adlon), as they make a pact to lose their virginity on prom night. The title is a shortened version of the slang phrase "cockblocking" and refers to the main plot obstacle wherein their over-protective parents try to stop their "sex pact." The majority of the comedic gags center on their parents interfering into their teenage worlds to disastrous (and often abject) ends. *Blockers* is far removed from the original script from 2012, *Cherries*, which followed three dads trying to stop their daughters from being sexually active (Kilkenny 2018). In the updated 2018 version there is no emphasis on purity or slut-shaming—in fact, it is quite the opposite; Kayla's mom explicitly calls out the other parents, including her husband, for their obsession with the three young women's virginity.

Like *Blockers*, the film *Booksmart* also premiered at South by Southwest festival. It showed there in March 2019, with a theatrical release in May of that year. It grossed $24 million (USD) globally and has a 97% rating on Rotten Tomatoes. While the production and creative team did not get nominated for any Oscars, Beanie Feldstein was nominated for a Golden Globe award for acting, and the film won "best female director" at the Hollywood Critics Association Awards and "best first feature" at the Independent Spirit Awards.

Booksmart follows two over-achieving best friends Amy (Kaitlyn Dever) and Molly (Beanie Feldstein), who have sacrificed their social lives to earn places at Ivy league colleges. Their worlds explode on their last day of high school when they discover all the cool kids who they wrote off as stoners and losers are also going to Ivy Leagues or six-figure jobs at Google. To reconcile their mounting regret at how they spent the last four years, they go on a one-night party adventure that includes awkward first-time sexual encounters, public fights, and one of them landing in jail.

These films re-imagine two longstanding narrative tropes within the coming-of-age subgenre of romantic comedies. The first trope positions teenage girls as sexually naïve and thus reaffirms heteronormative views of women's sexual passivity and men's active sexuality. The second trope frames date rape and nonconsensual sex as a teenage rite of passage rather than an act of sexual violence. Past eras of coming-of-age romantic comedy often used date rape as a punch line and portrayed young women as lacking sexual agency or a sense of their own desire. For example, in *Sixteen Candles* (Hughes 1984) the main protagonist Sam Baker (Molly Ringwald) reluctantly gives her underwear to nerd Ted (Anthony Michael Hall) as "proof" to his friends that they were intimate even though they were not. Romantic lead Jake Ryan (Michael Earl Schoeffling) later in the film encourages Ted to take advantage of his drunk and unconscious ex-girlfriend Caroline (Haviland Morris) when he drives her home.

That a film as enduringly popular as *Sixteen Candles* places the date rape of the "popular girl" as a punch line shows how far more recent films such as *Booksmart*, *Blockers*, and *To All the Boys* deviate from earlier teen comedy scripts. Two of these films even reference *Sixteen Candles* directly as a sort of revisionist gesture. In *Blockers*, a poster of *Sixteen Candles* hangs in main character Julie's bedroom, a subtle nod to the history of the genre and how it will be reconfigured as the narrative progresses. In *To All the Boys*, Lara Jean makes Peter watch *Sixteen Candles* at her house, where they engage in a productive conversation about the film's racist portrayal of the Asian character Long Duk Dong (Gedde Watanabe) from the perspective of Lara Jean and her little sister Kitty, as Asian American viewers. This scene switches the representational power of the original film's racism as it is actively addressed and negotiated by Lara Jean and Kitty.

To All the Boys, *Booksmart*, and *Blockers* model generative examples of young women protagonists engaged in consensual sexual relationships. These characters are comfortably in control of their sexuality and have supportive, respectful partners, solid friendships, and an open relationship with their parents. These are significant representational shifts within Hollywood that are connected to larger conversations around rape culture and youth culture in contemporary public discourse.

The Lives of Young Women On Screen Now

The three films I consider in this chapter reflect how women directors and writers are finding ways to imbue feminist intentions within the constraints of the big-budget studio system and traditionally sexist film genres. *To All the Boys* reimagines the protagonist of a rom-com as a grounded and thoughtful teen who feels accountable to herself and her family first before her romantic relationship. Unlike the more standard rom-com model of *To All the Boys*, *Booksmart* and *Blockers* are more vulgar R-rated movies about sex. The two films reimagine the raunchier coming-of-age script by refusing to sexualize girls and instead highlight the protagonists' desires and experiences as valuable sides of discourse. All three films explore with humor and grace the difficulties and realities of trying to maintain healthy connections *and* boundaries with friends and family. Like in *Booksmart* and *Blockers*, *To All the Boys* depicts sisterly solidarity and women's friendships, as well as the portrayal of high schoolers who actually like their families, creating space for relationships that aren't overly valued in traditional teen films (Shary 215).

In addition, fans and critics celebrate *To All the Boys* for its expanded representation of women and people of color as main characters within the genre. This is equally true of *Booksmart* and *Blockers*, although to differing degrees. All three films promote healthy models of consent and take a stand against racism, sexism, and homophobia. In *To All the Boys*, the representation of Asian American teenagers and multiracial families are distinct from previous, largely white, cinematic images of teenagers and family spaces in Hollywood film. The film expands who fits into our imagined (and real) social environments. Many fans and critics also appreciate how relatable Lara Jean is, applauding how her style and persona push back against whitewashed images of an idealized romantic lead. The fact that Lara Jean is a bit of an introvert who does not like parties and is a homebody is an accepted part of who she is. It is neither idealized as representing a pure and chaste exception to teenage life or something she has to overcome. While it does set out the crux of her narrative journey, the resolution to her introversion is not dramatic but rather is about her moving slightly out of her comfort zone.

Lara Jean complicates the existing stereotypes of Asian women onscreen; she is never depicted "as sexually available to the white hero" in order to cater to a "white, masculine gaze" (Marchetti 1993, 2–6). Nor does she need a white male hero to save her "from the evils or excesses" of her Korean culture (8). This is something her character shares in common with protagonist Kayla in *Blockers*. Kayla is a jock who has a white, hypermasculine, and overprotective stay-at-home dad Mitchell (Jon Cena) and a South Asian feminist mother, Marcie (Sarayu Blue). Kayla is self-possessed and confident, qualities she gained both from her mother as a feminist model as well as on the soccer field with her dad as her coach. While her dad is struggling with Kayla's entrée into dating life, her mom is vocally supportive of her daughter's sexual agency and explorations throughout the film—a marked contrast to her father's possessiveness. If there is a comment to be made on how his whiteness plays a factor in his possessiveness of Kayla it is subsumed by the more general trope of the overprotective father.

By foregrounding non-white characters in central roles, the two films refuse the troubling legacy of racist representation upheld by Hollywood for many decades. As Laura Hyun-Yi Kang suggests, we may want to question what *To All the Boys* and *Blockers* reveal "about racial, gendered difference as it is inscribed on an Asian female body and ultimately apprehended by white masculinity?" (Kang 74). Neither Kayla nor Lara Jean is depicted within the historically racist framing of Asian women as either predators through their excessive sexualized desirability or as victims that need a white male savior (Marchetti 218). To a degree, their narratives ensure that any current racial tensions within the United States are "reduced to the manageable realm of interracial, heterosexual romance between white male and Asian/American female" (Kang 74) insofar as narratively race is not a barrier to overcome. However, because race is not a barrier in these films, it also means the women protagonists are not playing into an "economy of white male desire" (Kang 74). Rather, the points of tension in the films center on familial conflicts and their own desires over those of their white male partners or fathers.

A larger historical trajectory of Asian American cultural producers offers the foundation for such reformulations in the two films. Gina Marchetti suggests that one way to critique dominant representations of Asian American women as love interests is for Asian American producers to explore interracial relationships on their own terms (217). This is what occurs in the source material for the movie, which was written by Jenny Han, who is Korean American. Han's original narrative productively used "these accepted images as part of [her] own critique of the media" (Marchetti 217). As Han notes, she had to actively resist a whitewashing of the script in her early encounters with Hollywood producers whose interest in making the film "died as soon as I made it clear the lead had to be Asian-American." Han recalls that "one producer said to me, as long as the actress captures the spirit of the character, age and race don't matter. I said, well, her spirit is Asian-American. That was the end of that" (Han). The *To All the Boys* film franchise intentionally takes the time to integrate Lara Jean's Korean culture into the narrative in both smaller ways (Peter brings her and her sister their favorite Korean drink) and larger ones (the opening of the second film shows them celebrating the Lunar New Year with her family). Kayla's relationship to her South Asian culture is not explored extensively in the film save for a nod to Indian sari fashion with her prom dress. While it would be great if the film did address her biracial identity more fully in *Blockers*, it seems to be overlooked in favor of exploring her negotiations with her burgeoning sexuality.

While Kayla and Lara Jean's biracial identities are not the focus of their narrative journeys, they do both end up with white romantic partners. Neither Kalya's nor Lara Jean's white boyfriend performs a stereotypical white knight role in their lives in order to assimilate them into dominant white heteronormative values and society. Lara Jean's main narrative arc requires that she be more forthright with herself and others about her relationship with Peter and confront the consequences it produces. This includes her being afraid of disappointing her older sister and her need to stand up to the mean girl at school who is bullying her. With Kayla, she needs to stand up to her dad, who is creating barriers to her self-directed sexual explorations. Kayla must articulate her desire for independence while maintaining a relationship, albeit a changing one, with her overprotective father. Her date Connor cannot do that for her. It is her narrative arc, and thus her task to complete.

In *Booksmart*, Amy and Molly are both white, and Amy is a lesbian. While there is a lack of racialized negotiations with these two characters, Amy's sexuality is equally integrated as a part of, rather than the defining element, of her identity. Further, in *Blockers*, the three popular boys in school are all racial minorities, but this too is subsumed by the dominant, upper-middle-class culture the three movies portray. Lara Jean and Kayla's biracial identities, like those of the popular boys in *Blockers*, are not whitewashed, but they are normalized within these largely white milieus. This is addressed most clearly in *To All the Boys* where Lara Jean actively negotiates her relationship to her biracial identity and is raised by her white father who has kept Korean traditions alive in the house since her mother died when she was young. The decision in all three films to not make race or sexuality a narrative obstacle but rather a fact of life is a critical reimagination of how to portray identity differences in teen comedy. I would question, however, if each film's replication of teenage worlds tied to wealth and privilege tend to maintain other cultural norms. Hollywood equally needs a more nuanced approach to incorporating difference that does not sexualize, whitewash, heteronormativize, or enact idealized class privilege.

Teenage Sex After #MeToo

I want to now focus in greater detail on how sex and intimacy, while key in the narrative plots of all three films, are catalysts for more profound self-realizations, rather than penultimate goals themselves. This refutes the standard Hollywood milestone of losing one's virginity within such teen comedies, as few of the protagonists considered here succeed in this particular goal. Instead, the films offer narrative space for young women to address their own personal growth both inside and outside of romantic relationships.

In *To All the Boys*, the male romantic lead is a down-to-earth teenager rather than a bad boy. He is a welcome shift in focus from films of the early 2000s, which romanticized abusive traits as desirable. This can be seen most clearly in Edward Cullen from the *Twilight* franchise (2008–2012), and the controlling playboy millionaire Christian Grey in *Fifty Shades of Grey* trilogy (2015–2018). Despite his popularity and traditional good looks, Peter Kavinsky is well intentioned, and models respect and care in the way he treats Lara Jean and her family. Peter does small things for Lara Jean because of his interest in her rather than grand romantic gestures that he expects her to reciprocate by being sexually available. The film has no one magical moment of falling in love but represents their relationship as a process of getting to know, share with, and trust each other. It presents the impression that friendship is the foundation of love.

This is put to the test when Laura Jean agrees to go on the senior class ski trip, which, she notes, is known as a place to lose your virginity. Instead of being with Peter, she hides out reading romance novels and putting on face masks in her hotel room with her gay friend Lucas (Trezzo Mahoro), who convinces her that Peter has a crush on her. Lara Jean finally goes after Peter and finds him waiting for her in the hot tub. An awkward conversation occurs in which Peter tries to make Lara Jean see how much he likes her. They are sitting on opposite sides of the hot tub, with Lara Jean perched on the edge still weighing her choices and sorting through her feelings. There is no invitation or pressure by

Peter for her to enter the hot tub. When she does, it is very clearly her choice; she initiates and directs the encounter. The scene is intimate and respectful. It does not glamorize the encounter but also doesn't avoid showing it. Afterward, they affectionately say goodnight as they part in the hotel hallway, and she goes to bed happy and alone. Lara Jean's first sexual encounter with Peter is framed as a positive experience of her own making.

The incident does yield consequences, as Lara Jean's mean-girl nemesis Genevieve posts a video of her and Peter in the hot tub on social media. The film carefully frames this so as not to play into slut-shaming or rape culture discourse. It shows the pain this bullying causes Lara Jean and how it impacts her trust in Peter and others. She is not punished by the film narrative for choosing to be intimate with Peter. Instead, she turns for support to her older sister, who gives a textbook example of how to report such breeches of privacy and have them removed from social media platforms. When Lara Jean returns to school thinking the worst is over, she is publicly embarrassed once again as photocopies of the video are plastered over her locker. Her best friend calls out Peter, asking why he isn't doing anything to stop the slut-shaming Lara Jean faces that he, as a man, does not have to negotiate. Thusly prompted, Peter clarifies to all those jeering at the photo that they did not have sex. While this shows Peter using his alpha male status to defend Lara Jean, it is significant that Lara Jean confronts Genevieve on her own without Peter's influence. Lara Jean is not being saved by her romantic partner, and he is not much of a hero in that moment. In the second film, Peter takes Lara Jean's cue on how intimate they will be. Lara Jean expresses hesitations to have sex because Peter is not a virgin and she is. The progression of intimacy is put on hold in the narrative as they work out their emotional conflicts as a couple.

In *Blockers*, the three best friends present parallel trajectories in their sexual explorations but to very different ends. Julie, the stereotypical blonde beauty, is the only one of the three friends in a committed relationship, with the handsome and wealthy Austin. She is determined to lose her virginity on prom night. She has grand visions of how the night should go and is the one who inspired her two friends to join the prom night sex-pact by emphasizing how meaningful the memory will be if they all share it together. She wants the experience to unfold perfectly and is seen carrying flowers and candles around the entire night for when the opportunity arises. Julie's hotel room sex encounter is the most recognizable from previous teen films. She is the one who is most invested in playing out the cinematic fantasy. Despite this overdetermined vision, Austin supports her and is content to go along with her vision. However, it is Kayla who sets up Julie's hotel room with flower petals, donuts, and condoms, as she knows what Julie likes better than her boyfriend Austin does. When Julie enters the room and loves it, Austin lets her know it was Kayla's doing. The sexual encounter between Julie and Austin is respectful and caring. Austin engages in all of Julie's requests. She is thus able to experience the encounter in ways specific to her desires. While this is an idealized scenario, it also models for younger viewers the value of such articulations. This is a valuable corrective to previous male coming-of-age films, which often promote rape culture and overlook practices of affirmative consent. If, as Lisa Funnell notes, the phrase "coming of age" is associated with women's first sexual experiences, then it should reflect "their clear and unwavering choice" (personal correspondence, December 19, 2019).

Sam is the more introverted of the three friends in *Blockers* and is still closeted about her developing queer desires. She agrees to get in on the sex-pact despite not being too interested or involved in her prom date Chad because she feels pressured to have a shared memory with her friends. The premise of Sam's narrative arc appears at first the most retrograde, as her desires toward the sex-pact are ambivalent, yet it ultimately models the safe exploration of her emergent queer sexuality as Sam keeps encountering Angelica (her actual love interest) throughout the night. At the start of prom, Sam asks Angelica how she knew she was gay. Angelica replies when she first touched a classmate's penis and said to herself "fuck no!" This conversation sets Sam up for her own similar realization when she tries to have sex with Chad later that night. Sam changes her mind about having penetrative sex, but while she is expressing this to Chad he prematurely ejaculates, offering comic relief to an otherwise uncomfortable encounter. This sets Sam up to then come out to her dad and then her two best friends and ultimately end the night kissing Angelica at the prom hotel after-party.

In contrast, Kayla is very direct with her desire, and her date Connor models a version of teenage masculinity that is not hung up on sex as the ultimate goal of the evening despite his interest. While getting high with Connor outside the prom, Kayla states very clearly that they are having sex that night. Connor is interested but keeps adding the caveat "if the opportunity arises." His interest in her continuous consent pushes directly against stereotypes of white men holding power in their sexual relationships with Asian women (Marchetti 1993, Kang 2002). Kayla's forthright sexual desire is all the more significant because it is not as readily seen or celebrated in teen sex comedies of previous eras.[2]

When Kayla brings Connor to a hotel room to finally have sex, she decides she doesn't want to lose her virginity without getting to know him better. Connor is supportive and agrees they should date first. He suggests instead they chill and do light journaling. Kayla says she'd rather have him perform oral sex on her, and he obliges. Kayla's agency to speak her own desire is significant and something director Kay Cannon pushed hard for throughout the production (Hasty). If previous teen comedies portrayed sex as largely a hormonal teenage male arena (Shary 210–214), these three examples from *Blockers* portray women as exploring their desire in a variety of ways. For Cannon, it was important to deviate from existing teen sex comedies because "it won't feel like we're equal until we can do the same things that the guys do without judgment or shame or disapproval" (Hasty n.p.). In *Blockers*, Kayla, Julia, and Sam do exactly what guys have been able to do from *Fast Times at Ridgemont High* (1982) to *Superbad* (2007) and the *American Pie* franchise (1999–2012): articulate their sexual desires to their friends in crass and funny ways with the support of their peers.

When Kayla's dad comes in and throws Connor against a wall, it leads to a fight between Mitchell and Kayla in which she shames him for thinking she can't make her own decisions. She asks him why sex is even bad. Mitchell admits he doesn't know and says that he just wants to be the best dad, revealing the social imperative he faces as her dad to disavow and actively fight against her sexual agency. Their story arc and the conversations he has with both Kayla and his wife Marcie are the most direct in countering rape culture and how it informs men's relationships to their daughters.

These representational themes are further supported by the plot trajectory of *Booksmart*, which is overt throughout in its referencing of feminist figures as role models for the two main characters. In their sexual explorations, both Amy and Molly try to awkwardly flirt with their crushes at a year-end party only to see their crushes end up together. This, paired with a huge fight between them (filmed by classmates for the world to see), sets them on different paths toward the end of the party. Molly sits alone at the party and is approached by Jared, a rich and nerdy guy who she ends up kissing the next day at the start of her valedictorian speech. Amy, on the other hand, finds herself in a bathroom where the beautiful, aloof mean-girl Hope is smoking. They exchange some barbed insults, and Hope calls her weak. Amy responds by kissing Hope, who returns the kiss. This begins a now infamous sex scene that is both endearing and awkward. The surprise in their desire is palpable, and their consent to be intimate with each other is very clear. As Amy has been out for two years and never kissed a girl, this is a momentous event that goes awry as she confuses parts of Hope's anatomy and then pukes on her in her embarrassment. In versions of the film shown by Delta Airlines in their in-flight entertainment programing, the bathroom scene was removed, alongside a scene discussing women's masturbation, prompting Wilde to critique the airlines censorship of queer storylines. The scene shows a version of queer teen sexual experience that is not overly romanticized or presented for the pleasure of the male gaze. It is honest, uncomfortable, and hopeful while maintaining a comedic tone. Amy's first intimate experience is a recognizable teenage rite of passage regardless of sexual orientation. And yet it also avoids the usual representational traps of queer sexuality as pathological, dangerous, or under threat. As such, it offers an important model for how to represent queer teenage desire in future youth-oriented Hollywood films.

Perhaps most importantly, *Blockers*, *Booksmart*, and *To All the Boys* do not end their narratives with these different scenes of first-time sexual experiences—arguably because these do not make up the crux of any of the narratives. In *Blockers*, the three best friends meet up to share their experiences with each other and then dance to their song "Gonna Love Myself" by Hailee Steinfeld. The teen anthem of independence and self-acceptance points to what they value as a group of friends and have all individually achieved in their separate narrative arcs. This is followed up by a final scene of the girls leaving on a road trip to drive Julie off to her university in California. Julie is not driving with her boyfriend, but rather her best friends, as well as Kayla's now-boyfriend Connor. This ending may be even more radical in its reframing of the teen comedy than the sex scenes themselves as it emphasizes how the girls' romances are secondary to their enduring friendship.

A similar scene is found at the end of *Booksmart* when Molly drops Amy off at the airport for her year-long trip to Botswana. The film does not end with each character interacting with their new love interests, but instead with them together, highlighting how primary their friendship is in their lives. The narrative arc is for them to come to a place of independence from each other while still maintaining their close connection. The takeaway from this and *Blockers* is how valuable strong friendships are for helping you navigate the transition to adulthood. While *To All the Boys* ends with Lara Jean and Peter kissing on the high school football field, it is ultimately Lara Jean's emergence from her introversion, the strengthening of her relationship with her sisters and her father, and her continued negotiation with the loss of her mother that provide the more meaningful narrative resolutions.

Conclusion

If the value of situating popular cultural texts as an "object of study" is that it becomes "a tool for thinking" about "the state of feminist politics" (Lumby 97), then *Booksmart*, *Blockers*, and *To All the Boys* offer insights into how Hollywood has started to accept more progressive representational politics within its framework. Each film's progressive politics reflect the parallel public dialogue around enthusiastic consent and equitable sexual agency prompted by the #MeToo movement. In particular, the films all move away from postfeminist tropes that favor individual success in both life and love. In contrast, the personal successes in *Blockers*, *Booksmart*, and *To All the Boys* are inextricably tied to how each protagonist exists in relation to her friends and family, suggesting that there is indeed more to life than a heterosexual happy ending.

The re-centering of women's agency is not unique to the teen rom-com genre. From melodrama, to action adventure, to dystopian sci-fi fantasy, women's agency is being re-centered in a variety of ways. This reflects a (re)emergence of feminism within film and television narratives, tracing a move from postfeminist themes to more politicized, or at the very least critically oriented, themes. I would argue this shift is aligned with contemporary sites of feminist rage, or what Sara Ahmed calls a feminist snap (2017), that has occurred across film and media industries, affecting both those producing and creating women-centered narratives and the audiences, who are increasingly vocal regarding feminist concerns. The #MeToo movement is perhaps one of the loudest and most far-reaching feminist snaps of the last several years. It is part of a timely series of political snaps, including #BlackLivesMatter and #IdleNoMore, that are aiming to foster greater social equity in our worlds. What we can hope is that cultural producers in Hollywood reckon with these snaps in meaningful and generative ways, offering a mirror to the movements in our film and television landscapes. The outcomes of the particular feminist snap that has informed the films considered in this chapter offer a sense of hope for our continued collective resistance to rape culture's presence in both the industry and the popular films and television it produces.

Notes

1. This list included Kathleen Kennedy, president of Lucasfilms and head of the *Star Wars* franchise; Diane Nelson, president of DC Entertainment; Debra Lee, CEO of BET Networks; Stacey Snider, CEO of 20th Century Fox Film; and Diane Gabler, president of Fox 2000, to name a few (Rushfield; *Hollywood Reporter*).

2. A precursor and exception to this is the character of Michelle Flaherty in the *American Pie* franchise, who is equally comfortable with being upfront about her sexual desires.

Works Cited

Ahmed, Sara. *Living A Feminist Life*. Durham, NC: Duke University Press, 2017.

Arthurs, Jane. "*Sex and the City* and Consumer Culture: Remediating Postfeminist Drama." *Feminist Media Studies* 3, no. 1 (2003): 83–98.

Brundson, Charlotte. *The Feminist, the Housewife, and the Soap Opera*. New York: Oxford University Press, 2000.

Coates, Tyler. "*Blockers* Director Kay Cannon Made the First Feminist Teen Sex Comedy." *Esquire*, April 9, 2018.

Cobb, Shelley. "I'm Nothing Like You! Postfeminist Generationalism and Female Stardom in Monster-in-Law and The Devil Wears Prada." In *Women on Screen: Feminism and Femininity in Visual Culture*, edited by Melanie Waters. New York: Palgrave Macmillan, 2011. 31–44.

Cobb, Shelly, and Tanya Horeck. "Post Weinstein: Gendered Power and Harassment in the Media Industries." *Feminist Media Studies* 18, no. 3 (2018): 489–491.

Debruge, Peter. "Netflix's 'To All the Boys I've Loved Before" *Variety*, August 16, 2018.

Fang, Marina. "Netflix Says *To All The Boys I've Loved Before* Is One Of Its Most Popular Original Movies Ever." *Huffington Post*, October 17, 2018. www.To+All+the+Boys+I%E2%80%99ve+Loved+Before+might+be+the+best+teen+

romance+of+the+decade.%E2%80%9D+&form=QBLH&sp=-1&pq=&
sc=8-0&qs=n&sk=&cvid=C8C0B8E531A04CC1ADD56AF934E199BB

Friedman, Jaclyn. "Yes Means Yes and Enthusiastic Consent" *our bodies ourselves.
com*, October 15, 2011.

Friedman, Jaclyn, and Jessica Valenti. *Yes Means Yes: Visions of Female Sexual
Power and a World without Rape*. New York: Seal Press: 2008.

Gerhard, Jane. "Sex and the City.' *Feminist Media Studies* 5, no 1 (2005): 37–49.

Gill, Rosalind. "Post-postfeminism? New Feminist Visibilities in Postfeminist
Times." *Feminist Media Studies*16, no. 4 (2016): 610–630.

Gill, Rosalind. "Postfeminist Media Culture: Elements of a Sensibility." *European
Journal of Cultural Studies* 10, no. 2 (2007): 147–166.

Grady, Constance. "Netflix's To All the Boys I've Loved Before might be the
best teen romance of the decade." *Vox*, August 24, 2018.

Han, Jenny. "An Asian-American Teen Idol Onscreen, Finally." *New York Times*,
August 17, 2018. www.nytimes.com/2018/08/17/opinion/sunday/crazy-rich-
asians-movie-idol.html

Hasty, Katie. "*Blockers*' Kay Cannon reveals what a female director brings to a
raunchy comedy.' *EW*, April 7, 2018.

Holmes, Adam. "The Shocking Line Director Kay Cannon Used to Sell *Blockers* to the
Studios." *CinemaBlend*, April 2, 2018. www.cinemablend.com/news/2396682/
the-shocking-line-director-kay-cannon-used-to-sell-blockers-to-the-studios

Kang, Laura Hyun-Yi. 2002. "The Desiring of Asian Female Bodies: Interracial
Romance and Cinematic Subjection." In *Screening Asian Americans*, edited
by Peter X. Feng. New Brunswick, NJ: Rutgers University Press. 71–100.

Kantor, Jodi, and Megan Twohey. 2017. "Harvey Weinstein Paid Off Sexual
Harassment Accusers for Decades." *New York Times*, October 5, 2017.

Keller, Jessalynn, and Maureen E. Ryan, eds. *Emergent Feminisms: Complicating
a Postfeminist Media Culture*. New York: Routledge, 2018.

Kilkenny, Katie. "How 'Blockers' Became a Feminist Trojan Horse." *The Hollywood
Reporter*, April 7, 2018. www.hollywoodreporter.com/news/general-news/
blockers-kay-cannon-how-movie-became-a-feminist-trojan-horse-1100262

Langone, Alix. "#MeToo and Time's Up Founders Explain the Difference between
the 2 Movements—And How They're Alike." *Time*, March 22, 2018.
https://time.com/5189945/whats-the-difference-between-the-metoo-and-
times-up-movements

Lumby, Catherine. 'Past the Post in Feminist Media Studies.' *Feminist Media
Studies* 11, no. 1 (2011): 95–100.

MacDonald, Shana. "Refusing to Smile for the Patriarchy: Jessica Jones as Feminist Killjoy" *Journal of the Fantastic in the Arts* 30, no. 1 (2019): 68–84.

McRobbie, Angela. "Post-Feminism and Popular Culture" *Feminist Media Studies*
4, no. 3 (2004): 255–264.

Negra, Diane. *What a Girl Wants?: Fantasizing the Reclamation of Self in Postfeminism*. Routledge, 2008.

Rivers, Nicola. *Postfeminism and the arrival of the fourth wave*. New York: Palgrave Macmillan, 2017.

Robinson, Joanna. "Unblocked: The Story behind *Blockers'* Unexpected Gay Romance." *Vanity Fair*, April 6, 2018. www.vanityfair.com/hollywood/2018/04/blockers-gay-romance-kiss-kay-cannon-gideon-adlon-ramona-young

Rushfield, Richard. 2017. "Women in Hollywood 2017: The Power List." *Elle*, October 19, 2017. www.elle.com/culture/a12468947/women-in-hollywood-2017-the-power-list-november-2017

Sandberg, Bryn Elise. "How Netflix Revived the Rom-Com Genre: "Nobody Was Making Them'" *Hollywood Reporter*, December 21, 2018. www.hollywood reporter.com/news/general-news/how-netflix-revived-rom-genre-1169776/#!

Shary, Timothy. *Generation Multiplex: The Image of Youth in Contemporary American Cinema*. Austin: University of Texas Press, 2004.

Willis, Jessica L. "Sexual Subjectivity: A Semiotic Analysis of Girlhood, Sex, and Sexuality in the Film Juno." *Sexuality & Culture* 12 (2008): 240–256.

Zeisler, Andy. *We Were Feminists Once*. New York: Public Affairs, 2016.

CHAPTER 12

Seeing What Isn't There

The Invisible Man and #MeToo

Michelle Kay Hansen

Leigh Whannell's 2020 iteration of *The Invisible Man* received mixed and contradictory reviews from critics and viewers alike. Negative critiques include a lack of character development, with *The New Yorker* review stating, "The characters don't exist between their scenes because they're given little identity, little personality within the scenes" (Brody par. 9). Michael O'Sullivan of *The Washington Post* essentializes the film as nothing more than a "supervillain movie" (par. 11). Others disparage the film for having a sense of confusion about its genre. Mark Mcgreal, in his review in UCLA's *The Daily Bruin*, states that the film's "identity crisis" is its "most glaring problem" (par. 10). He continues, "*The Invisible Man* starts out as a classic horror film—complete with an unknown monster and jump scares—before transitioning into a psychological thriller that drives the protagonist to a psychotic break" (Mcgreal par. 10). However, Mcgreal fails to note that this "psychotic break"—which is not a break, but an outright anger—is necessary to a story that is firmly rooted in the #MeToo movement. *The Invisible Man* is about the PTSD caused by abuse, the justified anger that comes from living in isolation, and fear as a consequence of toxic masculinity. The film uses this premise to make the meaning of the story transcend the film itself and resonate with contemporary audiences. On the surface, it's an entertaining, almost by-the-numbers horror flick, but for an audience steeped in the psychological dread that victims of abuse have endured—and continue to endure—*The Invisible Man* has reworked the 1933 classic Universal monster movie (directed by James Whale) with a #MeToo horror spin, using a premise to suit a 2020 outlook.

It is no secret that the #MeToo movement arose out of women's anger over being mistreated and not only unheard but silenced. In an Elle.com interview in 2018, Tarana Burke (originator of the #MeToo movement) and Patrisse Cullors (a cofounder of #BlackLivesMatter) discussed their respective motivations for activism. Burke affirmed Cullors's assertion that "most of us start this work because we are angry. We're angry about what's been done to us, we're angry about what we've witnessed, we're angry about what we continue to witness" ("Anger, Activism" par. 8). There is even a rhetoric of war around the movement, as when Sarah Jaffe writes that in the wake of the revelations about Harvey Weinstein's repulsive and long history of sexual harassment and assault, "a wave of people, most of them, though not all of them women, began to wield their stories like weapons in a battle that, for once, they seemed to be winning. Well, if not winning, then at least drawing some blood" (80). Anger has certainly become a progressive force, which can be seen as both pervasive and productive within the #MeToo era. In her book *Good and Mad: The Revolutionary Power of Women's Anger*, Rebecca Traister writes:

> On some level, if not intellectual then animal, there has always been an understanding of the power of women's anger: that as an oppressed majority in the United States, women have long had within them the potential to rise up in fury, to take over a country in which they've never really been offered their fair or representative stake. Perhaps the reason that women's anger is so broadly denigrated—treated as so ugly, so alienating, and so irrational—is because we have known all along that with it came the explosive power to upturn the very systems that have sought to contain it. What becomes clear, when we look to the past with an eye to the future, is that the discouragement of women's anger—via silencing, erasure, and repression—stems from the correct understanding of those in power that in the fury of women lies the power to change the world. (35)

Though anger as a progressive force can be seen as unsustainable in the long term due to the amount of energy it takes to remain in the emotional state, Traister's book is a testament to the way anger has continually worked as a catalyst for social change when it comes to women's rights.

Just as the anger fuels movements like #MeToo in an attempt to "change the world," the protagonist's anger fuels *The Invisible Man* in an attempt to change her own situation, which is presented as a microcosm that stands in for the contemporary world at large. The film centers on Cecilia Kass (portrayed by Elisabeth Moss), who has just escaped a toxic relationship. Having been abused and gaslighted by her tech entrepreneur husband, Adrian (Oliver Jackson Cohen), Cecilia decides she has had enough and escapes from their isolated, ocean-side mansion in the middle of the night. She finds refuge with her sister, Emily (Harriet Dyer), their childhood friend, James (Aldis Hodge), and his teenage daughter, Sydney (Storm Reid). Her trauma leaves her struggling with ever-present and paralyzing anxiety and agoraphobia, symptoms of her PTSD. After being informed of her husband's suicide two weeks later, Cecilia still refuses to believe her nightmare is over. She desperately seeks to prove she is being both haunted and hunted by her husband, but no one believes her, and she is written off as crazy. Sadly, dismissing Cecilia as mentally ill is not surprising since, historically, the concept of "hysteria"—linked directly to the female womb—was "undoubtedly the first mental disorder attributable to women, accurately described in the second millennium BC, and until Freud considered an exclusively female disease" (Tasca, Rapetti, Carta, and Fadda 2012, 110). However, because "we are in the era of #MeToo, with the once-protected monsters of the real world finally being exposed for what they are" (Laffly par. 2), Cecilia's anger is not only palpable, but justified, as she revolts against the undetectable authority and the patriarchy that ruins her life and controls her psychological well-being. As Owen Gleiberman points out in his review for *Variety:*

> The traumatic power of Moss's performance is that she acts out the convulsive desperation and rage of a woman who is being terrorized and, at the same time, totally not believed about it, even by those closest to her. *The Invisible Man* is a social horror film grounded in a note-perfect metaphor. It's the story of a woman who got sucked into a whirlpool

of abuse and now finds that she can't free herself, because
the abuse remains (literally) out of sight. She's every woman
who's ever had to fight to be heard because her ordeal wasn't
"visible." (par. 5)

The Invisible Man is a clear commentary upon the way women's concerns
are so often rendered invisible due to the patriarchy and other systems of
oppression designed to safeguard privilege. Women have gone unheard,
been dismissed as hysterical, and been challenged to prove their sanity,
even when there has been overwhelming evidence corroborating their
truths about abuse.

In an interview with *The Guardian*, the film's writer/director Leigh
Whannell stated, "I saw an opportunity to change people's perceptions
of what *The Invisible Man* was. He's very well known, but I think as
time has gone by that character has become almost comical: you know,
the floating sunglasses and bandages. The more I thought about it, the
more I realized *The Invisible Man* movie I would love to see has never
been made" (Lewis, par. 17). What makes the 2020 adaptation so significant is the change of focus from the male antagonist to the very real,
very human woman at its center. Whannell is known for his work in
the horror genre, as co-creator of the *Saw* series as well as the *Insidious*
trilogy. However, he had a particular challenge in attempting to produce
a female-centric message, taking on the role of an ally in an attempt
not to speak for the marginalized group but to amplify the voices of
oppressed women. Though he is writing from a position of privilege as
a white, heterosexual male, in an interview with *Screen Rant*, Whannell
openly acknowledged that "true female insight" was necessary to making
his script a success. He stated that he and Elisabeth Moss would "sit
in a room for hours" while Moss offered her female perspective on the
character and the elements of abuse, discussing situations "where she was
uncomfortable . . . where she's felt unsafe or she's felt that a person is
manipulating her or being verbally abusive. So, there was this firsthand
insight into it" (Hullender, "Leigh Whannell" par. 7). In a separate
interview, Moss also praised Whannell's willingness to listen and value
her opinion, stating:

he was really smart about understanding that he had written
this incredible script . . . and he already had this female character that was really interesting and fleshed out and layered.

But he also, of course, was the first person to say, "I'm not a woman. What do you have? What is your perspective? What is your point of view here? What can you bring to this?" . . . Rightly so, he asked for my opinion. (Hullender, "Elisabeth Moss" par. 4)

Though there is an oft-debated issue about whether men can write women characters as effectively as women themselves, and although women will always be considered experts when it comes to understanding female characters, it is "detrimental to both men and women to continue to promote the idea that male writers—or men, in general, if the writers are assumed to be representatives of their society—have not progressed since the Victorian Age" (Lange 6). Whannell has clearly occupied the role of a male ally in taking the initiative to listen to—and believe—that his female lead relates much more to the experiences her character is going through than he could ever imagine. And this relatability is inherent and essential within the #MeToo movement, since sexual violence has become a relatively normative condition for women.

There is irony in the title of *The Invisible Man* in its updated version. Of course, the film is first based upon H. G. Wells's 1897 novel, *The Invisible Man: A Grotesque Romance*, which was then adapted into the 1933 film by James Whale, focusing on a scientist whose experiments render him unseeable and murderously crazed. The "cleverly updated version of *The Invisible Man* plays with the different meanings of 'romance' by fusing the basic conceit from Wells's uncanny tales with the fallout of an abusive romantic relationship" (Dargis par. 2). In this version, Whannell "dares to turn a woman's often silenced trauma from a toxic relationship into something unbearably tangible" (Laffly par. 1). In other words, this film is much more about the "Visible Woman" than the invisible man. "Charged by a constant psychological dread that surpasses the ache of any visible bruise," Cecilia's pain is consistently amplified at every turn, "making sure that her visceral scars sting like our own. Sometimes to an excruciating degree" (Laffly par. 1). The film is about a visible woman who is robbed of options, allowing the audience to understand the main character's paranoia and the ways in which PTSD can turn the whole world into an untrustworthy place. However, even in living with her trauma, Cecilia is not viewed as fragile. There is "something both mighty and vulnerable" in Cecilia, as Whannell's script gives a woman in peril all the power (Laffly par. 4).

With this variation on power dynamics—flipping the emphasis from the original title maniac and the perils of science to a woman who learns that an abusive lover can be just as dangerous when he's nowhere to be seen—there is still the need for those around Cecilia to silence her and oppress her voice. Her oppression is not only from the words and actions of an individual but is systematic as well. The structure of the film silences Cecilia, even before the film begins. Whannell "likes to isolate Cecilia in the shot, surrounding her with negative space that at first seems to be just visually expressing her feelings of isolation" (Dargis par. 5). Whether purposefully or accidentally, the structural choices of the film could be interpreted as a reflection of the film industry at large and its history of overlooking the voices of women who have been harassed, assaulted, and oppressed. Often, films—especially those written and directed by men—present women more as seen but less heard given the limited proportion of dialogue they have historically had. This is reflected even from the opening credits. Before she is even on screen, the mansion Cecilia shares with her husband is shown on a cliff near the ocean, with no other lights around. As she is attempting her escape, views of the interior depict no evidence of Cecilia as even part of this home. Instead, the audience can see walls of Adrian's framed awards and degrees, and where there might be a picture of them as a couple, there is only abstract art. Cecilia is present in the house only physically and is otherwise completely undetectable. But she is certainly constantly controlled and watched by her husband, as evidenced by the amount of security cameras Cecilia must disarm before exiting the property.

Additionally, the first of a series of microinvalidations occurs when Cecilia is picked up by her sister on the road after running through the woods and away from her husband. She enters the car and urgently tells her Emily to "just go," but Emily hesitates and questions, "What is happening?" even after Adrian has aggressively approached the car, screaming expletives and pounding on the window (*Invisible Man* 00:10:10). These microinvalidations continue throughout the film, which is also pertinent to the story and Cecilia's character itself, since "microinvalidation aims to make people feel invisible" (Nguyen par. 12). Even when those around her are actually witnessing the abuse from Adrian, as Emily in this opening scene, they turn a blind eye, making Cecilia feel unseen from the outset.

After Cecilia's escape, she is able to voice the level of control Adrian has had over her to Emily and James, saying,

He was in complete control of everything, including me. He
controlled how I looked and what I wore and what I ate.
And then he was controlling when I left the house and what
I said, and eventually, what I thought. And if he didn't like
what he assumed I was thinking, he would [hit me] amongst
other things. (*Invisible Man* 00:16:15)

She also admits that Adrian wanted a baby, but she secretly took birth
control out of the fear that a child would force her to be forever bound
to him. Though a potentially small rebellion in the face of oppression,
this act is showing Cecilia's willingness to claim her own bodily autonomy
and to control her procreative abilities in spite of the patriarchal system
she finds herself in—where she is clearly valued primarily for her ability
to reproduce. Though she has had little control, and has been silenced
in her relationship through isolation, abuse, and pure fear, she at least
feels capable in governing her own body as a symbol of resistance.

This atmosphere of isolation and oppression continues through
the majority of the film. Cecilia is, of course, physically isolated when
she initially realizes someone may be stalking her and when she is first
actually attacked, making it easy for her support system to invalidate
her claims. The silencing of disbelief is potentially more damaging than
the actual attacks. When Cecilia first sees the footsteps of the invisible
intruder, for example, she immediately tries to tell James, who simply
replies, "Adrian will haunt you if you let him. Don't let him" (*Invisible
Man* 00:35:22). Even her closest confidante, the person she ran to in
order to feel safe, does not believe her. When she finally speaks the
words, "I know that he is invisible," followed by the sound logic that
Adrian is a world leader in the field of optics and has the ability to fool
those around him due to his technological savvy, Cecilia is immediately
silenced by Adrian's brother and estate lawyer, Tom (Michael Dorman),
who implies this idea is—naturally—all in her head. The oppression of
her voice continues, with even her sister claiming that she "needs some
medication" (*Invisible Man* 00:45:25). In a final effort to desperately prove
she is a victim, she screams, "You have to listen to me!" (*Invisible Man*
01:13:51) as doctors and nurses forcibly silence Cecilia by injecting a
sedative into her arm after placing her in restraints.

Cecilia is rightfully and justifiably angry about not only enduring
abuse but having her pain and fear go unseen and unheard, which can
be its own form of invisibility. As Emily Winderman writes, "Anger is

a notable way of both perpetuating and contesting epistemic injustices" (330). However, when that anger is silenced, it "exacerbates the harms of epistemic injustices because silencing neutralizes or renders invisible the knowledge speakers have of the injury their anger communicates" (Bailey 96). Often, anger—like Cecilia's—is a direct result of the lack of empathy, because when a person is "denied the attribution of a full range of human characteristics—including full emotional capacity—the ground becomes fertile for dehumanization to take root" (Winderman 332). In other words, by limiting Cecilia's ability to express her anger about her injustices, her own identity as a human being has become reduced. She is in a continuous search for acknowledgment of her own voice, and this is what becomes, perhaps, the most important aspect of *The Invisible Man*: the collective acknowledgment and belief that the audience itself has in Cecilia.

Two fundamental aspects of the #MeToo movement are listening to and, more importantly, believing women's voices. This desperation for belief is abundantly clear in *The Invisible Man* when Cecilia, about halfway through the film, urgently begs her sister, "I *need* you to believe what I'm about to tell you" (01:11:20, emphasis added). As the audience, who has been fighting alongside Cecilia from her initial escape, we are participating in the collectivity and solidarity that is at the heart of #MeToo, and proving that there is both safety and support in numbers. In her article "The Collective Power of #MeToo," Sarah Jaffe writes, "the thing I have heard the most from survivors (and we are all survivors, aren't we, that was the point of saying 'me too') is that they want acknowledgement of what happened" (82). She later asserts that "restorative and transformative justice hinges on the notion of community; that accountability can happen within and with the support of the people around us" (Jaffe 85). In *The Invisible Man*, Whannell relies on a common trope in psychological horror films featuring a female protagonist—the "crazy woman no one will listen to" cliché—involving a woman repeating incredible explanations to inexplicable events happening around them. But as Prahlad Srihari points out in his review of the film:

> Filmmakers often use this to play with our own ability to understand what is real and what is an illusion . . . Whannell uses the setting as a microcosm for a society which not only fails to listen to women's experiences of trauma suffered at the hands of abusive men, but devalues their testimony. *The*

Invisible Man thus condemns those unseen forces in society that have allowed the systemic abuse of women by taking the side of the abuser. (par. 3)

While those around Cecilia refuse to believe her, the audience is her collective community, longing for her restorative and transformative justice.

Even though Cecilia's isolation is consistently emphasized both in setting and in scene structure, the camera itself—and the audience by proxy—becomes an invisible observer, never allowing her isolation to stand. Since she is surrounded by the collective support of the audience, the film is an acknowledgment of her emotional and physical suffering. As Peter Travers writes in *Rolling Stone*:

> this story of a woman who needs to be heard and believed is as timely as Harvey Weinstein in handcuffs. Whannell has hit on a powerfully resonant theme: that the invisible scars an abused woman carries in her mind remain long after physical wounds have healed . . . Just as 1954's horror landmark *Invasion of the Body Snatchers* saw unfeeling duplicates of humans as symbols of conformity to anti-communist paranoia, *The Invisible Man* 2020 sees the scourge of turning a blind eye to domestic violence and the need for female empowerment. The dark universe of *The Invisible Man* doesn't need monsters to keep us up nights. The terror comes from a world that looks exactly like our own. (par. 5)

Perhaps one of the most outrageous terrors in the film occurs when Cecilia is told that she is pregnant, and that it must have been "very recent" (01:18:43). It is soon revealed that Adrian replaced her birth control pills with placebos, impregnating her without her consent, which is a form of sexual violence and further promotes the #MeToo tones of the film as a whole. According to the American College of Obstetricians and Gynecologists, this is known as "birth control sabotage" and is defined as "active interference with a partner's contraceptive methods in an attempt to promote pregnancy." Further, this sabotage is specifically defined as a "form of intimate partner violence and would make it a freestanding crime" (Plunkett 98). This is a "dark universe" indeed, and this terror is absolutely something that "comes from a world that looks exactly like our own," as Travers points out.

Jennifer L. Airey, in her article titled simply "#MeToo," gives historical and literary contextualization showing that "the story of sexual harassment and assault is, from its earliest conception, also the story of silencing," citing three foundational myths of rape (Verginia, Lucrece, and Philomel) as well as examples from Western literature that have shaped a "cultural understanding of rape" (9). In all cases, Airey points out, "the only 'safe' unchaste female body is the deceased unchaste female body; only in the silence of the grave can the truth of rape be conclusively established" (10). She continues:

> Today, we no longer insist ideologically upon the deaths of sexually violated women, but we silence them nonetheless—through rape kits that go untested, assaults that go unreported, and nondisclosure agreements signed under duress. We also silence them by the elevation of male voices over female, creating the widespread cultural belief that male voices are more trustworthy and more rational. (Airey 10)

When Cecilia realizes that she has been violated, and that her body really is no longer her own, she refuses to be silent any longer. In fact, in the very next scene, after being told that she is "mentally incompetent" by her former brother-in-law, Cecilia finally speaks up, saying:

> I used to feel sorry for you. The blood relative of a narcissistic sociopath. Permanent punching bag. Handcuffed to his wallet. But now, I can see you for who you really are. You're just the jellyfish version of him. Everything but the spine. (*Invisible Man* 01:21:15)

Cecilia has decisively reached a turning point, proven by her ability to find her voice. From this moment forward, not only does Cecilia take decisive action against her aggressor but those around her are able to finally see and understand that she was telling the truth all along. Her voice is acknowledged. And as the audience—who has believed her, listened to her, and confronted her pain alongside her from the outset—we collectively praise the refusal to remain silent. Cecilia acts and confronts the injustice of her situation, which is the epitome of what those of us who declare "me too" are attempting to accomplish.

In the first paragraph of its review, *NPR*'s Scott Tobias makes the following poignant statement:

When a man doesn't have to look at himself in the mirror, he divorces himself from the moral accountability that curbs his worst instincts. Arrogance and contempt are his defining character traits, and invisibility has the effect of weaponizing them, because his scientific genius has both isolated him from other people and heightened his superiority complex. (par. 1)

Essentially, this is not only what *The Invisible Man* is trying to portray, but what the #MeToo movement is about at its very core. Women are angry with men who no longer have to look at themselves in the mirror, and are demanding accountability for their egregious actions. There is a broader understanding—now more than ever—that individual actions by bad people are a direct result of systemic oppression. The "boys will be boys" attitude, for example, is no longer acceptable as an excuse, as this is simply a justification to train young boys that disrespecting women is how the world operates. Filmed entertainment (particularly in romantic comedies) continually uses the idea that "No" just means "Try Harder," but it is becoming apparent that even big, romantic gestures designed to win the heart of the girl are, in reality, quite creepy. *The Invisible Man* leaves no room for this type of thought process, and instead is truly a film that takes action against the systemic problems of male toxicity. As Airey writes, "The backlash to #MeToo has begun in earnest, with accusations of witch hunts, overreactions, and the criminalization of male sexuality. It is all the more important, then, that we promote women's voices and that we take women seriously as narrators of their own experiences" (10). *The Invisible Man* is a metaphor for this need to take women seriously, and now that this moment of recognition has arrived, it is time to transform mere awareness into tangible action.

Works Cited

Airey, Jennifer L. "#MeToo." *Tulsa Studies in Women's Literature* 37, no. 1 (Spring 2018): 7–13.

"Anger, Activism, and Action: The Founders of Black Lives Matter and the #MeToo Movement on Making Change." *Elle.com*. March 13, 2008. www.elle.com/culture/career-politics/a19180106/patrisse-cullors-tarana-burke-black-lives-matter-metoo-activism

Bailey, Alison. "On Anger, Silence, and Epistemic Injustice." *Royal Institute of Philosophy Supplement* 84 (2018): 93–115.

Brody, Richard. "*The Invisible Man,* Reviewed: A Horror Film of Diabolical Twists and Empty Showmanship." *The New Yorker.* February 27, 2020. www. newyorker.com/culture/the-front-row/the-invisible-man-reviewed-a-horror-film-of-diabolical-twists-and-empty-showmanship

Dargis, Manohla. "*The Invisible Man* Review: Gaslight Nation, Domestic Edition." *New York Times,* February 26, 2020. www.nytimes.com/2020/02/26/movies/the-invisible-man-review.html

Gleiberman, Owen. "'*The Invisible Man*': Film Review." *Variety.* February 24, 2020. variety.com/2020/film/reviews/the-invisible-man-review-elisabeth-moss-1203512835

Hullender, Tatiana. "Elisabeth Moss Interview: *The Invisible Man.*" *Screen Rant.* February 26, 2020. screenrant.com/invisible-man-2020-elisabeth-moss-interview

Hullender, Tatiana. "Leigh Whannell Interview: *The Invisible Man.*" *Screen Rant.* February 26, 2020. screenrant.com/invisible-man-2020-leigh-whannell-interview

Invisible Man, The. Directed by Leigh Whannell, Blumhouse Productions, Universal Pictures, 2020.

Jaffe, Sarah. "The Collective Power of #MeToo." *Dissent* 65, no. 2 (Spring 2018): 80–87.

Laffly, Tomris. "The Invisible Man." *RogerEbert.com.* March 20, 2020. www.roger ebert.com/reviews/the-invisible-man-movie-review-2020

Lange, Cheryl. "Men and Women Writing Women: The Female Perspective and Feminism in U.S. Novels and African Novels in French by Male and Female Authors." *UW-L Journal of Undergraduate Research* 11 (2008): 1–6.

Lewis, Maria. "Leigh Whannell on Reinventing *The Invisible Man*: 'I want to change people's perceptions.'" *The Guardian,* February 16, 2020. www. theguardian.com/film/2020/feb/17/leigh-whannell-on-reinventing-the-invisible-man-i-want-to-change-peoples-perceptions

McGreal, Mark. "'The Invisible Man' has unseeable monster but visible problems with the execution." Movie review. *The Daily Bruin,* February 8, 2020. https://dailybruin.com/2020/02/28/movie-review-the-invisible-man-has-unseeable-monster-but-visible-problems-with-the-execution

Nguyen, Kelly. "Microinvalidations Are Real and They Can Have a Big Impact." *Teen Vogue,* November 13, 2017. www.teenvogue.com/story/microinvalidations-are-real

O'Sullivan, Michael. "Rebooted *Invisible Man* Is One Giant Missed Opportunity." *The Washington Post,* February 26, 2020. www.washingtonpost.com. www.going outguide/movies/rebooted-invisible-man-is-one-giant-missed-opportunity/2020/02/26/c26930da-541f-11ea-929a-64efa7482a77_story.html?arc404=true

Plunkett, Leah A. "Contraceptive Sabotage." *Columbia Journal of Gender and Law* 28, no. 1 (2014): 97–143.

Srihari, Prahlad. "*The Invisible Man* Movie Review: Elisabeth Moss Brings the Chills in a Showcase of the Unseen Horrors of Domestic Violence." First post.com, February 28, 2020. www.firstpost.com/entertainment/the-invisible-man-movie-review-elisabeth-moss-brings-the-chills-in-a-showcase-of-the-unseen-horrors-of-domestic-violence-8097611.html

Tasca, Cecilia, Mariangela Rapetti, Mauro Giovanni Carta, and Bianca Fadda. "Women and Hysteria in the History of Mental Health." *Clinical Practice and Epidemiology in Mental Health* 8 (2012): 110–119.

Tobias, Scott. " 'The Invisible Man': When Danger Is Present—and Clear." npr. org. February 27, 2020. www.npr.org/2020/02/27/809316597/the-invisible-man-when-danger-is-present-and-clear

Traister, Rebecca. *Good and Mad: The Revolutionary Power of Women's Anger.* New York: Simon & Schuster, 2018.

Travers, Peter. " 'The Invisible Man': Monster-Movie Reboot As #MeToo Revenge Story." *Rolling Stone*, February 25, 2020. www.rollingstone.com/movies/movie-reviews/invisible-man-movie-review-elisabeth-moss-957734

Winderman, Emily. "Anger's Volumes: Rhetorics of Amplification and Aggregation in #MeToo." *Women's Studies in Communication* 42, no. 3 (2019): 327–346.

CHAPTER 13

Believable

Feminist Resistance of Rape Culture in Netflix's *Unbelievable*

Tracy Everbach

A police detective gently runs a cotton swab across the face of a twenty-two-year-old rape victim named Amber as they sit inside a car. Detective Karen Duvall explains that the test may help recover DNA from the rapist. Before touching Amber, the detective asks permission and after taking the sample, she thanks her. This moment featured in the second episode of Netflix's limited series *Unbelievable* is juxtaposed with scenes of another rape victim, Marie, a teenager whom two police detectives badger and berate into recanting her crime report.

Based on a true story published in 2015 by ProPublica and The Marshall Project, *Unbelievable* is a feminist deconstruction of traditional media rape and sexual assault portrayals. The eight-part series defies historical on-screen exploitative, violent, victim-blaming narratives and, in so doing, controverts rape culture. We see the repercussions of these crimes on survivors and watch women being believed and treated with fairness, empathy, and respect. By focusing on the work of two talented, intelligent, and powerful women detectives who team up to catch a serial rapist, the series also defies male-centered crime drama representations that construct women as victims and men as cops and criminals (Cavender,

Bond-Maupin, and Jurik 645). *Unbelievable* makes a powerful statement against rape culture by shattering rape myths.

Rape Culture

Both entertainment and news media are societal teachers about cultural norms. Socially constructed television and film depictions of rape and sexual assault influence and shape public perceptions of these crimes and who is to blame for them (Kahlor and Eastin 217). Culturally, women have been blamed for their own rapes and assaults, shamed for being victims, and disbelieved when they report these crimes (Gilmore 7; Issa 283). Although rape and sexual assault have been labeled "sex crimes," these crimes are acts of violence that occur when a perpetrator assaults a victim without obtaining consent or when a victim is unable to give consent. In addition, unwanted sexual activity occurs when a perpetrator coerces someone to engage in an act under threat, power differential, or to satisfy their own desires (Hust, Marrett, Lei, Ren, and Ran 1371; Wood 255).

Rape myths are untruths about sexual violence that are ingrained in our culture and perpetuated through news and entertainment media as well as societal institutions such as the family. These myths are socially constructed to remove blame from perpetrators of violence and hold victims responsible for their own assaults. In addition, in a patriarchal system such as ours, rape myths serve to protect men, specifically white men, from being seen as threatening, while Black men often are villainized as rapists and presented as sexually threatening, particularly to white women (Cuklanz and Moorti 118; Hayes, Abbott, and Cook 1542; Kahlor and Eastin 217; Lonsway and Fitzgerald 133; Wood 227). Rape myths, which contribute to a larger rape culture, can have negative long-term effects on victims, including psychological and physical damage, exposure to further violence, rejection by others, and other impairments (RAINN. org). They also serve to connect maleness with dominance and violence and to maintain cultural and societal beliefs that men are superior and women subordinate (Kahlor and Eastin 216).

Some of the most pervasive rape myths include (1) victims lie about rape, (2) rape is about sex rather than about violence, (3) women say no when they really mean yes, (4) men cannot control their desires so they are compelled to assault, (5) women provoke rape by their behavior or clothing, (6) rape is caused by visiting a specific location, (7) women want to be forced to have sex, (8) most rape is committed by strangers, (9) men cannot be raped, (10) substance-impaired people deserve to be assaulted, (11) victims "ask for" their own assaults (Benedict 14; Lonsway and Fitzgerald 133; Wood 259). Institutions such as families, law enforcement, language, religious institutions, and schools, as well as mass media reinforce these myths. Mass media, including film, television, music, video gaming, advertising, and news media normalize violence, including rape and sexual assault, as inevitable and even acceptable (RAINN.org; Lonsway and Fitzgerald 133; Wood, 259).

The truth is that one of six women in the United States has experienced an attempted or completed rape in her lifetime (RAINN.org). Eight of ten perpetrators are someone the victim knows. Ninety percent of rape survivors are women and girls. Trans* people are at higher risk for sexual assault than cisgender people. Native American/indigenous people are more at risk than any other racial group. Most rapists and sexual assaulters get away with their crimes; a majority of rape and sexual assault cases are never reported to law enforcement authorities. A minuscule number of cases ends in convictions. Fewer than 1 percent of rapists will ever be incarcerated (RAINN.org).

Although feminists and other activists have had some success in refuting rape myths, fallacies—mistaken beliefs based on unsound arguments—persist in mass media and in the public conscience. For example, news media coverage of abuse scandals by Catholic priests and by Penn State assistant football coach Jerry Sandusky have brought attention to the sexual assaults of young men and boys, yet sexual violence against them rarely is included in public discourse (Wood 257). Public messages instigated during the second wave of feminism have emphasized for five decades that victims are not responsible for their own assaults—perpetrators are—yet victims are still blamed and shamed (Gilmore 7; Issa 283). Women who report sexual violence and sexual misconduct continue to be labeled as untrustworthy, as liars, and as mentally unstable (Gilmore 170).

Societal denial of women's accounts of their own lives led Tarana Burke in 2006 to coin MeToo as an activist movement to show empathy, support, and encouragement to sexual violence survivors (Issa 282). The movement was elevated into public consciousness in 2017 and 2018, when a number of women as well as men and trans* individuals came forward to tell their stories of being sexually harassed and assaulted. Media attention to these reports and the prosecution of some perpetrators led to the downfall of some powerful and prominent (and predominantly white) men. Among those accused of sexual misconduct and removed from their jobs were Hollywood producer Harvey Weinstein, Fox News founder Roger Ailes, CBS chairman and CEO Les Moonves, NBC *Today* show host Matt Lauer, CBS *This Morning* and PBS host Charlie Rose, Fox News host Bill O'Reilly, actor Kevin Spacey, and comedian Louis C.K. (Carlsen, Salam, Miller, Lu, Ngu, Patel, and Wichter 2018).

By connecting sexual violence survivors with others who have experienced similar crimes, #MeToo has eliminated some of the shame associated with rape, sexual assault, and sexual harassment. As Gilmore writes, "#MeToo breaks down the isolation that sexual violence and its aftermath impose. It opens a pathway of identification and begins to replace shame and stigma with the possibility of new affiliations" (x). In much the same way, *Unbelievable* also breaks barriers by showing through its eight episodes how victims can be *believed* and criminals caught and punished.

News Media Coverage of Rape and Sexual Assault

News media, including newspapers and television, historically have sensationalized, misrepresented, or re-victimized survivors of rape and sexual assault (Benedict 4). However, some recent research has found that efforts by feminists and others to dispel rape myths may have influenced journalists to produce more factual and fairly framed reporting (McManus and Dorfman 43; Sacks, Ackerman, and Shlosberg 1244; Worthington 1).

News stories disproportionately focus on false accusations, even though false rape reports are rare, estimated at 2 to 8 percent of all cases (RAINN, 2020). Previous research has found patterns showing that news media blame victims for their own assaults by including in stories details of a victim's substance impairment, insinuation of a victim's "asking for it" by being present at a particular place and time, over-emphasis on stranger rape, allusions to victims lying to get money or fame (if a celebrity is the perpetrator), and/or provocative behavior or dress (Benedict 4; Franiuk, Seefelt, and Vandello 798; Sacks et al. 1240). This news framing emphasizes perceptions of reality that then are accepted by the public as common sense (Entman 51). News frames also repeat common myths portraying women as untruthful and unreliable, which serves to reinforce women's status as secondary in a patriarchal society (Hardin and Whiteside 321).

Some studies over the past fifteen years found that journalists may have developed increased awareness and sensitivity to rape myths. Worthington examined framing in local television coverage of a university sexual assault scandal and concluded that the coverage was more progressive than in the past. Worthington noted that the framing of the stories emphasized victims' perspectives, blamed perpetrators for the crimes, and criticized the university's culture for allowing violence to occur (14). Ten years later, Sacks and colleagues analyzed content in large, local newspapers from nine regions of the United States. The authors discovered that in most of the crime reporting, local journalists avoided rape myths. However, the authors pointed out that the stories reflected more sympathy for victims who were hospitalized because of injuries, for victims of assaults in which a weapon was used, and for victims assaulted by strangers. They noted these findings could indicate reinforcement of the myths that some victims "wanted it," "asked for it," or "deserved it" (Sacks et al. 1244).

Hurtful and harmful mass media accounts of sexual violence continue. Chanel Miller, who was sexually assaulted in 2015 while unconscious, said in her victim impact statement at her convicted rapist's sentencing that she learned the details of her own attack by reading a news story:

> In it, I read and learned for the first time about how I was found unconscious, with my hair disheveled, a long necklace wrapped around my neck, bra pulled out of my dress, dress pulled off over my shoulders and pulled up above my waist, that I was butt naked all the way down to my boots, legs spread apart, and had been penetrated by a foreign object by someone I did not recognize. (Miller 337)

The news story also reported "something I will never forgive," Miller continued. "I read that according to him, I liked it." At the bottom of the article, Miller, who identifies as Chinese American, was outraged to read her rapist's irrelevant college swimming times. News stories identified Miller's white rapist as an "All-American swimmer," prompting a backlash by people on social media to accurately portray him as a criminal. He eventually was convicted of three felony charges, but served only three months in jail.

Crime Drama Narratives

Sexually violent content is prevalent in film, television, and other entertainment media. For many years that content has emphasized rape myths by insinuating women enjoy violent sex and that they cause their own victimization (Bufkin and Eschholz 1327; Donnerstein, Champion, Sunstein, and MacKinnon 17; Sommers-Flanagan, Sommers-Flanagan, and Davis 745; Lowry, Love, and Kirby 90). Soap operas, music videos, crime dramas, prime-time television, and film are among some of the platforms studied for sexually violent content and found to have perpetuated rape myths. Starting in the 2000s, research about crime dramas, notably the *Law & Order* franchise, found that viewers of these shows are less accepting of rape myths and rape culture and more willing to intervene as bystanders to sexual assault (Cuklanz and Moorti 124; Lee, Hust, and Zhang 40; Hust et al. 1369). Researchers speculate this is because sexual consent often is a theme of crime dramas and mass media can teach viewers how to debunk rape myths.

Social cognitive theory asserts that people learn how to operate in the world by modeling behavior that is socially constructed in popular mass media (Bandura 265). Therefore, if audiences see victims of rape and sexual assault treated with respect and rape myths debunked, they may accept these practices as truth. Crime dramas also raise awareness about power differentials between men and women in sexual relationships (Hust et al. 1371).

A 2011 examination of the first five seasons of NBC's *Law & Order: SVU* found that the program refuted rape myths in a way previous crime dramas had not (Cuklanz and Moorti 117). The show portrayed women as survivors rather than as victims. The authors noted that the lead detective in the show, Olivia Benson (played by Mariska Hargitay) is a strong, empathetic, and dedicated woman and a female role model. *SVU* contradicts myths such as the belief that rape and sexual assault are about sex (they are violent acts), that sexual assault victims are "broken" (they are survivors), that sex workers cannot be raped (the show featured prostitutes as victims), that men are not sexually assaulted (they are featured as survivors, as well as transgender people), and that mainly people of color are criminals in interracial crimes (a falsehood) (Cuklanz and Moorti 118). The program depicts consent as crucial in determining a sexual assault crime, demonstrates that assaults may occur in public or domestic locations, that rape can happen to anyone regardless of sex, gender, race, or socioeconomic status, and that rape and sexual assault often involve ingrained societal power imbalances. "SVU storylines often go beyond offering an individual-centered explanation for sexual assault. They reiterate feminists' claim that violent masculinity is facilitated by society at large" (Cuklanz and Moorti 119). Another assertion that arises in cinema and television depictions of rape is that victims are "broken women." Actor Tatiana Maslany, known for the science fiction series *Orphan Black*, recounted that she played a number of roles early in her career that depicted women "marred by trauma" (Friedman 241). The storylines, consistently told from a male perspective, emphasized women as victims of sexual violence rather than as survivors with agency.

Streaming As a New Form of Viewing

By streaming drama series, Netflix has pioneered a new technological on-demand media experience that differs from traditional film or television. Watching *Unbelievable* is an immersive and active experience that audiences can absorb at their own pace during which they witness crimes committed, investigated, solved, and avenged. Unlike episodic television programs, viewers of Netflix and other streaming services have the choice to take in all episodes at once by binge-watching or viewing several at a time. This type of control over viewing has fundamentally changed the entertainment industry. In 2019, the *New York Times* declared, "the long-promised streaming revolution—the next great leap in how the world gets its entertainment—is here" (Barnes). Netflix also produces and releases its own series and films, rather than depending on large production studios and television networks. Instead of releasing films in theaters, Netflix and other streaming services have issued films such as *Roma*, a 2018 Academy Award Best Picture nominee, on their own platforms. With improved, high-definition technology available on home screens, the cinema is no longer the only place to view full-length motion pictures. Use of streaming content increased even more in 2020 amid the Covid-19 pandemic, when the use of such services boomed as audiences were stranded at home, theater releases were disrupted, and Hollywood productions shut down.

The Series *Unbelievable*

The eight-part Netflix series *Unbelievable* originated from journalism. "An Unbelievable Story about Rape," a 2015 publication from ProPublica and The Marshall Project, detailed the story of Marie, a teenager raped by a man who broke into her apartment. Marie reported the crime to police, who questioned her relentlessly until she was so demoralized that she said she invented the rape. Years later, two detectives who were investigating a serial rapist discovered Marie was one of his victims. Their hard work led them to catch the rapist, who eventually pleaded guilty to twenty-eight counts of rape and was sentenced to 327 and a half years in prison (Miller and Armstrong). Screenwriter Susannah Grant, along with writers Michael Chabon and Ayelet Waldman, later adapted the story into a screenplay.

The Netflix limited series, starring Toni Collette and Merritt Wever as the lead detectives, was released in September 2019 at a time when several women had been coming forward publicly about sexual misconduct by powerful men. The series also followed with the Senate hearings for Brett Kavanaugh's nomination to the U.S. Supreme Court, during which Christine Blasey Ford testified that Kavanaugh had sexually assaulted her in 1982. Public discourse was highly focused on #MeToo and on believing women who said they had been raped or sexually assaulted.

Grant, director and co-creator of *Unbelievable*, noted the comparison to current events, but emphasized that such stories are not unique. "Anytime you land a story about gender-based power imbalances, there will be a current event that's relevant," she told the *Los Angeles Times* (Blake). Critics praised the show for realistically portraying what sexual assault victims endure without taking a voyeuristic viewpoint. The show also focused on the survivors more than the rapist himself, who receives little screen time. The series was praised for its focus on two brilliant women detectives who solved the crimes (Blake; Gajanan; Gilbert). This nontypical approach can be attributed to the creative team driving the project. Women created nearly every aspect of the production. Grant directed two episodes and Lisa Chodolenko directed three. Ayelet Waldman and Grant both served as co-creators and executive producers of the series, along with executive producers Katie Couric and Sarah

Timberman. Grant said she wanted viewers of the series to understand how rape culture pervades society and to know how it feels to be violated and not believed. "I was conscious of how accustomed to the world of 'rape porn' we all have become—the voyeuristic view of quasi-violent sexuality. It's present in a lot of the images we're exposed to culturally," she said (Blake).

Frames of Resistance in *Unbelievable*

By contrasting two different ways to treat rape victims, *Unbelievable* dismantles rape myths. The series emphasizes empathy and compassion for victims of these crimes, empowers them with agency as survivors, and normalizes women detectives as smart, powerful, and strong—features usually associated in our culture as masculine.

Empathy for Victims

Unbelievable presents viewers with two types of investigators in rape cases: a pair of male detectives who botch a case by buying into rape myths and a pair of female detectives who work with a team of investigators to tie several cases together and catch a serial rapist. The women's work is marked by their empathy for victims, their belief of women's stories, their indefatigable work ethic, their intelligence, and their respect for others. The first episode of the series focuses on the aftermath of teenager Marie Adler's rape in Washington state. She repeatedly is forced to recount the sexual violence inflicted upon her: to police officers at the scene, in the hospital where she is poked and prodded for evidence, and at the police station where two male detectives grill her. The detectives make her relive the rape by retelling it while they point out inconsistencies in her story. They ask her if she dreamed that she was raped. Beaten down emotionally, she finally says the rape did not happen. The detectives are relentless, and they victimize her more by charging her with making a false statement. Throughout the series we see Marie tormented by peers and authority figures such as counselors, former foster parents, co-workers, and law enforcement, who call her a liar and fraud.

In the series' second episode, we encounter Amber, a Colorado victim who was raped in her apartment. Detective Karen Duvall immediately treats her with sensitivity and respect by speaking to her quietly and asking her if she will talk to her. She suggests they talk privately in her car, where the detective asks for permission to swab Amber's face for possible DNA evidence. Throughout their conversation, Duvall tells Amber that she does not have to explain anything to her, tells her to take her time, and thanks her repeatedly. It's a jarring contrast with the detectives who interrogated Marie.

Several times in *Unbelievable*, Duvall and her collaborator, Detective Grace Rasmussen, are shown empathizing with victims. They also make direct statements that contradict rape myths. For instance, Rasmussen comments that one victim "was blaming herself for leaving a window open." Duvall replies, "Like everyone in Colorado doesn't leave a window open at night." The detectives consistently show concern for victims by asking them how they are doing, whether they are eating and sleeping well. They tell victims they will not make them recount the crimes.

In one scene, Detective Duvall spots Amber at a local church service. Amber tells her she has been doing some out-of-character things: buying a gun and sleeping with different men. She says Duvall must think she is crazy. Duvall replies, "You don't sound crazy to me, you sound like someone who went through a trauma and is looking for control and safety." Through this statement and others, the detectives show that they take rape seriously as a violent crime. Duvall tells a co-worker: "This is not something people get over, it's something they carry with them, like a bullet in the spine."

Controverting Rape Myths

Unbelievable deliberately contradicts and debunks rape myths. As the detectives follow leads, Duvall questions a college student who spotted a flier on campus about police searching for a serial rapist. The young man says he knows another student named Scott who forces women to have sex. Duvall asks him how he knows that Scott rapes women. The student replies, "That's not what I said." Duvall fires back, "Yes it is. That's rape." On further investigation, Duvall discovers a woman reported to the campus police that Scott raped her, but later she decided not to pursue charges. Scott comes in for questioning and angrily accuses "that girl" of lying. He whines that "girls" make up rape charges all the time because "there's a status to being a victim. Then guys like me—normal guys—get accused of all kinds of crazy stuff." Duvall immediately corrects him: the woman did not lie; she decided not to press charges.

In another scene, a male detective who initially investigated one of the serial rapes tells Duvall he doubted the victim's account until he saw her physical condition. "I might have written her off entirely if not for her injuries," he said. He then is shown interrogating the victim as she lies in her hospital bed, badgering her about whether she had any alcohol to drink, took drugs, or if she dreamed the rape. "I know no victim likes to be asked if she imagined her assault. But I had to!" the male detective insists as Duvall stares at him, clearly disgusted.

In other scenes, Rasmussen talks about how easily society, media, and law enforcement ignore statistics on the impact of violence against women, including the strong connection between domestic violence and sexual assault. She admits that some police are lazy and some are misogynistic, contributing to a lack of rape prosecutions. She also laments that too many rapists receive probationary sentences. At one point, Marie's lawyer says that no one ever questions victims of robbery and carjacking and asks why we doubt victims of sexual violence. All these scenes feature characters directly resisting and correcting rape myths.

Agency for Victims

Although the serial rapist's victims, particularly Marie, are depicted as suffering from their assaults, they ultimately are shown achieving agency as survivors. In the final scene of the series, Marie, who has received a settlement check from the city for the bungled case and false charges against her, calls Duvall and thanks her for catching the rapist. She credits Duvall and Rasmussen for making a difference in her life by letting her know that two people were looking out for her and making things right. She says she finally is at peace—she wakes up in the morning thinking good things can happen to her. The survivors' recovery is emphasized at the rapist's courtroom sentencing, where several of them make victim-impact statements and watch the rapist lose his freedom.

Unbelievable's rape scenes are never explicit or exploitative; they are shown as flashbacks and fragments. The narrative does not focus on the rapist himself as a character. In a stunning jail scene, the defenselessness and humiliation the victims suffered is avenged when the rapist himself is degraded. A DNA technician orders the rapist to remove all of his clothes, leaving him naked, vulnerable, and exposed, then prods and pokes him in various orifices, plucks hairs from his body, and photographs him. He stands alone, exposed.

Rather than portraying survivors as broken victims, the series shows them as full characters with lives. Their victimization does not define them, and they tell their own stories. Marie, who is shown suffering more than any of the women, finally begins to heal when she gets a caring therapist who points out to her that she was attacked twice—by the rapist and then by police—and that none of it was her fault. Detective Parker, one of the original detectives who berated Marie and charged her with a false report, finally apologizes to her. In the final scene of the series, Marie drives her new Jeep, bought with a lawsuit settlement with the city, to the beach, the place where she always felt free.

Normalizing Powerful Women

Grace Rasmussen and Karen Duvall, the two detectives who solve the case, are perfectionists who work endless hours and revisit every detail to stop the man who is hurting other women. Although they work for two different police departments, they combine forces with a team of mostly women investigators. Duvall has high standards: she chews out a male member of the investigative team who she perceives isn't devoted enough to the case. But she also respects her co-worker's personal lives; in another scene, she tells a male co-worker who received a call from home during a stakeout, "Don't ever apologize for taking care of your family." Both detectives are depicted as multifaceted—we see their supportive spouses and their home life as well as their work life. Rasmussen is shown going for runs with her dog and working on vintage cars with her husband, who works for the attorney general's office. Duvall and her husband, another cop, are portrayed as sharing home duties such as child care and cooking, and working separate shifts.

The scenes serve to normalize women as tough, strong, fearless, aggressive, and intelligent—qualities often associated in entertainment media with male characters. Male cops in crime shows most often have been constructed as authoritative protectors who seek justice for vulnerable female victims (Cavender et al. 645). Yet Rasmussen and Duvall combine those characteristics with compassion, empathy, sensitivity, and humanity, traits often associated with femininity. These powerful women use their expertise and brilliance to solve the case on behalf of other women who gain agency by the end of the series. In one scene, Duvall uses her power and status to quell a creepy man who is leering at women in a diner where she is eating. She stands up to pay and as he ogles her, she flashes her gun and badge at him. He looks down and stares at his plate.

The show also repeats a trope often seen in male cop dramas—the older, more experienced detective (Rasmussen) mentors a younger detective (Duvall) to success and distinction in the field. But Rasmussen and Duvall clearly are women who embrace their femininity and often discuss the misogynistic treatment of women-identifying people by men cops. The relationship between the two detectives shows their power as well as their humility. When the suspect is identified and the investigators arrest him, Rasmussen, the mentor, lets her protegé, Duvall, put him in handcuffs while she stays behind at the station. Afterward, Duvall thanks Rasmussen for being a role model and mentor to her. In an extraordinary scene that lasts only one minute, a group of women investigators gathers in a bar, playing pool and discussing the status of their cases. Such a scene is a hallmark of male-centered crime dramas and here it is presented so casually that the viewer may not realize until later how groundbreaking it is.

Conclusion

Entertainment media are effective teaching tools that can influence public perception and beliefs by constructing narratives that become socially accepted as reality (Bandura 265). *Unbelievable* is a crime drama that works to counter existing rape culture by presenting scenes that upend rape myths, and in turn, deconstructing rape culture. The series' feminist approach to storytelling defies elements of established male-centered crime dramas, such as presenting women as victims and men as saviors or predators. By depicting powerful women detectives who display compassion and empathy along with ingenuity and strength, the series shows viewers complex women who crack the case of a serial rapist.

Unbelievable demystifies and deconstructs persistent myths about rape and sexual assault. Repeatedly the characters subvert rape myths by defining rape (forced sexual assault without consent), by placing blame on the rapist rather than the victims, and by stressing that women tell the truth about these crimes. The storyline about Marie exposes wrongdoing by police through its portrayal of male detectives' misconduct, and later highlights an apology by Detective Parker, who feels remorse for his treatment of the teenager. Also, by shining a light on the raw aftermath of rape, the series reveals how devastating and violent this crime is and emphasizes the physical and mental health toll it can take.

As a whole, the series questions why our culture accepts rape myths and rape culture and encourages viewers to accept a view of victims as survivors. It holds rapists responsible for rape. In addition, *Unbelievable* models ways to treat victims with empathy and to believe women's stories about sexual violence and misconduct. In an era of the #MeToo movement, this series takes an important and necessary stand to combat rape culture.

Works Cited

Bandura, Albert. "Social Cognitive Theory of Mass Communication." *Media Psychology* 3 (2001): 265–299.

Barnes, Brooks. "The Streaming Era Has Finally Arrived. Everything Is about to Change." *New York Times*, November 18, 2019. www.nytimes.com/2019/11/18/business/media/streaming-hollywood-revolution.html

Benedict, Helen. *Virgin or Vamp: How the Press Covers Sex Crimes.* New York: Oxford University Press, 1992.

Bufkin, Jana, and Sara Eschholz. "Images of Sex and Rape: A Content Analysis of Popular Film." *Violence against Women* 6 (2000): 1317–1344.

Blake, Meredith. "How Netflix's 'Unbelievable' Created Its Revolutionary Portrayal of Rape." *Los Angeles Times*, October 3, 2019. www.latimes.com/entertainment-arts/tv/story/2019-10-03/unbelievable-netflix-rape-representation

Carlsen, Audrey, Maya Salam, Claire Cain Miller, Denise Lu, Ash Ngu, Jugal K. Patel, and Zach Wichter. "#MeToo Brought Down 201 Powerful Men." *New York Times*, October 29, 2018. www.nytimes.com/interactive/2018/10/23/us/metoo-replacements.html

Cavender, Gray, Lisa Bond-Maupin, and Nancy C. Jurik. "The Construction of Gender in Reality Crime TV." *Gender & Society* 13, no. 5 (1999): 643–663.

Cuklanz, Lisa M., and Sujata Moorti. "Television's 'New' Feminism: Prime-time Representations of Women and Victimization," In *Gender, Race, and Class in Media: A Critical Reader*, edited by Gail Dines and Jean M. Humez. Thousand Oaks, CA: Sage, 2011. 115–126.

Donnerstein, Edward, Cheryl A. Champion, Cass R. Sunstein, and Catharine A. MacKinnon. "Pornography: Social Science, Legal and Clinical Perspectives." *Law & Inequality: A Journal of Theory and Practice* 4, no. 1 (1986): 17–49.

Entman, Robert M. "Framing: Toward Clarification of a Fractured Paradigm." *Journal of Communication* 43 (1993): 51–58.

Friedman, Jaclyn. "Innocent in the Face: A Conversation with Tatiana Maslany." In *Believe Me: How Trusting Women Can Save the World*, edited by Jessica Valenti and Jaclyn Friedman. New York: Seal Press, 2020. 240–254.

Franiuk, Renae, Jennifer Seefelt, and Joseph Vandello. "Prevalence of Rape Myths in Headlines and Their Effects on Attitudes Toward Rape." *Sex Roles* 58, no. 11–12 (2008): 790–801.

Gajanan, Mahita. "The True Story behind the Netflix Series Unbelievable." *TIME*. September 12, 2019. https://time.com/5674986/unbelievable-netflix-true-story

Gilbert, Sophie. "*Unbelievable* is TV's Most Humane Show." *The Atlantic*. September 19, 2019. www.theatlantic.com/entertainment/archive/2019/09/netflix-unbelievable-sexual-assault-revolutionary-competence/598411

Gilmore, Leigh. *Tainted Witness: Why We Doubt What Women Say About Their Lives*. New York: Columbia University Press, 2018.

Hardin, Marie, and Erin Whiteside. "Framing through a Feminist Lens: A Tool in Support of an Activist Research Agenda." In *Doing News Framing Analysis: Empirical and Theoretical Perspectives*, edited by Paul D'Angelo and Jim A. Kuypers. New York: Routledge, 2010. 312–330.

Hayes, Rebecca M., Rebecca L. Abbott, and Savannah Cook. "It's Her Fault: Student Acceptance of Rape Myths on Two College Campuses." *Violence against Women* 22 (2016): 1540–1555.

Hust, Stacey J.T., Emily Garrigues Marrett, Ming Lei, Chumbo Ren, and Weina Ran. "*Law & Order, CSI*, and *NCIS*: The Association Between Exposure to Crime Drama Franchises, Rape Myth Acceptance, and Sexual Consent Negotiation Among College Students." *Journal of Health Communication* 20 (2015): 1369–1381.

Issa, Sabrina Hersi. "Survivorship Is Leadership: Building a Future for New Possibilities and Power." In *Believe Me: How Trusting Women Can Save the World*, edited by Jessica Valenti and Jaclyn Friedman. New York: Seal Press, 2020. 278–290.

Kahlor, LeeAnn, and Matthew S. Eastin. "Television's Role in the Culture of Violence toward Women: A Study of Television Viewing and the Cultivation of Rape Myth Acceptance in the United States." *Journal of Broadcasting & Electronic Media* 55, no. 2 (2011): 215–231.

Lee, Moon J., Stacey J.T. Hust, Lingling Zhang, and Yunying Zhang. "Effects of Violence against Women in Popular Crime Dramas on Viewers' Attitudes Related to Sexual Violence." *Mass Communication and Society* 14 (2011): 25–44.

Lonsway, Kimberly A., and Louise F. Fitzgerald. "Rape Myths: In Review." *Psychology of Women Quarterly* 18, no. 2 (1994): 133–164.

Lowry, Dennis T., Gail Love, and Malcolm Kirby. "Sex on the Soap Operas: Patterns of Intimacy." *Journal of Communication* 31 (1981): 90–96.

McManus, John H., and Lori Dorfman. "Functional Truth or Sexist Distortion? Assessing a Feminist Critique of Intimate Violence Reporting." *Journalism* 6, no. 1 (2005): 43–65.

Miller, Chanel. *Know My Name: A Memoir*. New York: Viking, 2019.

Miller, T. Christian, and Ken Armstrong. "An Unbelievable Story of Rape." ProPublica and The Marshall Project, December 16, 2015. www.propublica.org/article/false-rape-accusations-an-unbelievable-story

RAINN.org. "Statistics" 2020. www.rainn.org/statistics

RAINN.org. "Criminal Justice Statistics," 2020. www.rainn.org/statistics/criminal-justice-system

RAINN.org. "Effects of Sexual Violence," 2020. www.rainn.org/effects-sexual-violence

Sacks, Meghan, Alissa R. Ackerman, and Amy Shlosberg. "Rape Myths in the Media: A Content Analysis of Local Newspaper Reporting in the United States." *Deviant Behavior* 39, no. 9 (2018): 1237–1246.

Sommers-Flanagan, Rita, John Sommers-Flanagan, and Britta Davis. "What's Happening on Music Television? A Gender Role Content Analysis." *Sex Roles* 28 (1993): 745–753.

Worthington, Nancy. "Progress and Persistent Problems: Local TV News Framing of Acquaintance Rape on Campus." *Feminist Media Studies* 8, no. 1 (2008): 1–16.

Wood, Julia T. *Gendered Lives: Communication, Gender, & Culture*. Boston: Cengage Learning.

Contributors

RALPH BELIVEAU teaches in the Gaylord College and is affiliate faculty in Film and Media Studies and Women's and Gender Studies at the University of Oklahoma. He co-wrote *Gramsci and Media Literacy* (2021), co-edited *International Horror Film Directors: Global Fear* (2017), and co-wrote *Digital Literacy: A Primer on Media, Identity and the Evolution of Technology* (2016). He has written about network society, women in horror, documentary rhetoric, *The Wire*, African American noir, Alex Cox, *Supernatural*, sin-eating, Richard Matheson, Shirley Jackson, and Paolo Freire and media literacy. Beliveau earned his BS from Northwestern University and PhD from the University of Iowa.

BRIAN BREMS is a professor of English at the College of DuPage. His academic work on cinema is varied, with numerous chapters appearing in edited collections. He is the co-editor of *ReFocus: The Films of Paul Schrader* (2020) and he publishes regularly in online film magazines and websites, including *Bright Wall/Dark Room*, *Vague Visages*, and *Film Inquiry*. He has also contributed to *Film School Rejects* and *Little White Lies*.

NICOLE BURKHOLDER-MOSCO earned her PhD in English litera-ture and criticism in 2003 and that same year joined the Lock Haven University faculty, where she is now a full professor. Her presented and published work traces roles of women and children in Gothic studies, examining marginal and subversive characters and the power shifts and boundary transgressions that accompany such roles. Her current teaching and research interests include an examination of Gothic constructions in the fairy tale and fantasy genres and the evolution of gendered motifs in fiction and film.

JULIA CHAN is currently the inaugural Postdoctoral Fellow at Carleton University's Institute of Criminology and Criminal Justice, where her research is concerned with voyeurism and surveillant looking. She holds a PhD in cultural studies from Queen's University at Kingston. Recently, she was a Mitacs Postdoctoral Visitor in Cinema and Media Arts at York University and the managing editor of PUBLIC: Art | Culture | Ideas.

TRACY EVERBACH is a professor of journalism in the Mayborn School of Journalism at the University of North Texas. She teaches undergraduate and graduate classes on race, gender, and media; news reporting; and qualitative research methods. Her research focuses on representations of race and gender in media, women's leadership in newsrooms, and sexual harassment in media. She is a former newspaper reporter, including twelve years on the city news desk at The Dallas Morning News.

LISA FUNNELL is associate professor in Women's and Gender Studies at the University of Oklahoma. Her research explores gender and geopolitics in the James Bond franchise, Hollywood blockbusters, and Hong Kong martial arts films. She is the author of Geographies, Genders, and Geopolitics of James Bond (2017), with Klaus Dodds. Her first monograph, Warrior Women: Gender, Race, and the Transnational Chinese Action Star (2014), won the Emily Toth Award for Best Single Work in Women's Studies. She has edited anthologies on gender and feminism in James Bond as well as the depiction of Asian identities in transnational cinema.

MICHELLE KAY HANSEN received her PhD in English with a literature focus from the University of Nevada, Las Vegas, in 2012. Her research interests are U.S. gothic and horror fiction and film, focusing on the concepts and definitions of "monstrosity," "art-horror," Kristeva's "Abjection," and horror and postmodernism in popular culture. She has been an active member of the Popular and American Culture Association since 2008, and her published work can be found in Adapting Poe, New Worlds, Terrifying Monsters, Impossible Things, Anthologizing Poe, and Shirley Jackson: A Companion.

KATHERINE KARLIN is an associate professor of English at Kansas State University, where she teaches courses in film and in creative writing. Her short story collection Send Me Work was published by Northwestern University Press. She serves as co-director of the Gordon Parks Digital

Archive at Kansas State and is currently at work on a book about singer and actor Etta Moten.

SHANA MACDONALD is associate professor in communication arts at the University of Waterloo, Canada. Her interdisciplinary research examines contemporary feminism across social and digital media, popular culture, cinema, performance, and public art. Dr. MacDonald is a director of the qcollaborative (qLab), a feminist design lab where she co-runs the online archive *Feminists Do Media* (Instagram: @aesthetic.resistance). She is the current president of the Film Studies Association of Canada (2020–2022). Her publications have appeared in *Feminist Media Histories*, *Media Theory Journal*, and *Feminist Media Studies*, and she is lead author on the forthcoming book *Networked Feminist Activisms*.

MICHELE MEEK is a tenure track assistant professor in communication studies at Bridgewater State University in Massachusetts. She regularly writes and speaks about representations of sexual consent for both academic and public audiences, such as articles in *Ms. Magazine* online and *The Good Men Project*; her TEDx talk "Why We're Confused about Consent—Rewriting Our Stories of Seduction" on TED.com; and scholarly essays in *Literature/Film Quarterly and Girlhood Studies*. In addition, she published *Independent Female Filmmakers: A Chronicle Through Interviews, Profiles, and Manifestos* (2019) which highlights fifteen legendary North American female filmmakers. For more information, visit https://michelemeek.com.

SABRINA MORO is a lecturer in media & cultural studies and French at Nottingham Trent University. Her research explores the complex interactions among gender/sexuality politics, rape testimonies, feminism, and contemporary celebrity cultures. In addition to her research, Sabrina designs and runs participative workshops aimed at an audience beyond academia and provides training and critical commentaries on contemporary media culture.

EMILY NASER-HALL is a doctoral candidate in English at the University of Kentucky. She earned a BA from Tulane University, a JD from DePaul College of Law, an LLM from Georgetown, and an MA from Northwestern University. Her research interests include post-1945 American literature, gothic narratives, and the intersection of law and literature. Her work has been published in the *Tulane Journal of International Law*, the *DePaul Journal for Social Justice*, and the *Proceedings of the Third Purdue Linguistics, Literature, and Second Language Studies Conference*. Her upcoming publications will be included in the *Popular Culture Studies Journal* and *Studies in the American Short Story*.

AMANDA SPALLACCI is currently an assistant lecturer in the University of Alberta's Department of English and Film Studies, where she received her PhD (2021) in English and was a SSHRC doctoral fellow and Killam Laureate. Amanda's research and publications concern contemporary Hollywood cinema, television, and life writing through the lenses of memory studies, trauma, affect, and critical race theory. She has published on sexual assault in journals such as *A/B Autobiography Studies* (2017), *Studies in Testimony* (2019), and *Arts* (2019), as well as contributing numerous chapters to edited collections. Her most recent work is a forthcoming edited book collection on digital memory cultures in Canada (2021).

BRITTANY CAROLINE SPELLER is an independent scholar who received her BA and MA in American history in 2014 and 2016. She later earned a master's degree in English from Auburn University. Her research interests lie primarily within the field of cinema studies, with a particular emphasis on the horror genre, and in American women's literature. Her forthcoming publications include a chapter *in ReFocus: The Films of Mary Harron* and an article on Shirley Jackson's short stories for a special issue of *Women's Studies*.

Index

Note: Book titles include the author's name(s);
film titles include the director's name and the release date.

Girard, René, 139, 141, 142, 143, 149

The Girl with the Dragon Tattoo (Fincher 2011): camera focus in, 164–65; compared to the Swedish film and novel, 163–64, 166–67, 172n11; concern for all women in, 156, 167; and disparities between genders in, 5; as introduction to Scandinavian Noir, 155; Lisbeth's character in, 163, 171n8; opening sound and imagery, 162–63; rape and revenge scenes in, 145–46; reversals of power in, 148–49, 166–67; sexual violence and capital in, 144; viewer response to rape scene in, 164, 165

The Girl with the Dragon Tattoo (Larsson): about, 155–56; change in title, 158; classlessness in violence to women in, 161; and focus on women's rage, 169–70; market impact of, 155; protagonist's revenge in, 161; role reversal in, 165–66; significance of tattoos in, 160–61; structure and sexual assaults in, 159–60

The Girl with the Dragon Tattoo (Oplev 2009), 155, 163, 164

Gleiberman, Owen, 211

The Godfather (Coppola 1972), 50

Godwin, Victoria L., 85

Goldberg, Evan, 184, 190, 195

Golden Globe nominations, 196

Goldfinger (Fleming), 14

Goldfinger (Hamilton, 1964), 19–21, 24–25

Goldman, Emma, 83

Good Boys (Stupnitsky 2019), sexual consent in, 5, 176, 184–85, 190

Goodstein, Lynne, 59

Gorney, Karen Lynn, 57

The Graduate (Nichols 1967), 187

Grant, Susannah, 232–33. See also *Unbelievable* (Netflix series 2019)

"Greased Lightnin," 151nn2–3

Greven, David, 76–77

Griffin, Susan, "The All-American Crime," 54

Guardian on celebrities against sexual harassment, 30

GWTDT. See *The Girl with the Dragon Tattoo* (2011)

Hale, Matthew, 82, 85; *Historia Placitorum Coronae* (1736), 80–81

Halpern, Emily, 182

Han, Jenny, 195, 199

Hargreaves, Stuart, 105

Hartwell, Judy, 81–82, 88

Haskell, Molly, 50; *From Reverence to Rape*, 77

Haskin, Sarah, 182

Heldman, Caroline, 163, 172n9

Heller-Nicholas, Alexandra, 119, 138

Henry, Claire, 138–39; *Revisionist Rape*, 119

heroism, sex-based. See James Bond films of the Connery era

Herzog, Amy, 67

Hewer, Elisabeth, 155

The Hills Have Eyes (Aja 2006), 120

The Hills Have Eyes (Craven 1977), 117, 120

The Hills Have Eyes II (Weisz 2007), 120

Hollywood Critics Association Awards, 196

Hollywood film: depiction of rape in, 18; expanding diversity in, 7–8; impact of pornography and horror in, 71; and perspectives of privilege, 1; potential for social commentary in, 77; and relationship with culture, 3; and serial on-demand dramas, 5–6; sex